LIVE THROUGH THIS

DEBRA GWARTNEY

LIVE THROUGH THIS

A Mother's Memoir of Runaway
Daughters and Reclaimed Love

HOUGHTON MIFFLIN HARCOURT

BOSTON   NEW YORK   2009

For information about permission to reproduce selections from this book, write to Permissions, Houghton Mifflin Harcourt Publishing Company, 215 Park Avenue South, New York, New York 10003.

www.hmhbooks.com

Library of Congress Cataloging-in-Publication Data
Gwartney, Debra.
  Live through this : a mother's memoir of runaway daughters and reclaimed love / Debra Gwartney.
    p. cm.
  ISBN 978-0-547-05447-6
    1. Runaway teenagers—West (U.S.) 2. Teenage girls—West (U.S.)
  3. Mothers and daughters—West (U.S.) I. Title.
  HV1435.W4G93 2008
  362.74 — dc22
    [B]   2008013751

Book design by Melissa Lotfy

Printed in the United States of America

DOC 10 9 8 7 6 5 4 3 2 1

Note: Some names have been changed to protect the privacy of individuals.

Excerpt from "Birches" from *The Poetry of Robert Frost* edited by Edward Connery Lathem. Copyright 1916, 1969 by Henry Holt and Company. Copyright 1944 by Robert Frost. Reprinted by permission of Henry Holt and Company, LLC.

Portions of this book previously appeared in a somewhat different form: "Far Away, So Close," in *Salon,* "Mothers Who Think" column, November 23, 1998; "Tenderloin," in *Creative Nonfiction,* no. 16, 1999, pages 21–30; "Tent," in *Fourth Genre,* vol. 3, no. 1, Spring 2001, pages 20–27; "Out of Gas," in *Tampa Review,* 33/34, 2007, pages 19–27; "Runaway Bus," in *Portland Monthly,* January 2006. "Runaway Daughter" was included in the anthology *I Wanna Be Sedated,* published by Seal Press, March 2005. And a segment related to this book was broadcast on *This American Life,* Chicago Public Radio, March 29, 2002.

For my daughters

Prologue

THE GIRL NEXT TO ME ON THE PORTLAND CITY BUS IS bone thin and has mouse-brown hair. Her crooked horn-rimmed glasses—the temple on my side held together with oily Scotch tape—hang at the end of her nose. The coat she's wearing is two sizes too big, three sizes, so she's rolled the sleeves halfway up her arms and she's using ragged fingernails to pick at an exposed knob of wrist. I'm guessing she's sixteen years old, give or take a year, and I know she's coming off a drunk. Either that or a bad high. She's got sallow skin, half-shut eyes, hunched shoulders—but mostly it's her smell. When I lowered myself onto the vinyl seat next to her, I got the first whiff, the air around her so pungent it tasted of drugs and booze and smokes and daze. The dried-urine, stale-ashtray stench of a binge.

I turn away and glance around the crowded bus. Is anyone else troubled, disgusted even, by this girl, this child, and her obvious downfall? It's twilight outside, and the others squeezed in the seats and aisles are only pointed home, lost in themselves, not noticing the girl next to me huddled in her soiled parka tent. But I notice. I take in every detail; I fume over my bad luck at getting stuck next to her. I slide to the far edge of my seat and try not to glance in her direction.

And there, staring out the window across the aisle, I start to wonder about myself. About my suddenly prickled skin and hands knotted in my lap. Why am I revolted by everything about this girl:

her puffs of shallow breath, the scab she's opened on her arm that's now steak red and glistening, the white crust that formed on her lips while she slept in a train station chair or a building's frigid alcove?

Of course I know why. Of course this stranger has stirred memories of my daughters when they were no more than sixteen and fourteen years old. My own girls, who'd show up at home looking and smelling something like this on the days they bothered to show up at all. The child I'm sitting by has also reminded me of something else I don't like to think about: the mother I was back then who couldn't manage the trouble that had landed on my family.

It's been ten years since Amanda and Stephanie stopped going to school, stopped coming home; a whole decade since they joined those on the street who gave them access to beer, dope, tattoo ink, every circus shade of Manic Panic hair dye, metal spikes, and the best corners for getting money from strangers—*spanging*, they called it. I've let myself believe the passage of time and my daughters' turns for the good have washed me clean of most old aches and pains, but then I get ambushed: by the girl next to me and others like her at bus stops and on street corners and sleeping on benches in the hallways of the university where I work. When I see such kids, when I get up close, I'm inevitably shoved back into my daughters' old life and into mine, and right up against the question that can't seem to leave me alone: why?

When my daughters got tired of having their mother search for them on the streets of Eugene, Oregon, and then drag them home again, where we'd scrap and yell and accuse and blame, they jumped a freight train to Portland, two hours straight north up the West Coast. I found out they were in that bigger city a few days after they'd left—friends had spotted them panhandling in the downtown Pioneer Courthouse Square. I drove a hundred miles north to look for Amanda and Stephanie in the nooks and crannies of a strange town; the lack of a single sign of them sent me back home. Years later, the girls told me they'd heard I'd been asking for them, heard I'd stopped at youth shelters and the police station with their photographs. So they'd hopped another train to get farther away, this one to the Tenderloin District in San Francisco, where the drugs were meaner and the cold wind off the bay drove them to accept about any comfort. My daughters had disappeared.

Amanda was gone for three months; I didn't see Stephanie for a year. For nearly a decade, I thought I wanted to forget everything about that empty expanse of time. But those kinds of memories don't just get wiped out, they don't get swept away. Instead, now I find I must wander through the worst of it again—where my daughters went, what they did. How I, every day, handled or failed to handle their absence. I have to face it, although until recently our past has felt too thick, too dense, and, somewhere at its heart, too implicating of me.

I've been wary of getting on a bus in Portland, or in any town, and sitting next to a girl like this, with her familiar odor, someone who can yank me backward and who can fill my throat with sour heat before I have a chance to steel myself against memory's rush. The girl who's now made me take a look at myself: Where is even the smallest surge of concern for her? Why do I feel more like slapping than hugging her? What's wrong with me, still, after all this time?

I'd like to be one of those women who can confront the past's reminders—like this young seatmate—with nothing but compassion. But apparently, I'm not there yet. Something tangled and sore remains unsolved in me. After years of trying to decode and dissect our history, of picking over episodes with my daughters (a fight over a concert, a note found under one of their beds, the nights and nights and nights they didn't come home), and crawling through the muck again to discover the origins and escalations of our troubles, I want to move on. I want to forgive—Amanda, Stephanie, myself, the times we lived in—so we can stop looking backward.

Now the girl on the bus sits up straighter, pulls a wrinkled plastic bag from between her feet. I'm relieved by these getting-ready-to-disembark moves. She'll go away and I'll calm down. I'll get off near my cozy home with its stocked fridge and good music. Except it's not going to be that simple; when I stand to let her by, grabbing a silver pole to stay steady, she looks straight at me. "Could you spare a couple dollars?" she asks, pushing the glasses closer to her face. "For something to eat?"

I'm about to say *no* into her cloud of bitter breath, but my right hand has another idea—it begins reaching for the wallet buried in my purse. And why not? Maybe giving this girl money is a flinch, a gesture in the direction of peace. A reconciliation with the turmoil still inside me. Then I remember how I've long railed against those who gave my daughters everything they needed to stay on the streets—blankets, pizza, sandwiches, drugs, alcohol, tampons, medicine, a bed for the night, and money. My daughters stuck their hands out, coins and bills landed in their palms, and that was one more day they didn't have to come home.

Murky as I am about the giving or not giving, I shake my head in refusal, a nearly invisible movement. With her own small shrug, she clambers off. The bus rumbles ahead again. That's the end of it, I think, though I can't help looking out the window, straining to see her one more time. She's gone. Disappeared that fast. I turn back to press my fingers against a rib that tends to devil ache at moments like this. It's a pain that reminds me of memory's snarl and its potency. The pain reminds me, again, how sometimes the past simply refuses to be finished.

One late autumn night a few weeks after the freight train dropped her in San Francisco, my fourteen-year-old daughter Stephanie wandered in the Tenderloin District. It was 1996. She was by herself except for the puppy following her on a rope leash. She had on a tank top, worn through, and a pair of double-kneed Carhartt's that were dirty from the train yard and dirty from the train she'd ridden in. She also wore a stained orange necklace, a string of about twenty pointed teeth she'd pried from the jaws of dead nutria, a strange cousin of the beaver that tended to get smashed nearly flat on the rails that ran along the Willamette River. High on whatever was smoked and handed out that night in the Tenderloin and on too many forty-ounce cans of beer, Stephanie staggered through clusters of the stoned and drunk—people who inhabited this corner of the city after dark. The crack cocaine users were out in the public square—a crackhead fair, I'd hear her call it years later. They'd spread ratty blankets on the concrete plaza near the library and lay out broken watches, bottle caps, toys dropped from tourists' baby strollers, parts of toilet-paper dispensers stolen from department-store bathrooms. Shiny things, she said, as if deposited there by crows.

Stephanie stumbled to one of these displays glowing under a streetlight and squatted to the ground to have a look. She reached over to pick up a metal box, thinking that she'd trade the crackhead for the out-of-fuel yellow lighter in her pocket, but the second she lifted the box off the blanket, rolling it from her fingers to her palm, its owner leaped out of the shadows with a bowie knife in his hand. He yelled at her to get away. He ran toward her, shouting, scattering his stuff as he slipped and slid to get to her. Stephanie dropped the box and was up fast, but the knife was already pointed at her chest. She jumped back as he took a swipe. A line of blood popped up on the inside of her skinny arm, the one she'd raised to protect herself, four or five straight inches. Stephanie watched the cut drip blood as she turned from him and hurried through the hazy crowd toward her friends, the puppy under her good arm. She made her way to her older sister, Amanda, who'd stayed with the group my girls had hooked up with after they'd left our house in Oregon, a group they called travelers. Travelers who followed certain music (punk, grunge, Johnny Cash) and certain weather (sunny days, tolerable nights), and certain drugs, getting from one city to another on rumbling freight trains.

"You need stitches," one guy said when Stephanie slumped down into the circle of friends who were wrapped in cheap blankets, caked with dirt, surrounded by smoke.

"No way," Stephanie insisted. "They'd want my name." And that was that.

Someone had loose cloth, a ripped shirt or an old sock. He tore it up and cinched it around Stephanie's bloody arm and handed her another beer, another forty, to ease the pain.

When I heard this Tenderloin story, about Stephanie knifed in the square, she and Amanda had been off the streets for two or three years. They were back in school, clean of drugs, getting by. That helped, but I still walked around the house and through our back-yard with this scene from my daughters' past erupting like disease in my mind. I realized (realized again) that too much had hap-pened, that we could never go back to what we'd been before the girls left, even though I had, for so long, harbored the image of an ideal family life that would poof magically into existence once they returned.

But I'm the one who'd rushed my daughters away from our life in Arizona and moved them to Oregon in the wake of a divorce that had felt bitter enough to me and, blind as I was to this at the time, catastrophic to Amanda and Stephanie (they must have picked up on the fact that once the papers were signed, I planned to for-get their father had ever existed). The two of them stopped doing homework, stopped going to classes, began failing math and even English (stunning for girls who often had books in their hands). Okay, I thought then, that's what happens sometimes when fami-lies come undone, fly apart, when parents split up. I figured my old-est daughters—as symbiotic with each other by then as the red and green strands of a DNA illustration in a science book—would get over being steamed and disaffected and distant. They'd learn to live far from their dad. A few simple corrections and we'd be fine again: meetings with teachers and school counselors and the family ther-apy sessions I dragged us to. I insisted on family trips to the coast and dinner at the dining room table. I waited for the phase to pass. But Amanda, followed quickly by her sister, got deep and deeper into the grunge/punk/spikes-and-purple-hair scene in our town, and I couldn't pull them out. Why couldn't I? Because I waited too long to take it seriously? Or because I wouldn't allow myself to believe anything or anybody could take my daughters away, not until they vanished?

Even after Amanda and Stephanie were gone, I pretended with my younger girls that this was a phase, a fit their sisters would get over soon and then come bounding home, looking for food and beds and hot showers. Except eleven-year-old Mary would wake up crying in the middle of the night because rain was driving against our roof and I couldn't promise her that Amanda and Stephanie were warm and safe. Or Mollie's teacher would call to tell me they'd found my fourth-grade daughter crossing the bridge over the highway again because she had to go search for her sisters. That's when I'd realize that the same images that were in my mind filled my younger daughters' minds too. Amanda and Stephanie out there somewhere, asking for money as strangers passed by, eating food pilfered from garbage cans or gathered up at shelters. The drugs whistling through their bodies. The dirty corners they were sleeping in, the trains they were jumping to get from town to town. The railroad security men who beat them with flashlights and chased them with dogs. Where did they go to pee? Where did they find toilet paper or soap or clean underwear or socks without holes? How were they getting by without us, without me—the shelter of our roof and a mother who, though I was worn-out and short-tempered more often than I should have been, wanted more than anything to take care of them?

While they were gone, the other three of us went about a normal life. Or tried to. I'd put another pot of beans on the stove, fold the laundry, help Mary make a costume for Lewis and Clark Days at her school—she and Mollie and I would sit cross-legged on the living room floor wadding and flattening brown grocery bags until the paper was as soft and pliable as leather, and then I would fashion the wrinkled bags into a pseudo-buckskin vest. I'd drive Mollie to gymnastics practice and watch her balance on the beam; stew about my empty bank account; beg the electric company to keep my power on for another few days. I'd get up at first light to make lunches; work eight hours at my job; go to bed after staring out the living room window for an hour, for two hours or three, hoping this might be the night Amanda and Stephanie would come home. Not knowing the hour-to-hour habits of my own children, or how to locate them anytime I wanted to, was beyond what I could comprehend. I was mad at them and mad at me, angrier every time a grocery clerk overcharged me for an avocado or some distracted guy cut me off in traffic. I plodded through the mundane, hung on to my little corner of home, and kept pretending with Mary and Mollie that this would be over soon and we'd be us again.

During this time I grew fond of cuddling with the cold stone in my bed—the boulder I'd conjured that let me feel wronged and betrayed by my own daughters. They had hurt me. They had damaged us. That's what I got to believe as long as they were gone. I couldn't learn to love these girls differently or admit to my own role in our problems if they wouldn't talk to me, if they wouldn't come home. So I remained hard. And they remained hard.

Yet during the months Amanda and Stephanie weren't anywhere around, I also tried to hold my daughters in suspension, the same ploy I use to stay awake on an airplane, afraid the plane will fall if, even for a second, I quit willing it to stay in the air. I hung my daughters somewhere like billowy clothes on a line. Safe, untouched, and clean. Sometimes Amanda (though never Stephanie) called me, and my mind allowed this daughter to exist in a phone booth for the minutes it took her to say "We're okay." And then "Nowhere" to my "Where are you?" And "No, Mom" to my "Please come home." The second she hung up the phone, I put Amanda in that suspended state again. With Stephanie. Up where they couldn't get hit or sliced or stabbed or raped or killed. Up in the heavens, in the air, in the heavy autumn mist that fell over our valley. Someplace my daughters could stay whole.

LIVE THROUGH THIS

1

AMANDA WAS CUTTING HERSELF.

The five of us at a picnic at the riverfront park in Eugene on a Sunday afternoon when Amanda was fourteen and Stephanie twelve, the younger girls nine and seven, three years after my marriage to their father had ended. Mollie was showing me how many times she could cross the monkey bars without resting—without the briefest stop at either end to ease any strain on her arms. She went back and forth, her hands a bright pink, her too-long bangs hung up in her eyelashes, her lips a straight, determined line. I followed her, sidestepping over layers of prickly tree bark put down to cushion falls, keeping my arms scooped under my youngest daughter, sure that her muscled shoulders would give out and that her fingers would slip. But they didn't. She powered along, jutting her hips and kicking her legs to help her grab one bar after the other.

Mary was on a nearby swing, pumping hard, toes aimed toward some perfect weekend clouds. After Mollie jumped down, satisfied by her display of monkey-bar prowess, she ran to the swing next to Mary's and was in an instant competition to see who could go higher. I walked across the sandpit, over the remnants of our chicken and potato salad meal on a blanket laid out on the grass, and toward the bench where my two oldest daughters sat glued together, the hoods of their black sweatshirts pulled up, hiding their faces. Concentrated as they were on a patch of skin above Amanda's kneecap, which she'd exposed by rolling up her canvas pants, they didn't notice me coming. A few steps away, I caught a glint of what Amanda had in her hand—an unbent paper clip, which she was using to carve into her leg, deep enough that beads of blood bobbed on the surface of her skin.

"What the hell?" I said, swooping in to grab the thin piece of metal but missing.

Stephanie looked up at me with black-lined eyes, ghoulish eyes, while Amanda hurried to roll down her pants as she tossed the paper clip in the grass. "What are you doing?" I said.

"Nothing," Amanda said, pulling herself deeper into her hood, into her sweatshirt, and into the shaded back of the bench.

I wanted to believe her. I wanted to believe it was nothing. I would have liked to keep thinking it was no big deal when I spotted long, scabby lines on the inside of her forearm a few days later. I wanted to convince myself that this slicing of skin wasn't a sign of danger even after I'd dragged her to a therapist to talk about why she cut and cut and kept cutting. I sat in the tiny waiting room and fake-read *Architectural Digest,* stewing about what Amanda was saying to the middle-aged woman with expensive shoes and gleaming teeth. Complaining about me, that I had hardly any time for her, that I was often impatient? Or worse: saying she wanted to live with her father? I couldn't stand for her to want that.

After nearly an hour, the counselor called me in and had Amanda wait this time with the pile of tedious magazines. "It's not dangerous," the woman told me, her soft hand flitting through the air between us. "It's just something girls do when life feels too painful and something has to be released. Think of it like that, a release."

I might have eased into this line of reasoning, assuring myself that a little bit of cutting was getting the devil out of my angry daughter, but it didn't make sense. Amanda was getting more sullen the more she sliced her own skin and spilled her own blood, becoming a faint and frightening presence in our household—dark and sultry as a storm just over the mountain. I knew the cutting was more than a release. And yet I didn't seek out another therapist, another expert, who might give me a different opinion or offer a solution. I simply told myself that my daughter would get past this soon. Then it was too late.

The questions that crowded my mind: Why was Amanda so angry? What had pushed her into a black corner that she couldn't or wouldn't emerge from? And why had Stephanie become her constant sidekick, her doppelgänger, giving up her own friends and perfect report cards and the gushing praise of her teachers to join her sister's budding rebellion?

Part of my daughters' fury and consternation stemmed from my divorce from their father, Tom, who'd remained in Arizona when the rest of us moved to Oregon. On the phone and, during the girls' visits to his house, in person, he often reminded them that *I'd* left *him*, that he'd wanted to work things out, keep the family together, but that the mother of the family had smashed the family apart. I could see on Amanda's and Stephanie's faces how hard it was: they loved their mom but at the same time hated me for hurting their dad. A quandary they couldn't work out. Easier to back away, get isolated, stay isolated.

Again, the accounting. Another nail of self-recrimination pounded in as I scramble for do-overs, the way I used to when I was a kid playing Horse in the driveway with my brother, who was the far better shot. I comb through what I could have done differently: this path instead of that path; these words instead of those words. How could I have moved away so soon, away from their father and to a town where I had not a single acquaintance? I shouldn't have taken a second job after we arrived in Eugene. I should have been less proud about asking for help. And yet what I did, I did. Worried myself sleepless trying to prove I could manage without their father and plowed ahead without measuring or assessing the damage behind us. During these first months, years, after the divorce, the strain across my face and in my voice and the weariness in my body must have upset all four of my children. Other parents have a way, it seems, of conveying that *This stress you see in me has nothing to do with you.* But in the early days after my divorce, I sent signals I didn't mean: that I was too depleted to fully love my daughters; that they had become a burden to single-mother me. That it was their responsibility to keep me upright and soothed. And, after such tension had eroded us for too long, maybe even that running away was the only thing left to do.

Amanda and Stephanie remembered their parents' marriage better than the younger girls did, and they longed for the family of six—for their father—years after the two of us were finished with each other. Stephanie wrapped Tom's picture in the soft clothes of her underwear drawer. Amanda wore one of his old college T-shirts to bed. I loathed my ex-husband for promising to call the girls and then forgetting; I hated him for using the calls he did make to complain that I'd robbed him of his children, even though he'd made no move to stop me from going and in fact had agreed that Oregon was a good place for them to grow up. I condemned him for coaxing our girls to side with him, while I somehow ignored the fact that I was doing the same: to speak about him in our house brought a stern look from me; their mentioning his name caused me to grow stiff and silent. I waged my own campaign to win the girls' loyalty—mostly I pushed them to see the five of us as family and him as interloper. When he remarried and had another child and withdrew further from his first four daughters, well, that fit my projections nicely. And, lost in my own transformation to single woman, I missed my children's heartache over being shoved to the periphery, hardly noticed by their dad.

In the last months of the marriage, in Tucson, I kept the girls busy enough that they didn't notice (I told myself) the first dust and crumble of the coming dissolution. Starting with Amanda. One Saturday that spring, she, ten years old then, and I stood in a long, hot line in a parking lot outside a downtown performance hall; black asphalt stuck to the bottoms of my sandals and the day's heat frying a hole in the top of my head. I'd read in the paper a few days earlier that a traveling acting company from New York was coming to town to put on eight days of performances of *Annie,* and they were looking for local girls to play the orphans. I'd talked Amanda into trying out, since she'd always wanted to be in a play; it had seemed like a great idea until we were sixty-seventh in line for the audition and I realized I had three hungry kids at home with a father who often forgot about lunch and about checking regularly on the whereabouts of the younger ones. Besides, every dressed-up-pretty and sweetly curled child in Tucson, most of whom held professional glossy photos and blue folders of sheet music, twittered around us. I'd dragged my daughter into something that could end up embarrassing her—that was my worry. I should have figured out that Amanda herself was ambivalent about getting into the play, and that part of her buoyant pleasure at the moment was simply this chance to spend time alone with me without a sister or two along. A whole afternoon. (I'd often promise myself that I'd make time for each daughter alone—a lunch, a walk, a shopping trip—but then I'd quickly revert into my old pattern of taking the whole set of them, or at least half, to whatever function we had to attend or on some errand or grocery trip.) I'd tucked away in my purse the two snapshots of Amanda that we'd taken in the backyard, and I reached over now and then to clean dirt off the bottom of her chin with my shirt. That morning, before we'd left, she and Stephanie had crawled around in our big cactus garden, as they often did, searching for scorpions and spiders. Amanda hadn't swept the mud off her knees or pulled all the twigs from her hair. But no matter. I took another swig of water and passed the bottle on to her, draping my arm across her bony shoulders. We'd get inside, Amanda would sing her audition song, the people in charge would thank her for coming, I'd tell her how proud I was of her for trying, and we'd go home.

But Amanda made the first cut. And the next cut, that evening, nine hours after we'd arrived. The third came Sunday afternoon: she was in the final group of almost-orphans. Late Sunday night, I was drying the last of our dinner dishes when Tom picked up the ringing phone. I could tell by his grin, his flash of glee in my direction, that Amanda had made it. He hung up to tell me that she'd been cast in the role of Pepper, the rascally, tomboyish, ill-

5

tempered orphan, the one most longing for love and acceptance who hid her quivering need behind a scowl.

I don't know how much my daughters had sensed by that soft April night about the slow dismantling of their parents' marriage, which we'd not yet spoken to them about but which was in every molecule of air between us. I pushed away the issue constantly on my mind, to leave him or to stay, as Tom and I climbed the stairs to wake Amanda. We sat on either side of her twin bed to tell her the news about the play, Stephanie resting on her elbow in the other bed to listen in. I remember the glow on Amanda's face and Stephanie's shriek as she leaped over my lap to crawl under her sister's covers. The four of us squeezed together in celebration of this strange acting thing that would soon pull our daughter into its center. The break soon to come—Tom's and mine—wasn't part of anything that night. All of us realized that the months of rehearsals and costume fittings and cast parties, and then the eight-night run of a show that would put Amanda in front of three thousand people at a time, were going to bind us like nothing had for a long time. For me, it was a temporary fix, the marriage too far gone by then, but now I understand: every day Amanda clung to the show as a way to save her family.

The evening of the final performance that warm summer, with Amanda in her lemon yellow dress and black saddle shoes, cheeks pink from makeup and with the flush of this night's fame, signing autographs in the greenroom where Mary and Mollie slept on our pile of coats under a table topped with ice sculptures and bowls of cold prawns—I saw it then. The firm line of her jaw and the taut muscles of her neck. The all-engulfing run of performances was over. Done. Now her sisters would stop the hundred-times-a-day rendition of the "Hard-Knock Life" dance and the "You're Never Fully Dressed without a Smile" song. Now her parents wouldn't have this daughterly activity around which to be united. *Annie* was finished and we were finished.

The August night Tom and I sat in the living room of the house where we all still lived together to tell our daughters about "the

6

separation," not yet "the divorce," Amanda was the one most wiped out by the news and flattened by what she, more than others, had known was coming. It was Stephanie who actually cried the hardest and the longest, though, wailing as she could as a child, a sound to pierce the heart, and holding her father's arm as if he'd float away if she let him go. Just out of the shower, Stephanie had a blue towel wrapped around her shoulders, her arms and legs the warm color of cinnamon popping out from a terry-cloth robe. Her long blond hair dripped down her back. The second I'd said the words—*Dad and I are going to live apart*—to our daughters, who were scattered around the room, Stephanie had flown to Tom's lap and stayed there, her arms gripping the towel to her chest, her lips and face wilting. When I said, *We're going to live in different houses, but you'll see both of us as much as you want,* Amanda turned her face to the horsehair couch's scratchy fabric and refused to turn back. Mary and Mollie were six and four years old. They pressed themselves into my lap, crying too, dampening the front of my shirt, though I could tell neither knew what was happening except that a sadness had washed through their family like the flash floods from monsoon rain that filled the arroyos at their father's family ranch in the hills above the city.

I'd said what had to be said. I held Mollie to my chest with one hand and rubbed Mary's back with the other, waiting for the sobbing around me to pass. I couldn't afford to enter this weeping with the rest of my family. Someone needed to get the little ones to bed, finish the dishes, fold the laundry. Move on. Suck it up, get going, don't look back. I had no idea how to make this change, this reconfiguration of my daughters' lives, better for them. Since I couldn't make it hurt less, I made myself still and silent and withdrawn.

Then Stephanie's nose started to bleed. First a bulb of red at one nostril, then a gush from both. I stood up, leaving the little girls on the seat without me, and stepped to the edge of Tom's chair. He'd tipped Stephanie's head back and held the bridge of her nose; his neck and the front of his shirt were covered by a bloom of blood. His bloody hand stuck to her bloody cheek.

"I'll get a washcloth," I said and rushed down the narrow hall to our one bathroom at the back of the house. Once in the little space, I stopped rushing. Without flipping on the overhead light, I turned on the sink's tap and laid a square washcloth in the cool dip of the basin and sat on the toilet to watch the water soak into the green cotton fabric. From the other end of the hall, I heard Tom's mutterings to the girls, though not his words. I stretched out my leg and nudged the door closed so I'd hear nothing at all.

Balanced there with my knees against the edge of the tub, I thought about a dinner we'd had at Tom's family ranch, forty miles into the Catalinas, a few weeks earlier. As we'd passed platters of enchiladas and bowls of black beans and rice around the table, Tom's mother had—out of nowhere, if I remember—told us a story about her husband arriving home hours late one evening from his work as an engineer. She was irate, she said, about having been left with the evening chores for their children, several saucy teenage girls and three wild, uncontainable boys.

It turned out that her husband and a few friends from work had stopped at a carnival in one of the small towns they'd traveled to that day, and while they were walking among the neon-lit rides and game booths, my husband's father gave in to a whim—he stepped behind a curtain and let a palm reader tell his future. Once home with his wife, he sat on the living room sofa and, under soft lamplight, showed her the lifeline that the fortuneteller had suggested was shorter than most. There wouldn't be all that much time left, the woman had told him. He should live it up. He'd pulled his hand back from his wife's and laughed at the story, standing up to pour his evening toddy. But my mother-in-law hadn't taken it as a joke. Thirty years later, fork in hand at our family dinner, she trembled a little over the memory of that long-ago conversation with her husband. She took a sip of her wine and gave me a long stare. Or I felt her stare was directed at me, anyway—that night, I probably couldn't have imagined it pointed anywhere else. I sat at the far end of the table with Mary in my lap—my six-year-old's earache (which she heard back then as *ear-egg* and couldn't understand why I didn't reach in and pull out the offending egg) had made her feverish and fussy, her heat pouring into my chest. Now my own

8

face turned red. Tom's family had, no doubt, picked up on my un-happiness, which I'd made quite a show of that night with drooped shoulders and something of an overproduction in the care of my sick child.

At the table, Tom's mother went on with the story about her husband's palm. She said that every time she'd felt fed up with him —the man who'd died suddenly of a heart attack in his early seven-ties—during the five decades they spent as a couple, she'd remem-bered that short lifeline and forgave him.

An hour later, I sat on the closed toilet lid in the upstairs bath-room of my mother-in-law's house with Mary still in my lap. I was taking her temperature—my excuse for stepping away from the dinner and from my drunk husband, who'd already pulled one of his favorite late-night family stunts. Just after dinner, and more wine, he'd jumped on his chair and stripped down to nothing, then leaped off the seat, leaving a rumpled pile of jeans and shirt and boxer shorts, to run white-bare-assed through the living room, out the front door, and into the pool while his sisters and brothers scattered chairs across the tile floor and tittered with laughter and while the group of child cousins who'd been playing in front of the fireplace, our daughters included, stopped what they were doing and watched, stock-still and stunned. We moved from the table, the group of us, though I straggled behind the others with Mary in my arms and Mollie wrapped around one leg. The adults and the children all peered out the giant picture windows in the living room that faced the unlit swimming pool, trying to see Tom rise and fall through the dark water. A sister-in-law, the oldest, wan-dered in close to me, as if to challenge my moodiness. "Isn't he just so much fun?" she said into my neck.

I closed my eyes, wondering why I felt no joy about my husband anymore, no surge of humor over his boyishness and revelry. I'd known he was this way since the day I met him—but at that mo-ment I resented the hell out of Tom for the one attribute I was al-ways claiming I wanted more of from him: consistency.

In the bathroom, the thermometer sagged at the corner of my daughter's pink mouth. I held it to make sure it stayed inside her gums and under her tongue. Mary's eyes were closed and her cheek rested against my sweat-soaked arm. A minute later, I pulled it out —101 degrees. Now I could insist we go home. I could load her up with baby Tylenol and wrap her in blankets, pack the car with the rest of our kids and our things, and leave this ranch—Tom's most beloved place, where he could be as wild as he desired—behind.

I recapped the thermometer and set it on the countertop, but before I got up, I readjusted my daughter so I could take a quick look at the flat terrain of my hand. I held my right palm still beneath the bathroom light. I knew my mother-in-law's story was supposed to have stirred in me compassion for my husband, but it was my own skin I peered at. My outstretched palm had a series of intersections and grids and crevices, its own mysterious geography; I looked for the lifeline, whichever one that was. I was thirty-three years old and figured in this moment that if a prophetic indentation in my skin suggested I had decades and decades to live, maybe I should force a few more years of making do with my marriage for our children's sake. Except maybe the short line in the middle, the one starting between my first two fingers and swooping below my pinkie, was telling me to hurry up and get out before I'd damned near wasted my life.

Two weeks after that dinner, and two weeks after telling Tom on the way home that I couldn't stay with him any longer, I sat alone in the dark bathroom at the end of our own house, watching the water in the sink run over the washcloth, afraid to face my own kids. I didn't want to go back into the living room, where they would stare at me, wondering why I'd done this—why I'd announced the split from their dad and caused the breakup of our family. When the water was about to run over the sink, I shut it off and used the wrung-out cloth to make a quick rub of my own face, around my eyes, under my chin, across my dry lips. I rinsed and squeezed the cloth again, then I turned and opened the door. I would have spent the night, a couple of nights, in that bathroom if I'd thought I could avoid the consequences of what earlier that evening had felt like my only choice—telling the girls I was leaving their father.

Blood equals hurry. When mothers see their children bleed, they rush to help. And though every other time my daughters had bled I'd scurried to fix them, the last thing I could do this evening was hustle. I didn't want my daughters to be anguished because of me, to be angry or confused because of me—but they were. I moved through the hallway back to the living room, wondering if they'd all be bleeding because of what I'd done. Red on the chairs and red on the old sofa and stains on the brown oak floor.

But when I stood at Tom's seat again I saw that Stephanie's crying had turned into hiccups and the blood on her cheeks was already becoming crusty. The coppery smell no longer rose from her skin. I handed Tom the cloth and he touched it to her neck, though Stephanie buried her face into the side of his shirt so she could avoid looking at me. My husband did look, though; straight at me, his own moist eyes meeting my dry ones. "I don't get it," he said. "I really don't." He shook his head, staring at me. "When did you get so cold?"

Tom and I had met in college—when I was a sophomore and he was a junior. I considered him a wildly mysterious set of contradictions, not yet realizing that contradiction was actually my own disguise at the time. My name was on the dean's list, and I studied for hours each night in the student union building's smoking section. I was vice president for mental advancement for one of my clubs. I chain-smoked Marlboro cigarettes and loaded myself with ten-cent cups of coffee, eating maple bars for dinner while writing about the sod images in *My Ántonia*. But sometime around eleven, when the student union closed, I'd make my way to a bar where the English majors congregated and where for long stretches I drank too much beer and became overly boisterous and flirty, and we all tried to impress one another with talk of books and writers and by reciting "Thanatopsis" by heart. I drank and drank some more, blushing at attention from boys I believed were too smart, too good, for me, and yet tipping in to press against one or another's shoulder for a few seconds, getting close enough that he could smell the dark hollow of my neck.

When I heard about Tom, I suddenly wanted his attention too —wanted it a lot—though for reasons I couldn't decipher. I'd been warned about his antics, the bottle of whiskey he often carried in the pocket of his down vest, and the chewing tobacco he'd sometimes squirt through his front teeth, making a liquid brown arc that would land near others' feet. One day, after hearing about how he'd been arrested again, this time for trying to climb the brick and ivy walls of the administration building to break the minute hand off the giant clock—and falling into the bushes below—I decided I had to meet this guy who had such nerve and could demonstrate such badness. I had to find out why he didn't care about disappointing parents or professors or university administrators, how he did only what he wanted anytime he wanted to do it.

I waited by his baby blue 1960s Ford pickup truck until he came out of the house he lived in, and I started up a conversation with him about nothing. We ended up sitting on the wheel wells in the bed of the pickup for five or six hours, talking. His voice, I remember, was soft. Shy even. He was tall and thin, wore dirty Levi's and a pair of scuffed cowboy boots. His two front teeth were marked with small brown squiggles that I'd later learn were caused by fluoride. That first afternoon, those teeth stains were another sign of his vulnerability, instantly making me want to take care of him and allowing me to form in my mind a defense of what I'd decided that day was his misjudged character.

After that, I was known as his defender and he was known as my boyfriend. That is, others started calling him that because it was common knowledge that we were sleeping together, and after some months I began calling him my boyfriend too, though it wasn't a label or relationship he wanted. The weekend after I graduated, three years after we'd met, we got married because I'd convinced Tom this was the natural next step, the right thing to do now that we were college educated and had entered adulthood. Besides, my own parents, married practically as children and now in the middle of a divorce, were each calling me regularly to complain about the other. I couldn't imagine a better way to slip from the grip of their unhappiness than to make a tidy little family of my own.

During our college romance, Tom and I didn't go out to dinners or movies, we didn't imagine a future with a mortgage and a station wagon and towheaded babies—instead, on a Saturday night he might knock on the dorm window some hours after the bars closed, waking the other girls, who'd bark at me to get rid of him. I'd yank on my sweatpants and a T-shirt and meet him in the alley. Throwing his arm around my shoulder, he'd sip the last of a pint of Wild Turkey out of a paper bag or smoke a joint as we walked back to his house, the metal edges of his boot heels sparking off the sidewalk. Those nights, we had sex in his small, musky room, Willie Nelson's *Red Headed Stranger* the soundtrack, Tom's whiskey breath hot in my hair. Sometime before dawn I'd sneak back to my own place, hoping no one would notice any evidence of what I liked to think was a secret life. Of course they did; girls reporting to other girls that I was not the straight-and-narrow student I pretended to be, going to my Phi Beta Kappa meetings every third Thursday and my Mortar Board meetings each first Tuesday, delighting my parents and my teachers and the foundation officer who wrote out my scholarship check. I couldn't stop seeing this boy. I couldn't tell him to leave me alone or even to take me out to a restaurant like a real boyfriend. I couldn't convince myself that I should have a plan for the years ahead. Instead, late at night I waited for a sign from him that he wanted me, that I was wantable by someone who wanted nothing. He'd drawn no lines limiting what he did or to whom he did it, a freedom I couldn't even imagine but could try to absorb from him when he was around. This resolve of mine to be with him was beyond my understanding then, only slightly less fuzzy now. For some reason, he was the mystery—horrible and exciting at once—that made me feel most alive.

As these college years went on, I refused to admit what was obvious to everyone else: Tom and I were a lousy match. I waited jumpily for him to call, to come by. He drove around in his old blue truck, the bed full of whiskey bottles and straw bales. He pulled all-nighters to barely pass classes he'd ignored all semester, somehow getting assignments done in the very nick of time. Just before

13

he graduated, he was arrested again for driving on downtown side-walks and for smashing beer bottles on a college building's stoop.

After that last one, Tom phoned to ask me to visit him in the county jail. Without telling my friends where I was going, I rode the bus to the distant side of town, underwent a search of my purse and pockets, then stood behind the glass that separated visitor from inmate, my back resting against a wall of exposed brick. I hadn't known what to expect—but this visit already was no fun, no good, not even fodder for a story I'd want to tell my English-major pals later. I shivered. I didn't know why I was there; I didn't belong. Did I belong? Later I'd believe that this period at jail was my penance, my sentence—or at least one last piece of glaring evidence—for failing to listen to the side of myself that knew our union was no good.

At the jail, Tom, skinny, pale, jumpy, someone I didn't particu-larly want to be connected to but to whom I was irrevocably con-nected by then, like it or not, told me they'd just eaten hamburgers and freshly cut fried potatoes, and that he'd made friends with the other men even though they gave him crap about being a college boy. He pulled down his pants to show me his jail-issued under-wear, stamped with a thick black number across the rear, while I looked out the sunny window and over the rolling fields of golden wheat trying to pretend I didn't know him.

When he wasn't in trouble, or when his wealthy father wasn't making calls to keep him out of trouble, Tom was bored. Bored, he'd jump on a train. I'd realize I hadn't seen him around for two or three days and then I'd know he'd gone to the rail yard with alu-minum-foil-wrapped potatoes in his pocket and a pint of whiskey in his pants. He'd hop a freight car. He knew the regulars, hoboes who emerged from the train smoke as if from a Waylon Jennings ballad, and together they'd ride to Montana or Washington State, sleeping under bridges at night and cooking the potatoes in small fires for dinner. Or so he told me. And maybe later told Amanda and Stephanie. Somehow, anyway, they became aware of the allure of their father's train-jumping past.

At the end of my senior year I was busy panicking about graduation, about leaving the campus, the town, where I'd had the kind of contained success I could recognize. A safe, predictable success. But then my Romantic poetry teacher handed back a major exam on which I had earned a B–, my lowest grade in the past several years, and that knocked me out of the running for the golden cords worn at graduation by the most accomplished students. I stumbled to my apartment, humiliated by this dash of failure in an academic environment I'd believed would never fail me. I pledged to avoid anything that could make me feel that way again. I talked myself into focusing on our wedding, which was planned for the week after graduation. On the pretty bridesmaids and the abundance of roses and gardenias. I sat in my little apartment with my face resting on the cover of *Riverside Shakespeare* and told myself that marriage was good and right and that I must now enter it.

Twelve years after that wedding day—a parade of pastel-gowned girls and tuxedoed boys that my mother had executed to perfection, followed by a feast of salmon and champagne I couldn't eat or drink because I was newly pregnant and queasy—I moved my children and myself out of our Tucson house and into an apartment nearby that was mine and not Tom's. In that decade-plus of matrimony, I'd gotten what I'd thought I wanted. Tom had gone to work and soon enough started a business of his own. We took our pink-clad girls to church, where we taught the seventh-grade Sunday school class. We made hordes of young-parent friends and often crammed them into whatever Craftsman house we were fixing up at the time for wine cocktails and baby spinach quiches. Tom still liked to wander down the street to smoke pot at his friend Pete's house rather than help me get the girls bathed and put to bed, but that was no big deal. I fought with him about chores for the sake of fighting, but I secretly wanted to be in charge of the sweeping and cleaning and child-tending, and usually redid any of his domestic efforts anyway. What upset me more were the times I'd come home to find him building a bonfire in our suburban backyard, our hyped-up and ash-covered daughters throwing scrap wood onto the flames. Or hammering another tree house into the big maple, a structure the electric company later tore down after chewing me out for posing a danger to the neighborhood kids. The wildness that flared in Tom was milder, yes, and not as threatening as it had been in college—I knew for sure that it no longer thrilled me. Now his rebel self, when it emerged, was irritating. I was irritated at him and he at me, and it wasn't long before the girls noticed our divide: a mother who wanted to play it safe, and a father who thrived on danger.

Before Tom and I got married, we'd borrowed my father's Audi sedan and drove to Arizona so I could meet Tom's family and get the first long gander at the utopian ranch he talked about endlessly. He'd promised me we'd hunt for scorpions with a black light in the cracks of the exterior adobe and in the interior closets in the house and take hikes around rattlesnake dens while skirting the inch-long thorns on the cat-claw bushes. About three o'clock one morning during that trip, when we'd just crossed the Arizona border, Tom pulled the car over to pee. We'd reached the deep, broad, and very white bowl of the Hoover Dam, gleaming like a giant skater's park on the mountaintop. I got out of the car to stretch and watched as my boyfriend hopped onto one of the retaining walls then scrambled to the top of one of the highest barriers, teetering there at the edge of a maybe six-hundred-foot fall to the bottom. I didn't move. I didn't cry out or shout or even breathe, worried that even the slightest air out of my mouth would be wind enough to topple him from the skinny perch and frantic already about whom I'd call after he fell. Weaving and bobbing, Tom unzipped his jeans and a second later sent an arc of yellow urine—glittering a bit under the towering mercury vapor lamps—into the scoop of the dam.

It occurs to me now to make this episode a pronounced emblem of our marriage. Tom on the edge, whatever edge, while I'm standing back, cautious and often very afraid. As our girls were growing up, he'd often say, "Don't listen to her—she's scared of everything," to my "Back up, you're too close," to my "Leave it alone, it's too dangerous." Repeated and repeated. We had hardly any interest in common, nothing to say to each other except for the distracting chatter about our daughters, how funny they were and how cute.

And now I understand: soon after Amanda's birth Tom started to become irrelevant to me, each subsequent child made him matter less. I had daughters to love, to mold, to adore, to bring through childhood as I wanted. This boy-man's antics were in my way.

As for Tom, he didn't like that I was gone so much after Mollie had finished nursing and I had begun to take classes and get into some paid work of my own. Mostly he didn't like that I had new friends who had little to do with him. During this year, the last of our marriage, Tom often fled to the ranch, appearing at home every few days to argue with me again about our lack of money, my lack of concern and care for him. By then, I was done with my husband, done with our nattering fights that had no beginnings or ends but looped one into the other until they were a dissonant buzz around my head. As if the marriage were a fuel-dense forest on fire, my attitude was *let it burn*. It was the dawn of the nineties and I was the cliché of the dawning-nineties woman—sure I could leave my husband and get it all, have it all, whatever "it all" was.

The day I moved us out of our house, I did so in secret. Tom was off at the ranch for the day, and an hour after he'd left, I'd jammed every inch of our van with the girls' belongings and mine. I drove both giddy and scared a few miles toward the bone-dry river and, at the apartment complex, turned into the parking-lot slip—number 6. But before I'd even yanked the car's emergency brake, I spotted him—Tom—sitting on the front porch of my new apartment. I still don't know how he found out where I planned to live, but he had. For a few seconds I stayed in my seat, heat rising into my face and bursting out the top of my head while the air conditioner blew one cold line across my sweaty neck. I yanked the van into reverse, ready to pull out of the spot, ready to drive down the street to find another apartment to rent. I felt my husband's smugness through the metal and windshield of our family's car—if his message was that he could always find me if he wanted to, I got it. And now I had to run again.

Then I remembered the money—the thousands of dollars my parents had given me for the deposit. The landlord had told me that once I'd accepted the keys, the sum was nonrefundable. The money is what got me to turn off the car, to open my door. Even so, I avoided glancing in Tom's direction. I walked around the back of the van instead of the front, slid the side door open, and buried myself in the dark space inside, resting my forehead against the edge of Mollie's car seat until I was ready to move again.

I pulled the biggest box from the interior and carried it in front of me across the overly lush lawn so Tom couldn't see my face. I wanted change to be easy—I wanted him to let it be easy. But there he was, muddying the smooth transition I'd counted on. His body was sprawled over the white, hot concrete steps, keeping me from the front door that was mine. Behind my box shield, I felt him, maybe I smelled him—the familiar scent of his glistening sweat rising in the hot air.

I'd told him that if I lived without him for a while, I'd have distance to think about our marriage and about him and what I could and could not commit to. I told him that if he would get out of my sight, out of my path, out of my way for a few weeks or months then I could find my clear head and work out what was best. But when I set the box on the sidewalk Tom was every bit there, grinning, his elbows resting on the concrete steps and a set of keys dangling from one index finger.

He wore a T-shirt he'd owned since college and a pair of cutoff jeans from which his long legs, coated in a fine layer of blond hair, angled down the stair steps, ending in a worn pair of red flip-flops, one of which he slapped, slapped, slapped against his heel.

"Where'd you get those?" I asked him, pointing to the keys hanging from his finger.

"Easy," he said, squinting in a way that made the crow's-feet around his eyes deepen. He jingled the keys, which had its desired effect—I was even more irate. "I told the manager that I'm the husband."

I reached for the keys but he jerked his hand away. "It's not a bad place," he said, standing up and brushing the dust from the back of his pants. "I left a drawing on the table to show you where to fit the furniture." Shoving my keys in his pocket, he slid on the sunglasses that had been hanging from his shirt's neck and walked past me to his car.

"Don't come back here!" I shouted at him. He smiled, waved, and then he drove away.

I talked the landlord into changing the locks on the doors, but that didn't keep Tom from appearing all the time. There he was in the pool delighting the girls with four new squirt guns when we went out for a swim. There he was parked in my space when my daughters and I arrived in the late afternoon, inviting us out for green-corn tamales and cheese quesadillas. At night, he'd phone me five or six or ten times to ask when I was coming back, when I was going to get over my bad stage, my crisis, my fit of selfishness.

Five days before Halloween in 1991, a few months after my move into the apartment, I drove to the elementary school to pick up nine-year-old Stephanie from basketball practice. I pulled to the curb and slid open the door, and she climbed in over sacks of groceries, past Mollie, who was strapped into the middle seat of our van, past the box of clothes I'd been intending to drop at Goodwill for weeks, and into the far back corner. Stephanie wasn't speaking to me at the moment. During a costume-buying trip the day before, I'd declined to rent her a real cheerleader's uniform for $24.99. Yes, it came with thick pompoms and had a fat blue *S* sewn on the peppy red sweater. And it had a swingy skirt that flashed a blue satin lining when she danced about. But it was $24.99. That was too much when we could throw one together at home that would be just as good, I told her: she already owned a skirt and a too-big red sweater. I could pick up football pompoms at the university's bookstore, and bows for her hair. I was sure, I said, that we could find an old school letter at a thrift shop to sew on the front of her outfit.

Now Stephanie buckled herself into the farthest bench seat back and stared out the window. Amanda had stayed home to play with a friend from the other end of our apartment complex—the first of the girls to enter this new circle of apartment friends—Mary was in the passenger seat next to me, while Mollie sat behind us in her car seat. Stephanie was alone in the far reaches of the van, sighing out her disappointment. "Is that belt on tight?" I said, watching her in the rearview mirror. Another sigh, this one louder.

Fine. I had enough on my mind. I preferred silence over the morning's argument about the costume. Stephanie hated the homemade idea, and Amanda was her champion in dissent. Didn't I know how important it was for Steph to look right when she hit the trick-or-treating with her fourth-grade friends? With everything they were going through, the two girls as a unit told me, the least I could do was make sure Stephanie had the perfect costume.

I drove the school's circular driveway and turned sharp out onto the street, tipping over a couple of grocery sacks. Cheese, toilet paper, a package of hamburger, and apple-strawberry juice boxes tumbled onto the floor. "I want one! I'm thirsty!" Mollie cried when she saw the drinks. I ignored her plea and Stephanie's silence and raced home to get Amanda to afternoon theater rehearsal—off to her new play.

Soon after the girls and I had moved into that apartment several miles from their dad's house—and many weeks post-*Annie*—the same troupe of New York actors came back to town. Their director called Amanda and asked her to be in the new production—*Jesus Christ Superstar*. She spoke on the phone with him for only a minute, giving him a quiet answer of *yes*, as if the theater were a tedious habit now, the fun wrung out of it. Her separated parents, who lived in different houses, would juggle the rehearsal schedules and the performances in which she would play a leper, a child at Jesus's feet, and an angel in the afterlife. Opening night would fall on Halloween.

In the evenings after rehearsals and dinner and homework, Amanda went over her dance steps and songs for the musical, Stephanie a skinny shadow behind her and Mary and Mollie watching from the doorway. The dark and strange un-*Annie* songs sank into the girls' imaginations, and a steady stream of musical questions floated through our house: "What's the buzz?" "Who are you, what have you sacrificed?" "Why'd you let the things you did get so out of hand?"

The play confused Amanda. In *Annie*, right and wrong were cloyingly obvious. But what was Judas, she asked me, a good guy or a bad guy? She brought me a Bible from our bookshelf, asking me to locate the part about the betrayal, the blood money. I rifled through the pages and read a couple passages that seemed to relate while she slunk down next to me and laid her head on my shoulder. "What does it mean?" she said. She couldn't put the Scripture together with the rowdy scenes on stage: Judas wailing in the disco afterlife.

I set the book on the floor and pulled her closer to me. Maybe the play was too sad, I said, running my fingers through her long hair. Maybe it was too big a load of sadness and darkness in the middle of my separation from her dad. "It's not too late to quit," I told her.

She sat up straight and turned to me. "No way," she said. "You can't make me quit."

"I didn't say you had to, only if you want to," I said to her shaking head, her outstretched hands that were pushing me away.

No matter what, she'd stay with it. She was too enchanted by the dazzling Mary Magdalene, who'd promised to help layer on the gray leper makeup and attach the angel halo once performances began. And she couldn't leave Jesus, who gently touched the top of her head every time he passed her on stage.

I was thinking about all this driving back to the apartment after I'd picked up Stephanie. I'd promised cookies for Mollie's preschool class and it was my week to cart Amanda back and forth to the rehearsal hall. Tom's phone calls were coming in a steady stream every night; if I couldn't think about him, he said, then think of our children, who would soon come unglued without both parents in the same house.

In the rear storage section of the van I'd stashed a plastic bag I'd picked up earlier at a friend's house. In it was an orange jump suit, the type made for an industrial cleaning team or a highway flagger. A friend had bought it for me because she and her boyfriend were going to a costume party that night and wanted me to go along; the three of us would dress as Biospherians, the faux scientists who'd been sealed up in a giant glass terrarium outside Tucson the month before. On their 3.2-acre replica of Earth, these orange-clad Biospherians were to spend two years learning to "harness nature," as the PR person told me at the sealing-in festivities. I'd covered the party for *Newsweek,* a job I'd landed only because the magazine's editor had called one of my old journalism professors in a panic and he'd given her my name. The press badge granted me access to the private gathering, to Timothy Leary, to the cast of *Cheers.* That night after the Biospherians were locked in tight, I went back to my apartment, the girls at their father's house for the weekend, and wrote a story that was faxed to New York by midnight. Now my friend wanted to celebrate my first national story—even though my name appeared only at the bottom in six-point italics—at this party. I didn't know if I should, or even could. Still, the idea of a party flooded my mind. Standing in a group of adults, holding a cold beer, talking to people who weren't thinking about how to pay for cheerleader's uniforms and who might want to ask me what it felt like to write for a real magazine. Was that what would make me happy?

Fuming about Stephanie's mood and about Tom's ire if I went to a party without him, worrying about cookies due in the morning, and my wedding band that tapped, tapped, tapped against the steering wheel, I never saw the car. And the car's driver didn't see me. He raced through the intersection, blowing through the stop sign, and slammed into our silver van. His sports car was so low to the ground that it slid under us. I felt a slight rise and suddenly heavy, as if we were in an airplane whose wheels had just left the runway. The van tipped, pitched hard, and leaned in a way that no car should. I turned my head to try to see Mary next to me, thinking that keeping my eyes on her would prevent this daughter from getting hurt, but I was pressed into my seat as if by the gravitational force of a carnival ride, the tilt-a-whirl or the space rocket. Mollie behind me and Stephanie behind her were a million miles away. It was dead quiet inside as we rolled like a steelie down the street: first sideways, then upside down, skidding, a screech of metal against roadbed. I listened for some sound of the girls above all that noise while the seat belt tightened across my chest and my ribs collapsed inward toward my stomach—hair flying in my face—but there was nothing. Nothing human, anyway. The movement of the car was slow and without human protest, as if we had already resigned ourselves to what was happening. What I knew was that we couldn't stop moving—because I couldn't face what was at the end of this when we did.

Still upside down, we did stop, the force of nature and a jutting sidewalk curb taking care of that. I was able to move my arms, enough to push my dangling hair out of my eyes and turn to look around. Mary, hanging toward the top that was now the bottom, reached over to press the button on my seat belt, but it was jammed shut and wouldn't budge. Mollie whimpered. I twisted harder, enough to see my youngest child suspended from her car seat, and then to see the rear seat—the rear seat was empty. The window that had been next to Stephanie was gone, disappeared as if it had leaped off and run away like the gingerbread man I had read about to Mollie the night before. I shouted Stephanie's name and then I screamed it. Mary said, "There," and I looked out her window, my head now so full of blood I felt as useless as a tick. I saw Stephanie lying on the road, curled into herself, the way she had looked once at the park when she'd fallen wrong off the monkey bars and sprained her ankle. Maybe that was all it was, an ankle or a shoulder. I called her name again. "Get up, Stephanie, get up!" I yelled. I knew those were the worst instructions possible to give a hurt child, but I had to see her move.

She did sit up, legs spread in front of her and blood streaming down her face and hair. Onlookers gathered, pouring out of their houses and cars. "My mom and sisters!" she shouted at them. But no one stepped forward. "Somebody help us!"

A woman's voice from far away: "Tell your mother to turn off the engine." I pawed the space in front of me, what I thought was the dashboard, but I couldn't find the ignition. The steering wheel was cockeyed, staring at me blankly. Nowhere could I locate the metal jut of the key. Outside, the wheels of the van turned while the engine raced, as if the car were trying to find some way to escape through the air. My head was bulging now, or felt like it was; I was dizzy, and my body, like Mary's and Mollie's, hung in angled suspension from the seat belts. Five years of dust and grime crawled up my pants and covered my glasses, wove itself into my hair. I'd feel all of it later, the itchy dirt, the bruises and broken ribs. But right now, I needed to get my kids far from this car. I had to reach Stephanie.

"Get us out of here!" I shouted at the people beyond the shattered windshield. They stood on the sidewalk, held at bay by the car whose engine roared and kept roaring.

Stephanie stood up and moved toward the van. She pushed herself back through the hole from which she'd been thrown, first her head, then her chest, then her legs. "What are you doing?" I said, more alert by now, smart enough to know she needed to keep still until someone checked her out. "Sit down, don't move. Tell someone to call an ambulance."

But she squeezed through the interior of the car, through the spilled milk and broken eggs, the bricks of cheese and smashed bread, blood dripping from her face and down her arms and legs, until she got to Mollie. I heard rather than saw what happened next: Stephanie pressed the button of her sister's seat belt and caught her as she fell free.

"I want Mommy," Mollie whimpered.

"She's coming," Stephanie said. "She's right behind us."

A minute later I saw upside-down Stephanie and Mollie on the sidewalk, and an upside-down woman with a topknot of hair and a green facial mask hardened across her cheeks, chin, and forehead rushing toward them with an open blanket. I turned to Mary. "We'll be out in just a minute," I said, my head throbbing now. "I promise."

A bare-chested man appeared at my window. He was huge, muscled, and had inky tattoos on both upper arms. He was talking to me but I couldn't tell what he was saying. He was on his knees, reaching toward me through the opening, pushing his wide body in the broken window until I saw rivulets of red across his skin. With the knife in his hand, he started to cut me loose, but I reached out and grabbed his wrist. "Get my daughter first," I said over the still-roaring engine.

"I'm here already," he said with an exaggerated shrug, which for some reason made me furious at this person who was trying to help when no one else would. "Get my daughter first," I said through clenched teeth. He sighed and pulled himself out the window and walked far enough around the car that he didn't come anywhere near the spinning tires, and in a minute he'd cut Mary free—she braced her knees and palms against the floor of the van to hold herself steady while he moved her toward the blanket he'd packed across the jagged base of the shattered window. He lifted her out. Then he came back for me.

The next day the girls stayed home from school, and I called the director to say Amanda wouldn't be at rehearsal that afternoon. A few hours later Jesus phoned to ask about her. I told him she hadn't been with us during the accident, and he let go of the air I could tell he'd been holding in his lungs. The hospital had released Stephanie, stitched back together, jagged black threads poking like buried insects from her face and arms and kneecaps. Hair shaved in patches for more stitching, a purple ring of bruise around one raccooned eye. The doctor had pointed out the long dark streaks under her skin; he called them road tattoos and said that over the years as she grew and her skin stretched the wounds would reopen and gravelly remnants of that skid across asphalt would squirm out, the way shrapnel eventually worked its way out of a wounded soldier.

My husband's mother, who'd not spoken to me since I'd left her son, came to sit with sleepy Stephanie and vigilant Amanda while Tom and I, along with Mary and Mollie, went to check out the car and to sign the papers for its dismantling. We drove to the lot on the outside of town where the van had been towed. It had rained in the night, the sharp smell of creosote and new mud puddles attesting to the recent moisture. I held Mary's hand, and Mollie sat on her dad's shoulders, while we walked up and down the gravel rows, battered automobiles on either side, looking for the one that belonged to us. "There it is," my husband said, pointing to a smashed and twisted hunk of silver metal squatting on four flat black tires. Mary yanked at me as she came to a stop on the path.

"What's wrong?" I asked her.

She stared up at me. "Who turned it over?"

"What do you mean?"

I picked her up and she buried her face in my shirt. "Tell them to put it back," she whispered.

And then I realized I agreed with her: if force and speed and gravity came together to create such havoc, it ought to have been left alone. At least until we could make some sort of amends with our rolled-over car.

The sliding door had broken off and was resting against the van. During the rainy night, coyotes had smelled the groceries, the hamburger and butter and big ripe tomatoes, and I suppose Stephanie's blood, and had squeezed through the fence to consume what they could and to tear everything else into slimy bits. Their paw prints were everywhere, floor, ceiling, seats.

Tom climbed in to have a good look around. "It couldn't be more wrecked," he said when he stepped back out.

When we arrived at the apartment an hour later, papers signed, I went upstairs to check on Stephanie and Amanda while Tom and his mother muttered to each other in my living room. She left without telling me goodbye, which didn't make me seethe as it might have before; I was willing to concede that from her point of view my desire to be rid of her son was appalling. On the outside of Stephanie's closet, I hung the cheerleading uniform wrapped in plastic. I'd asked Tom to stop at the shop on the way home and I'd run in to pay for it.

Amanda sat in a chair on the other side of Stephanie's bed, her legs curled under her. She looked at the costume without a word.

The evening before, after we'd come home from the hospital and were reunited with her, after I'd assured her that everyone was okay—even the out-of-control boy in the sports car had walked away unscathed—Amanda told me she knew what would have happened if she'd been in the car with us. She would have been sitting on the other side of the rear seat, opposite Stephanie. The point of impact. She'd probably be dead. That's what she said as I tucked her into bed. *I'd probably be dead.* I sat down next to her and put my hands on either side of her head. "No," I insisted, "that wouldn't have happened. You'd be okay."

"I feel like a ghost," she said.

But she was not a ghost and she was not an orphan. She wasn't a leper or a child at a master's feet or an agent of heaven. She was a child, wondering, I was sure, what was to become of her and her sisters after I ended this marriage for good. Whether we could keep surviving collisions and mishaps and all the dangerous things that might sneak in while I was too busy to notice. I wanted to tell her we were going to be fine without her dad, maybe even better than before, but I managed, for once, not to say anything.

A few days before the accident Amanda had announced that she finally understood the play. At least in the rock-opera version of the story, Judas was fed up with Jesus. They'd made a plan together that Jesus wasn't sticking to. Jesus had bigger ideas and wanted to do his own thing. Judas insisted that Jesus rein himself in and get back to business, but Jesus refused. That's why Judas had gone to the church leaders, a self-serving lot, and unwittingly created a disaster. As Amanda told me about the meaning she'd gleaned from the big drama that now included her, she scrutinized my face. I stepped back from her. What was going on here? Had she already cast me in one of those roles? If so, was I the one desperate to keep the plan in place or the one who'd blown the plan apart?

Why'd you let the things you did get so out of hand?

The night of the accident, I left the little girls in their room playing and Stephanie with Amanda and found my husband on the front steps drinking a beer he'd pulled from the refrigerator. I sat next to him, the porch firing up the ache in my bruised body.

He reached over and took my hand in both of his and gazed at me like he used to when we were young, not yet able to imagine the love and despair we would take on because of the four girls in the house behind us. "Doesn't this prove to you how important it is to stay together?" he said. "Everything can change in one second and all we have is each other."

I might have given him a different response if I'd been able to see the ways in which my daughters would be torn apart in the years to come because of the battle between their parents, two people who didn't belong in a marriage together but who couldn't manage to find a decent way to split up. If I could have imagined, even, Amanda on a park bench gouging a boy's initials into her skin with a paper clip. If I'd been smarter then, I might have asked Tom if we could find a way, both of us, to cloak our daughters from pain and confusion while we pulled this thing apart and found our way to be done with each other. I might have said that I couldn't stay married to him, but I'd try — try — to be his friend.

But instead I said this: "I need more time."

He sighed and got to his feet and set the beer bottle on the porch. "I'm going home," he said, which surprised and relieved me at the same moment.

At the bottom of the steps he turned and said the words that confirmed for me once again that I was finished with the marriage, with our house in need of repair, the unruly cactus garden planted in front, and with the way we'd been with each other since we were teenagers. I thought then that the reason I could walk away from Tom was that he was still, in so many ways, a boy. What I couldn't see was how I was still, in my own way, a girl, one who didn't understand how deeply my daughters needed me to keep them at the center, to make them the focus of everything, while I unwound my life from their father's.

"I would have seen that car coming," Tom said. "I would have swerved out of the way."

"How can you say that? You weren't there."

"Listen," he said. "I know you and I know myself. If I'd been the driver, there wouldn't have been an accident."

He ignored the sidewalk and walked instead across the grass, still wet from watering, leaving a line of dark footprints between my porch and his car. He got in and sat for a while without starting the engine. A few seconds later Mary and Mollie came to the door and asked me if we could go for a swim. I told them to get their suits and I'd get mine. "Mom's going swimming!" one of them called out as they ran into the house to collect their things.

I turned to see an escaped sliver of light stream through the trees and sweep across the lawn in front of me. The grass, refracting that light, shimmered as eerily as the shiver that tended to climb my back whenever I was scared or excited, either one. I stood to go in, bending to pick up the empty beer bottle. By the time I rose again, my husband had pulled out of the parking lot. His car was on the street now, a trail of exhaust puffing behind him. The footprints in the grass in front of me were gone too. In a matter of moments, all signs of him had vanished.

2

THE DAY MY DIVORCE WAS FINAL I DROVE AWAY FROM Tucson in a battered Volvo station wagon bought with insurance money from the car accident. We settled in Eugene, Oregon, a town about an hour from the ocean, because I'd been offered a job there, and because Tom had said he wouldn't fight my move back to the Northwest, where I'd been raised. The girls and I found a rental house that was walking distance from my university office and their schools, too many miles from their father, my ex-husband now, for me to worry that he might show up and pound on our door in the middle of the night as he had been those last weeks in Tucson, shouting and demanding to be let in. Too far away for him to appear on the porch when I was away at work, pushing past the scared babysitter to ransack the garbage, print out my computer files, tear apart my bed.

One night, about ten months after we'd landed in Oregon, it was not Tom but Amanda who hovered in the doorway of my room. I put down the book I'd been reading to catch the expression on my oldest daughter's face—she was about to take me on. I drew in a deep breath and the scent of a tired body and sour sheets, which a few minutes before had smelled of comfort and rest. My mind spun, trying to figure out what this was going to be about before she started to talk.

Earlier that afternoon I'd picked up the girls at the airport; they'd arrived home from a weeklong court-decreed visit with their father—he'd taken them on a spring camping trip in Mexico. The four of them had argued and punched each other on the two-hour drive to our house, Mollie slapping Mary, Stephanie grabbing Mollie's arm hard enough to leave a purplish bruise, and Amanda yelling at all of them to leave her the hell alone. This is how it went when they weren't quite parted from him, weren't quite back with me: two or three days of short tempers and scraps over the slightest transgression until they got oriented again.

Once inside, they'd opened their suitcases and the smells of baked sand, insect repellant, rotting fish, and, mostly, a sharp, sweet chemical stench poured off the dirty clothes. A can of kerosene had tipped over in the back of their father's truck on the way from Tucson to the campsite in Mexico, Amanda told me—news that instantly sent me into a rage about Tom's jackassness, his endless irresponsibility, his refusal to be a grownup. The girls slunk into their rooms and closed their doors as I began complaining about their father, and I found myself standing alone in our living room, not yet getting how utterly predictable this was—not yet seeing how I was encouraging my daughters to believe, again and again, that they had to choose between the carefree father and the fastidious mother.

The gas-soaked shorts and tank tops and bathing suits they'd carted home were now airing on the back porch railing. The stench had jammed in my nose and the back of my throat and a headache had set in behind my eyes. It had taken us to nearly ten o'clock to get dinner eaten, baths done, packs and homework located, lunches planned—and now this. Amanda at the door, wanting, I guessed, to duke it out with me.

"What's going on?" I said, patting the edge of my bed.

She stepped closer, but didn't sit. She wore an oversize T-shirt that hung to her knees and made her look younger than fourteen, though her bright red toenails glittered the color of adolescence. Her face, sunburned from Mexico, showed every line of the scowl set across her forehead. It was quiet for a few seconds between us; I sat with my hands around my book, while she moved a couple of things around on my dresser, rocks I'd picked up on a hike, a photo of my grandmother. Then she turned toward me. "I need to go live with my dad," she said.

I sat up taller in my bed. "Why would you need to do that?"

"Mom," she said. She dropped her hands to her sides, grabbing up handfuls of T-shirt. "He's alone. He doesn't have anyone there and he can't stand it. One of us has to go."

I got out of my covers and stood in front of her in my cotton nightgown and scrubbed face that suddenly felt dry and older than thirty-five, cheeks and lips tightening as I spoke, as if my skin itself were trying to keep me from saying too much—how he was remarried now, for example, as well as surrounded by his sisters and other family. "It's not your job to take care of your father," I said, resting my hands on her shoulders a little too heavily with a desperation I didn't want to recognize—my desperation for her to stay with me and not disturb the picture I had of my own new and improved family.

"Yes it is," she answered, staring me down. "He needs me to take care of him."

"Amanda," I began, but I stopped there. Anything else I said would be taken as criticism of her dad, would *be* criticism of her dad.

"You don't care about him, but I do," she said, pushing my hands away.

She whipped around to leave the room and I let her go. Back in bed with the covers to my chin and my book fallen to the floor, I thought about getting up again to follow her upstairs and talk until we hammered something out about her jumbled heart. I should have done that. But instead I let the urge wither—I didn't have the energy for soothing and solving; I wasn't sure I had energy enough even to climb the steps. Besides, she'd forget about the whole thing in a couple of days, wouldn't she? She'd get back to school, to dance lessons and art class, to the mission of finally making a couple of friends, and drop this fresh-from-daddy insistence.

But I was wrong about that.

• • •

The next afternoon I answered my office phone to hear from the middle school secretary that Amanda was being questioned by the police in the principal's office.

"For what?" I said, reaching over to close my office door so my coworkers couldn't listen in.

"No reason for alarm," she said, a statement that in fact alarmed me. "There's a group of girls waiting to talk to the officers and your daughter's one of them. Can you get over here?"

At the school a half-hour later, I looked for the group of girls in the principal's office, but the square space was strangely empty, oddly silent—blank chairs and shut-down computers. The vice principal's door was open a crack and through it I saw Amanda sitting at a table, her hands flat on the surface in front of her. I pushed the door open. Two cops stood up, as did the vice principal. "Are you Amanda's mother?" that official asked me.

I sat in the empty chair next to my daughter.

"What is this?" I asked her, but she only shook her head, her hair hanging in her face.

"There was a fire in the locker room," one cop said, "and we've charged your daughter with arson."

"A fire?" I set my soft purse in my lap, squeezed it.

While the vice principal told the story, Amanda kept her hands pressed against her eyes like a blindfold. He said that Amanda had skipped math class with another girl that afternoon. They'd hid out in the locker room behind the gym. The other girl had a lighter in her pocket, which she'd used to try to set fire to the loose laces on Amanda's Converse shoes. The shoelaces didn't catch, barely smoldered in fact, and that's when the girls really got going—determined to set something, anything, aflame. Amanda picked up a garbage can and dumped the contents on the ground. She took the paper—towels, wadded-up homework, candy and gum wrappers—and made a pile in one of the sinks. The other girl, the owner of the lighter, claimed that Amanda had called to her, "Toss it here," and reached out her hands to catch it. The girl said she had looked on as Amanda lit one edge of the paper mound, then another, until flames shot as high as the mirror.

A few seconds later, Amanda twisted on the water faucet to douse what was left of the embers, but not before a sixth-grade girl had swung the door open to see what was going on in the locker room, which would soon be jammed with other sixth-graders getting ready for afternoon PE. She shut the door and ran to the office to report: fire.

"We had to take the appropriate course of action," the vice principal said as if reading a prepared speech, his hands folded on the table. "This is for the police to handle, not the school district."

The only students questioned were Amanda, the girl who'd been with her, and the sixth-grader who'd reported the fire (and who would be mercilessly dogged by Amanda and Stephanie for the rest of the year). For whatever reason, the secretary had made up the part about a group of suspects—did she think she was making it easier on me? Because it wasn't easier.

The girl with the lighter was charged with damaging school property, a misdemeanor. My fourteen-year-old was charged with first-degree arson. A felony.

When the vice principal finished talking, Amanda put her head down on the table and wrapped one arm around the top of her skull, as if to make sure she couldn't rise again. I wanted to scramble into her self-made cave. Or take her hand and pull her under the cheap oak furniture with me and hide until these men with their heavily starched clothes and buzz haircuts went away. I wanted to curl up until I could make some sense out of this fire she'd started and whatever was going to happen next, which I already knew was beyond me.

Instead I glared at my daughter with a parental scorn I thought the men would approve of. At the moment that's all I could think to do: show that I was in control, that I was disappointed, that punishment would be delivered. It wasn't a lie; I was beyond furious, though not sure at what or whom, and I put on a display of rigid contempt I didn't actually feel. I did this rather than what was best for Amanda—best would have been to turn whatever tender attentiveness I could muster to the frail daughter next to me. I was racked with remorse about our talk the night before, but I didn't want to admit to any part in her confusion or heartache, especially in front of these authorities across from me or even to Amanda—I couldn't handle admitting weakness in the middle of being weak. These men expected me to show the "tough love" that was the parenting rage in those days, and I did my best to sit straight in my chair and look tough.

I felt nowhere near tough. How would I tell the other girls what had happened? How was I going to tell Amanda's father without hearing for the thousandth time that I couldn't handle raising our kids on my own after all and without his getting Amanda on the phone to say, *See? Your mother doesn't know what she's doing.*

I wasn't even certain what it meant for a fourteen-year-old to be arrested for a felony. The cops handed me paperwork telling me whom to call, where to appear. Amanda wouldn't be taken into juvenile custody that night but she was suspended from school for two weeks and would be prevented from attending any student activity deemed enjoyable for the rest of the year. We'd meet with a court counselor the following day and schedule a hearing in front of a judge. The judge would decide her sentence. *Her sentence.* The permanence of that rang in my head.

I took the papers and folded them into my purse, refusing to believe what was going on in this room. This was something that happened to other people. To people with bad kids, not to parents with kids like Amanda, a tender and sweet girl who wanted to help and who wanted to please.

Once a week or so Mary and Mollie and I dragged in tired after work and daycare and found the two older girls, who'd walked home from school, all decked out in the old thrift-store prom dresses I'd bought them for Halloween, one mint green, one sea blue. Stephanie, who had a gift for coming up with colorful adjectives and for drawing fleur-de-lis, had written and decorated menus, which she handed to me, and the delighted little girls as soon as we got our coats off and seated ourselves at the dining room table. *Creamed peanuts on crispy toast wedges, $1; Melted cheese on crackers, $1.50; Tea with cream and sugar, free with any purchase.* The ink bled down the edges of the paper in long strands of yellow, blue, orange.

Amanda held a tray spread with tiny sandwiches and barely brewed tea. The ripped seam of her dress's waistline tore open another few inches as she walked toward us, her milk-white belly skin peeking through the separated fabric as she balanced the rose-covered china cups I'd inherited from a great-great-aunt. Amanda hurried back into the kitchen for plates and napkins and silverware, which were supposed to have come out first, while Stephanie turned on the Bach Concertos. I smiled at my oldest daughters, tamping down the impatience I tried desperately not to show—I had laundry to do, bills to pay, I smelled cat pee somewhere in the living room, and now there was fine if chipped china to wash by hand. I had no idea what to cook for dinner or how much homework stretched out in front of us before I could finally collapse on the couch and prepare myself for the next day's early rise. I didn't have time to stop everything to sip Earl Grey laden with sweet milk and chew on half a peanut butter sandwich, and yet it was ridiculous to be anything but thrilled, silly to be anything but relaxed—Amanda did this and Stephanie did this because they wanted our everyday life to include some possibility of elegance, or at least to offer a good dose of ease among us.

Now here I was, a few months after the last tea party, surrounded by three men who wanted me to believe that my oldest daughter was a criminal. That she deserved to be punished by the state. That she had to be slapped with a sentence. "I'm sure she wasn't trying to burn the school down," I said, finally finding a few wits with which to defend her, mild as that defense was. I couldn't tell if Amanda had heard what I'd said. She'd sat up again, her face blank.

The cops stared at me. The vice principal cleared his throat. "Give me a call in a few days and let me know what's happened," he said, nodding to us, releasing us from his office, leaving us to sort out our own disaster.

. . .

36

In late August, five months after Amanda's arson arrest, I waited again at the end of a passenger tunnel that led from plane to terminal. Post-divorce, I realized how often I'd find myself in this very spot, ready to catch my daughters as they swung from one life to the other and not knowing what to expect. This time I was even more nervous than the others. This time Amanda had threatened not to come back from her father's house.

"You can't just decide to ignore the custody agreement," I'd told Tom the night before, our last talk before the girls left Tucson. I still believed, despite his often-expressed opinion that all rules were made to be broken and that he was the right guy to do the breaking, that the expensive divorce documents bore some weight.

"It's ignored," he said. "She wants to stay with me and she's going to."

Still, standing there at the airport, I had to think he wouldn't go through with it. I couldn't believe he'd actually keep her from me. How would he wedge Amanda into his new family? Besides, she'd done her community-service hours, paid the fine, attended droning fire-prevention and anger-management classes, caught up on her schoolwork, and, worst of all, sat in a cold empty room at the middle school while the rest of the eighth-graders went off to a graduation celebration from which she was banned. The only thing she would prove by not returning was that she'd been chased away—that was my argument when I spoke to her, that she needed to walk back into the school, head lifted high. What I couldn't think too much about was the panic that stirred in me every time I contemplated living without one of my children. I certainly didn't consider for a moment that Tom could ever feel the same terror. It was sharp and mean and unrelenting.

"You can live with your dad when you like your school again, not when you hate it," I'd told Amanda the night before, after her dad had handed her the phone. This was my last plea.

"Do you know how crazy you sound?" she said.

Now at the airport, I could tell by the slump of Stephanie's shoulders when she came out of the tunnel that her big sister wasn't with them. Steph wandered into the waiting room, Mary and Mollie behind her. I studied the face of every passenger, but there was no Amanda.

"That's it?" I said when the three came over to me. Mollie wrapped herself around my leg, held on. "She isn't here?"

Mollie started to whimper and I picked her up. Mary took my hand. Stephanie was crying too, but with no sound. The bright red rims around her eyes and the sag and tremble of her bottom lip gave her away. She slung her orange-flowered bag across her shoulder and took off in front of the rest of us, heading toward the baggage claim, her ponytail slapping her back. Stephanie's gloom wouldn't ease, I'd realize soon enough, until she was with her sister again.

In December, Amanda came home to Eugene for Christmas. She was subdued but glad to be at our house — to my delight, she said so many times. Then she and the other girls flew to Tucson for the rest of their winter break. Stephanie, Mary, and Mollie arrived back in Oregon on the second day of January to start school.

On January 3, after her first day back at Tucson High, Amanda rode her bike home as usual. Over the coming weeks and months I pieced together the details of that day's story, until the scene became as vivid as if I'd been there, unable to stop what she'd set out to do. This is how the reel runs in my mind: No one else in the house. It's about three thirty in the afternoon; Tom and his wife, Ellen, will get home after five. Amanda has watched television for a while and has eaten a microwaved corn dog. Now she goes into the bathroom and dumps a bottle of Tylenol on the counter. She pushes the bright pink capsules into the palm of her hand. Thirty-two pills. She fills a glass of water and swallows them.

Later that evening, Stephanie handed me the phone and said she'd called the Tucson house to talk to her sister and had been told by one of Ellen's children that Amanda was in the hospital. They didn't know which hospital. I dialed until I found the one that had admitted Amanda several hours earlier.

I spoke to the doctor. He told me that Tom had discovered

Amanda unconscious when he went out to her room—a shed in the back that they'd turned into a spare bedroom, which I'd complained to Tom was exactly wrong for a child who needed less isolation, not more—to get her for dinner. At the emergency room, her stomach was pumped and she drank a charcoal solution to decrease the effect of the Tylenol, but the drug had likely already damaged her liver. "We won't know for a day or two what shape she's in," the doctor said.

I spent the rest of the evening arranging for people to watch my three girls. The next morning, Stephanie shouting at me from the front door that she had to go too, that I couldn't possibly leave her behind, I left to fly alone to Tucson.

One thing I wasn't ready to face during those days at the treatment center, where Amanda had been transferred after the doctors decided that her liver was compromised but would continue to do its job, was that good parents don't stretch a daughter so tight between them that she has no recourse but to unscrew a medicine bottle cap and dump the contents into her belly. Though I did notice that from the moment I walked in, when the woman at the reception desk glanced over my file, lifted her gaze slowly, arched her eyebrows in disapproval, and tapped her pen smartly against the page, I had felt nothing but scorn from the center's staff. A hidden-away part of me welcomed their disappointment—the part that desired the castigation and punishment a bad mother deserves. The bigger part of me, though, wanted to blame what had happened entirely on Tom.

Over the week I was there, I spent much of my time adding up the ways he was at fault, while he and Ellen spent much of their time adding up the ways I was at fault. We were each allowed two hours a day to visit Amanda, no more. Other chunks of the day, I filled counselors and nurses and doctors in on Tom's neglect and irresponsibility, portraying myself as the real parent to Amanda and her sisters. I'd bought a house, and, in need of repair though it was, it gave my daughters a stable place to live. I had a job and health insurance. I'd found daycare, took them to music lessons, bought many gallons of milk a week, cooked every meal at home, served dinner at the table and not in front of the TV, met with their teachers, drove them to friends' houses. I laid it all out to the professional counselors: didn't this prove I'd done the job of mother?

Not once did I suggest to the teams of doctors and nurses and therapists trying to put Amanda back together that I was willing to deal with my ex-husband in taking care of our daughter. Nor did I address the ways I could have helped her love her dad without inflicting stabs of guilt. In fact, by the Friday morning of my stay—I would fly home on Sunday—I'd told anyone at the clinic who would listen how right I was and how wrong he was in regard to our children. *This* child, Amanda, the one he'd talked into moving to Tucson, who'd become miserable and lonely enough to want to kill herself. Hadn't I said it to Tom a hundred times? The girls couldn't be parted from one another, nor could they be parted from me.

During that week in Tucson, I'd calculated Tom's visiting schedule down to the minute so I could avoid having to see even the faint hint of his shadow down the hallway. Or his wife's. And they did what they could to avoid me. Linda, Amanda's main counselor, had already told me that because of my "inability to communicate" with Tom, and his inability to communicate with me, she and the others would decide where Amanda would live after the month-long treatment. That suited me. I had no doubt that they'd send her home to Oregon. I'd already told Stephanie that Amanda would soon be with us, at our house, going to the right school, belonging to the right family.

My last Friday morning there, I went past the nurses' station and down a narrow hallway painted with aqua-greens and blues of a seascape most of these kids would probably never see in real life—dancing dolphins, smiling lobsters, breaching orca whales—and spotted Amanda in the unit's common area. A pungent mix of sweaty feet and Lysol drifted from the doorway of the institutional space posing as a living room, with a few soft chairs and worn sofas and untouched jigsaw puzzles on round tables. I stood there and took her in. Amanda was curled at the end of one of the couches wearing the clothes she'd been issued by the clinic: white cotton pants with no belt or drawstring, long-sleeved T-shirt, flat slippers, no socks. Her hair was in a tight ponytail, and with fluid gestures of her hands, she spoke with a like-dressed girl on the other end of the couch.

They both fell silent when I came in, which made me sad. They'd seemed like such normal teenagers before they were aware of me. The other girl hurried away, leaving Amanda and me alone. I sank into a battered cushion next to her and put a volume of Gary Snyder poetry, which she'd asked for, in her lap. She reached over to hug me, her bony hands resting lightly on my shoulders, and her chin burrowing under mine. When she'd nuzzled her face deep in my neck—an embrace that would last only a second, I knew— I told her I loved her, a statement that, as it had all week, made her recoil. She pushed herself into the far corner of the sofa, away from me. My arms and hands cooled, suddenly emptied of my daughter. She yanked pillows in front of herself and huddled in the corner.

"Why can't I say that?" I said, reaching over to push a strand of hair behind her ear. "Why can't I say I love you? Don't you know how many people love you?"

Knees to her chest, she lowered her head then raised it again. "That makes it worse," she said, "not better."

We talked, a little, in between silences I'd almost grown used to. Then, five minutes before my visit was to end, I kissed her good-bye and slipped into the dim hall, sure that if I hurried I'd miss Tom and Ellen, whose appointment to see Amanda began at noon. But heading straight toward me was Amanda's counselor Linda, tightlipped as usual, with Tom and his wife walking right behind her. Ellen's cantaloupe breasts bounced under her skimpy tank top, her peasant skirt flowing from generous hips. I had on a pair of cords, a long-sleeved T-shirt, sandals, my usual getup. No matter how I tried to talk myself out of it, Ellen made me feel like a pencil-shaped little kid.

I slowed down, wondering if I could turn around and walk off in the other direction. Stopped dead and heart pounding, my hands in midair as if trying to decide how to react, I remembered a bathroom a few doors away I could slip into before they reached me. But then Linda called my name.

"Can we step in my office for a minute?" she said.

My throat was too constricted to answer. I couldn't stand the idea of being in her small, cramped space with Tom and Ellen, but it seemed impossible to get out of it. Once there, I paused, then lowered myself into the metal chair closest to the exit, right foot angled toward the door, determined to slip away as soon as I could.

Linda placed her bag under her tidy desk, a splotched banana sitting on the corner. She cleared her throat and riffled through papers, while I imagined her peeling the banana after the three of us had left, breaking off small chunks of gooey fruit and chewing on them until they were mush. She started talking then, getting my full attention when she said that the staff had put together notes from their interviews with each of us, including Amanda.

"We plan to make a decision about where she'll live in the next week or two," she said.

"Why can't you decide now?" I asked her. "I'm leaving day after tomorrow."

Tom interrupted me before I could argue that he'd try to sway things his way once I was gone and he had the staff to himself. "Amanda wants to be with us," he said, leaning forward in his chair and pointing his index finger at me. "You'd better learn to live with that."

I remember wondering—in one quick flash and no more—how things had become so vicious between us, especially since everyone, from doctors at the hospital to this stiff-backed counselor across the room, had urged us to get along for the good of our child. All of our children, in fact. Why couldn't we do that, get along? But the fleeting thought to do better by our daughters, to take on the mantle of this parental responsibility, was obliterated by my need to fight with the man I was sure had driven Amanda to despair. I'd be sorry for it later, but at that moment I could not rouse a spirit of cooperation when it came to Tom.

. . .

During our first winter in Oregon, two years before Amanda's Tylenol overdose, Tom had flown up for Thanksgiving weekend. We all six hiked in the wet, mossy woods, Mollie riding on her dad's shoulders, while the bird I'd stuffed that morning roasted in the oven at home. The path up Mount Pisgah was damp and muddy, and the girls slid over the slick Douglas fir tree roots that rose from the black ground like miniature whale backs. Mollie, who hung on tight to her dad's neck with one hand, picked strands of gray-green moss off the trees with the other to make a wig for Tom's head. She was, she called out to me, turning him into a troll; she stuck twigs behind his ears for horns. When I got around one corner, Amanda, Steph, and Mary ahead of us on the path, I turned to look at the man I was once married to, surprised in that instant that he was there and that I was tolerating the heft of him around us again—the sound of his voice, the weight of his footsteps, the way he'd left a scattering of his whiskers in the bathroom sink that morning as if planting seeds. He lowered Mollie to the ground, putting an end to the game. She scampered off toward her sisters while he shook off the long shreds of moss-hair, brushing his shoulders and the front of his jacket. He looked up and saw me watching; he smiled, showing those same brown squiggles on his front teeth, and pulled at a few last sprigs stuck in his short, graying hair. I whipped around fast, calling for the girls to slow up and wait for me, keeping a distance from the person behind me I'd now firmly relegated to the past.

After dinner and pie and cleanup that night, Tom and I got the girls to bed as we had in the old days—reading stories, watching over teeth-brushing—then sat in my living room to talk. The week before, my guts had churned every time I'd thought of him in my town and in my house, but things had gone okay the first night. He was leaving Saturday, so we only had one more full day to get through. My shoulders relaxed a little. I pitched off my slippers and tucked my stocking feet under my legs. I remembered the old days in a way I hadn't for a long time—the two of us as young parents with barely enough money, lying side by side on our living room carpet while Amanda and Stephanie galloped My Little

Ponies down our legs and across our chests, baby Mary napping between us. The train-hopping hard drinker from college had become someone else—a man trying to make an ordinary life, with a job and a house and a family. He'd get fed up with the tedium of that life and would quit his job or get a speeding ticket or empty our savings account for some insane purchase—or build another tree house or bonfire to terrify me—but in those early years, I had to admit now, he mostly tried to keep it together.

I drank a mug of tea on the sofa, nearly forgiving him for not becoming the man I'd wanted as a husband and almost forgiving myself for not being the right wife for him, realizing again that the marriage between us was simply a bad idea from the start, and I let down my guard. He began to tell me about a new woman in his life, Ellen. They'd met at work. She'd kept making excuses to come by his office and had scheduled meetings that included him. They started having lunch together. He met her kids. "She thinks I'm wonderful," he said, grinning into his own cup.

A weight I hadn't even known was strapped across my back lifted when he said that. *She thinks I'm wonderful.* The first sentence having to do with his emotional life or mine that wasn't some kind of ammunition. *My God,* I remember thinking, *we might actually be able to do this.* We might be able to be divorced and not hate each other.

Yet that moment of hope crumbled soon after his Thanksgiving visit as we fought endlessly on the phone about our differences and our objections over the raising of our daughters, and it was now utterly gone. In Linda's crowded office, I lifted my arm to block Tom's pointed finger. "Why would she want to be with you?" I said. "What she did means she can't wait to get away from you."

"What she did—" Tom began, leaning harder, nearly poking my chest. When he tipped in I noticed how much he'd aged since I'd last seen him. At thirty-eight, he was no longer the eternal boy, his family's Puck. His hair was gray and spiky, his square face dented with lines. I bent away, but he came in so that he was only an inch from me and said: "She did what she did because of the guilt you heap on her."

Tom turned to Linda and started to tell her a story that made me stand and put my hand on the doorknob. But Linda raised her flat palm in my direction to tell me to stop, and, reluctantly, I did. A few weeks earlier, Tom was saying, Amanda was making a cake in their kitchen and accidentally dropped the bowl and spilled the batter across the floor. Ellen walked in as the bowl fell and dough oozed out across the linoleum. Tom, glowering now at the counselor, went on about how Ellen was surprised when Amanda leaped back, cowering, sure she was in trouble.

"Amanda told us she couldn't believe it—that she wasn't getting yelled at, that she didn't have to be scared. She couldn't believe Ellen got down on the floor and helped her clean up," Tom said, getting up and stepping close to his wife, putting a hand on the back of her chair.

Ellen leaned against him and piped up before I could defend myself about this cake story—before I could admit that, sure, I'd snapped a time or two over a spill, but I could also recount dozens of other baking days when Amanda and I had made a cake or bread or muffins or cookies without harsh words or hurt feelings. I'd been stretched since we'd moved to Eugene, but not every minute, not every day; not, I had to believe, to the point that my children considered me the kind of tyrant Tom was creating in front of a counselor who was about to decide our daughter's fate.

Ellen spoke then, directing the words at me but mostly looking at Linda. "You're going to have to accept that Amanda thinks of me as her mother," she said, picking up the edge of her skirt and dropping it again.

Before I got myself far away from the room and from that clinic, I took two big steps over to Ellen, a strand of my hair stuck across my chin. "You can fuck yourself," I said.

That brought Tom around the chair and Linda to her feet. He grabbed my arm and spun me around. "Don't you talk to my wife like that," he yelled.

The counselor stepped between Tom and me, pushing us from each other while the shouting continued. "You know what?" Linda said to the ceiling, her dark eyebrows knit together and her hands fisted. "If I was your daughter, I'd want to kill myself too."

Two weeks after I returned home, Linda called me late one evening to tell me that a decision had been reached. I happened to have a glass of wine in my hand and took a gulp as I waited for her news. She told me the unanimous vote of the team was that Tom and Ellen were the more stable parents. Amanda, after the last week of her treatment, would go back to their house.

I set down my glass and reached over to grab a cloth from the sink, wiping off the counters as Linda dribbled on, a few more comments I couldn't hear over the ringing in my ears. I scrubbed the circles of dried milk and swept up the toast crumbs I'd missed after dinner. I cleaned around the flour and sugar canisters and knelt down to get the fingerprint-smudged front of the stove. "What are you talking about?" I asked her, breathless. "Is this because of that day in your office? You didn't even let me explain about the cake — is this about the cake?"

"It wasn't anything Tom said," she told me. "It's just what we think is best for your daughter."

I hung up and flung the damp cloth across the room; it dangled from the sink's faucet. I stood still in the middle of the quiet of my house. I had to tell someone. I needed to find someone equally as disdainful of and furious over this misguided and wrong-headed decision made by people who hardly knew Amanda and who surely didn't know me. I wanted to bake ten cakes with my daughters, letting the girls spill egg yolk and flour all over without a single reaction from me and then send the cakes to smug Linda, but instead I hovered there in my kitchen, fed up, indignant, crushed.

Then I realized: the person I could spill my troubles to was Stephanie.

I stumbled to her room, the one she once shared with Amanda, an empty twin bed across from hers waiting for a sister's arrival that now wasn't going to happen. I ached for sympathy, a longing that let me convince myself that Stephanie would see things exactly as I saw them. I didn't stop to think how this news would hit her, reshape her, pull her from me in yet more ways. I moved in greedily to be close to her. This second daughter's schedule, since I'd been back from Tucson, had become almost dangerously rote: up and dressed for school with little said between us. She caught her bus, went to her afterschool program, waited for me to pick her up after I'd retrieved the little girls. She rode home staring out the window, and she lived only for the nightly telephone call she was allowed with Amanda.

I sat on top of her covers and rested my hand on her narrow waist. She opened her eyes and looked over, but instead of reaching for me as I'd expected, she sat straight up, wagging her head from sleep. "Amanda," she said. "What happened? Where is she? Is she okay?"

I wrapped my arms around her. "She's fine," I said, hugging hard and waiting for the tension in Stephanie's body to fall away and for my daughter to give in to my need for comfort, and to give in to her own need for comfort from me. "But she's going to stay with your dad. They say she has to live with them."

Stephanie sank back, away from me, all angles and stiffness, and I saw a plan flit across her face that was unmistakable: She, too, would move to her father's house. She'd go where Amanda was. As soon as she could. I reached for her again, terrified now and planning to squeeze the desire to leave me from her skinny body, but she drew farther apart. She lifted her covers, forming a cloth barrier to keep me separate. She pulled the blankets and sheets up to her neck as she rolled to face the wall. I rubbed her back through the blankets until she cried herself to sleep, neither of us admitting to the other what was already set in motion, both of us frightened — she would not be without her sister, and I would not lose another child.

It was a rainy February night a few weeks after Linda's call, and I was making dinner for the girls. Mary and Mollie were in their room pitting the elephant family against the polar bear family. Stephanie was making a mix tape for Amanda of Madonna's most angst-ridden songs. The phone rang and I answered. The voice on the other end was Linda's, which surprised me. Once I'd lost the competition for our daughter, I'd figured there wasn't much more she had to say to me. I certainly had nothing to say to her.

"Things didn't go as well as we hoped today," she told me, with a slight—was it?—tone of contrition.

I immediately began to gloat. I felt it in my arms and legs, in my chest, in the tingle of my scalp. "Did Tom do something?" I asked. Linda cleared her throat, and I knew he'd messed up. This was the day he was to take Amanda out of the clinic and to his home, and on his first chance to get things right for his daughter, he'd failed. This, I have to admit, made me very happy.

"What happened?" I asked her.

It was several days before I put the whole story together—Linda gave me only the skeletal version that night about why Amanda had been removed from her father's house and taken to a state group home for teenagers. What I got later from Amanda was that she and Tom had arrived home from the treatment center to find Ellen waiting in the house, ready to continue an argument they had apparently started the night before about which room was to be his daughter's—Ellen wanted her back in the outside cottage; Tom wanted her inside the house.

The fight was going full-bore a few minutes later, and Ellen threw the coffee from her mug into Tom's face. Tom went after her in the kitchen and that's when Amanda ran to the bathroom in the hallway and locked herself in. Ellen called the police. When they showed up, one arrested both Tom and Ellen for domestic violence, handcuffing them and loading them into the police cruiser. The other talked Amanda into opening the bathroom door—once she'd cracked it, the officer found the sink and counter covered with blood. Amanda had dug a razorblade out of the drawer and used it to make zigzag cuts down the inside of both arms, from wrist to the bend of her elbow. "Surface wounds," Linda called them.

"Where is she?" I asked, sitting in a dining room chair, my free hand half strangling my own neck, the self-satisfaction that had risen up a few seconds before gone, chased from the room and from the house.

"No one seems to know that right now," she told me. "The police took her to a state home, but I can't tell you which one or where. I don't know where she is. They said they'd call in the morning, once the paperwork is sorted out."

I'd been waiting the whole conversation to give her my *You should have listened to me about him,* my *I told you so.* But when I opened my mouth to start in on her, the desire was dead. The gloating was gone. Maybe I was the winner, but the winner of what? Amanda was stuck in some stranger's dwelling or in yet another center for lost and empty kids, wondering why no one was coming to get her. After all our fighting over who got to have her, our daughter had ended up alone.

Once Amanda was found, in a downtown group house in Tucson where social workers stashed kids temporarily for all kinds of reasons, Linda went to pick her up. Amanda had to stick around the clinic for another couple of days after that—the staff wouldn't send her to me until I'd made appointments with a psychologist, for regular talk therapy, and a psychiatrist, who could prescribe drugs. Getting the latter appointment turned out to be tough. Even when I explained I was calling about a suicidal fourteen-year-old, I got each receptionist's ho-hum. Her so-what. Her *Get in line with everyone else's same sad story.* Finally, I managed to schedule an appointment with a board-certified child psychiatrist brand-new in town; he'd see her once a week. (I'd have to take afternoons off work; hours to be made up when I had no extra hours to give.) James Grim was the doctor's name. Jim Grim.

A week to the day after the police carted her away from her father's house, Amanda met me and the three girls at a Denny's near the Portland airport. Linda had said Amanda couldn't fly alone, so Tom had brought her home. Mollie and Mary, penned into one end of the red vinyl booth, ordered pancakes, though neither ate a bite. Tom sat next to them. Stephanie held Amanda's hand on the tabletop, their silverware scattered to the side. Amanda, white and thin and folded into herself, said little. I, across the table, sipped bad coffee and watched her, counting the minutes until her father was once again headed south, and I could show him how much better I was at taking care of our daughter.

"Guess what?" Tom said, dragging Mollie to his lap, her tummy squeezed against the too-close table. The bright light over us threw a scaly shadow over both of their faces, and the smell of fake maple syrup and fatty bacon rose from the girls' plates. "You're not going to be the baby anymore."

Mollie grinned, but I could tell she had no idea what he was talking about. "What do you mean by that?" Stephanie said, with just enough strain in her voice that I was sure she knew exactly what he was saying.

"What do you think it means?" Amanda said. One sister looked hard into the other sister's face. Stephanie gripped Amanda's hand and Amanda gripped back.

Then he was gone. Flown south. And in the days that followed, the thing I'd not known to prepare for when I'd insisted she come home showed its face, reared its head, made its presence known: Amanda's despair. I was left on my own to deal with a planet-size and utterly unreachable sorrow in my daughter, a hole in her I could make little sense of. It stemmed, I knew by then, from the divorce and how her parents had become with each other because of the divorce—but it had to be more than that. It was too big to be just that. Whatever its multipronged source, I didn't have a single clear idea about how to deal with its magnitude.

A couple weeks after she'd arrived, Amanda called me at work and asked me to come home. "Please," she said. "Please get here."

"What's going on?" I asked her, the hard metal edge of my desk digging into my ribs. I already knew what this was about—it was the fourth, fifth, sixth time I'd had such a phone call from Amanda telling me she needed me to scrape her together again. To hurry and get to her. The sound of her voice this time sent exasperation through me that nearly displaced compassion or anger. Tired was all I was, though that included a jittery fear, a pinching anger, and mean twists of shame over the intensity with which I wanted Amanda to stop behaving this way. "Why aren't you at school?"

"Mom, stop it," she said. "Get home."

It took me fifteen minutes to reach my car, even though I ran most of the way. Ran with my keys in my hand, nearly out of my mind over what I was about to confront this time. I'd sorted through every drawer, taken every knife and scissor and razor and sharp thing out of the house, gathered up every bit of medicine, benign and otherwise, and padlocked it all in a cupboard. But precautions were useless—I'd soon enough figured that out. The image of what the cop had seen when he opened the bathroom door back in Tucson ripened in my mind. Blood everywhere and my daughter collapsed on the floor. Amanda could have stopped at the store down the street this very day to buy more pain pills or a package of razors. She could be hanging or drowning or falling into an irretrievable sleep.

If I did get there this time, what about the next? How long could we keep doing this? Mary and Mollie were ragged. Stephanie hovered, fretted, every day. And I was getting shaded comments at work about projects not done well, about not showing up where I needed to be. How many afternoons could I leave without somebody finally saying that the job wasn't mine anymore, not with these distractions and interruptions and disappearances? I was the one bringing in the money, the one with the health insurance paying for the pile of Amanda's drugs meant to help her sleep and calm her down. I couldn't lose my job. But I couldn't not go to her.

I pulled my car into the driveway and ran in the front door calling her name. "Amanda!" She wasn't in the living room or in the kitchen. I tossed my bag aside and hurried down the hall to her bedroom. The tiny space that used to be my office was now her room, so she'd have at least a little privacy and quiet. It hadn't mattered, though—Amanda spent most nights in Stephanie's bed, the two of them entwined, a tangle of legs and arms.

Now I found my daughter in her own room, sitting on the wood floor, leaning against her bed, legs straight out in a V. Drawers were pulled out of her dresser, dumped clean. Blankets and sheets torn off the mattress, wound in a heap. Slatted blinds yanked from the window—they had landed on the floor like plastic pick-up sticks.

I knelt down in front of her, dust motes rising between us as she pulled her legs to her chest. A plastic container rolled toward me, and I picked it up. Her bottle of Prozac, full this morning, now empty. In one of her hands she held a ballpoint pen. I unclenched her fingers and took it into my own hand.

Amanda had used the pen to draw circles around her eyes, thin black trails of ink, round and round and round again. Lines that ran through her eyebrows, up to her forehead, across her nose, into her hair.

I pulled her to her feet to get her to the hospital. One more time. More black, sticky vomit that would smear across her face until she looked like a baby eating mud out of the garden. Another scowling visit from the psychiatry resident, who would call Jim Grim to tell him Amanda had crashed and who would send us home with nothing more than another bottle of drugs that might work better than the last or that might make her worse.

I led her to the bathroom and began scrubbing her face with a wet, soapy washcloth while she flailed under the grip of my arm. "Leave me alone," she cried. "Get away from me." She shoved me with her flat hands, but I tightened my hold on her, the sweat from her armpit glossing my palm, and her knob of shoulder hard in my chest. I glanced at myself in the mirror while I washed my daughter's face. The woman who peered back wasn't the conqueror of anything, she wasn't the winner of anything. Far away, Tom was starting over with a wife and a baby-to-come and, I was sure, a newly minted story about how he'd done his best with Amanda but that it hadn't worked out. He could tell himself and others that he'd given me exactly what I wanted, because he had. I'd insisted on being the only one who could save her; I'd given him all the room he needed to release himself from the day-to-day care of a scared, lost girl who believed she wanted to be dead — or as far as possible from parents more interested in squabbling with each other than in taking care of her.

Amanda had drawn a hundred circles on her face, and no matter how hard I scrubbed, I couldn't get them off her skin.

3

ON CHRISTMAS DAY THREE MONTHS AFTER THE FIVE OF US were together again—Amanda returned to our house from her time living with her father—I opened a big box that had come by mail from Idaho, sent by my sister Cindy. The gift underneath the candy-cane wrapping was a tent. Olive green with a rain fly, it was the kind you erected with long, flexible poles and kept in place with metal stakes tapped in the soft ground of the woods. The cardboard box, from Sears, had a picture of Sir Edmund Hillary on one side. On another side was a list of the tent's best qualities: its waterproof coating, its sturdiness, its roomy interior that comfortably slept five.

When I tore off the last of the paper and saw the family photo on the front—mother, father, kids, all in ironed shorts and smooth tank tops, lolling around a pristine campground with burgers on the grill and a tent in the background—I let myself imagine my family that way. Except my fantasy had no dad involved, and it took place at night with the girls cocooned in sleeping bags, my own bag smack in the middle, all of us surrounded by the walls of our tent from which wafted a particular odor—the smell of brand-new canvas that had soaked up sunshine all day and campfire smoke all evening. In the cool, damp darkness, Mollie would roll closer to me, complaining about a rock under her sleeping pad and asking about the sound of yipping coyote pups calling for their hunting mother. Mary would say she had to pee, and Amanda would stand up to pull back the skylight flap so we could see the stars and so

53

Stephanie could point out Cassiopeia. We'd hear crickets and frogs in the marsh, the creek gurgling by, the soot of wood smoke and the campsite's dust caking our bodies and hair.

It had once been sweet like that among us—if I forgot about the sister squabbles and bee stings and sunburns and the melted marshmallow stuck to the bottoms of our shoes and the endless dirt—but those days were long over. At least I'd given up on living any more of them.

"A tent," I said, holding the box up in front of my kids, the picture of woodsy togetherness vanquished. I set the still-sealed box on the floor and shoved it aside with my bare foot, tired of how things that used to be so simple—going camping with my children, for one—had become impossible and distant.

I was settled in the big, soft wing chair in our living room, with Mary on the floor in front of me leaning against my legs. Mollie's pink-nightgown-covered bottom popped out from under the tree as she sorted through the couple of dozen presents left, counting and recounting her stash to make sure she and Mary were perfectly even, while Amanda and Stephanie sprawled on the long tan couch, one at each end, their wool-socked feet tangled in the middle. We wore rumpled nightclothes even though it was past noon—nobody had bothered to get dressed.

Our tree, perky green the evening before, had started to slump under the weight of salt-dough snowmen, feather angels, decade-old paper chains, and the dozens of lovely and fragile ornaments my mother had sent the girls over the years. It didn't even smell that good anymore, this five-footer that Mollie and Mary and I had picked out a few days earlier from the lit-up lot on the corner. The sinus-opening pine scent that had filled our car that evening had ebbed away as soon as we set the tree in the corner and poured water around its amputated trunk. The branches had been raining needles ever since, and now some of those needles dropped on Mollie's head and cascaded down her shoulder.

I scanned the five separate piles of presents Mollie was tending and guessed it would take us another hour to get through the package-opening. I wanted this part to hurry along. Once we were done eating our holiday breakfast on holiday china and once Amanda and Stephanie had slipped away with their new black-clothed and Technicolor-haired pals, as they'd been antsy to do all morning, my plan, if the little girls didn't protest too much, was to pull the decorations off the limbs and yank the tree from its stand, then toss it into a wet corner of the backyard where raccoons might use the branches to hide from winter rain. I was itching to sweep the room clean of every last piece of tinsel and green waste, wind up the lights, and wrap up the star for another year. Shove everything to the back of the storage closet. Just get it done, over with, finished.

I doubt I was the only one out of steam, faking a happy Christmas.

Mollie laid a package in Stephanie's lap, and Stephanie—a few days from her thirteenth birthday—stared at it for a long beat before she groaned as if attending to some tedious task, math homework, say, rather than a Christmas gift. She swung her feet to the floor, sitting up with her long T-shirt twisted around a body thin as a drinking straw. She picked at the bow atop the box and sighed.

"If you don't want it, I'd be glad to send it back," I said, thrusting my hand toward her.

"What did I say?" Stephanie asked me, holding the bright red package to her ear and shaking it, and shaking too her crop of chopped hair—a chemo cut, she called it. Amanda laughed from the other end of the sofa. "Did I say I didn't want it?"

"You don't have to say anything," I said.

"Jesus," Amanda said, her hands under her head, chin pointed to the ceiling. "Get off her back."

I reached down to scoot Mary out of the way—suddenly, I had to get out. As soon as I touched Mary, I felt the hardness in my third daughter's shoulders as her sisters and I went at it again, like we did every day, ten times a day. I gave this daughter's back a quick rub, as if that were enough to soothe her worries, and headed into the kitchen. I was glad to be away from the scene I myself had concocted, glad to be away from the two older girls who wanted nothing to do with a family holiday anymore. Mary was ten and Mollie eight—they deserved a Christmas with stockings stuffed to the hilt with candy and new socks and sparkly tubes of lip-gloss. It was for them that I'd sprung for the tree and baked trays of star- and tree-shaped cookies, which we'd decorated with frosting and sprinkles, and mixed up my great-grandmother's recipe for gooey cinnamon rolls, now slipped into the hot oven. But maybe I should have skipped every last one of the old traditions. Maybe I should have stunned Amanda and Stephanie by heading to the coast with the little girls and checking in to a hotel with sixty-three cable channels and the roaring ocean outside the door.

Things, in other words, were bad at our house, getting worse by the day. Just when I'd think the bar was set—*This is as awful as it's ever going to get*—I'd have to push it higher. This hopelessness, which I felt as a burned patch on my tongue and as pressure behind my eyes, was first stirred one night in October when Amanda and Stephanie didn't come home—the first time they'd flat-out failed to show up. Amanda, seemingly done with the idea of hurting herself, was now determined to go where the hurting could be done to her—and to Stephanie. That night, when they hadn't returned by the time we'd agreed they would—ten P.M.—every bad thing that could happen to teenage girls rolled one after another through my mind. Every horrible thing. I stared out the living room window at the rain, the phone silent in my hand. If their new friends had telephone numbers, I didn't know them. I waited until two A.M., until three, then started calling hospitals and police. No reports involving a fourteen- and twelve-year-old; no one offered a single idea about where my daughters might be.

Early the next day, a Saturday, I got up after no sleep and drove Mollie to her horseback-riding lessons in the country, up the winding hills that rose from our lush, green valley, dappled sunlight trickling through the car's window and over us. The lesson, offered by the city for a low enough fee, was what Mollie most looked forward to every week. While she rode the tall paint horse who'd become her best pal, I waited in the car under a cluster of maple trees, unable to read the paper I'd brought along or swallow the hot coffee from my thermos, or even think. If I didn't move my arms and legs or take my eyes from the waving pasture grass in front of me, I could manage not to feel anything. I could stay that way until my sweaty and glowing youngest daughter slipped into the car and I had no choice but to shake myself from torpor and head back to town.

How could my children not have come home? I knew they'd been skipping school—I'd had plenty of calls about that—and I figured that even though they told me they'd be at this girl's house or that girl's house, my daughters had been hanging around a certain pack of boys I'd seen lingering in our downtown mall; boys nearly through their teens, into their twenties, who wore skin-tight black pants and black T-shirts with anarchist *A*'s painted on the front and jackets covered in patches and wooly hats on their heads; boys who no doubt gave the girls beer and drugs and showed them how to Dumpster-dive and beg for spare change, and who offered them a place to settle in and be part of the edgy coolness of the street scene. I was no competition for any of that.

I drove toward home, Mollie quiet and worried about my worry in the seat next to me. I wondered what I would do if Amanda and Stephanie still weren't there. Wondered what I would do if they were there flopped in their beds in clothes stinking of beer and smoke—how I could impress on my own children how anguishing it was not to know where they were for a whole night? Mostly I wondered this: How do you get any kind of control back once it's utterly, totally gone?

I rounded a sharp curve and looked off the edge of a cliff to the wide, flat valley floor, the long scratch of a river meandering through. It would have been so easy to miss the turn and drive straight—shift into neutral and fly my car into empty blue-morning space. That had to be simpler than figuring out how to keep my tattered family from falling apart any more than it already had.

I thought that would be the worst day—the first time they didn't come home all night—but it wasn't. By that Christmas Day when I opened the tent from my sister, the girls had made a habit of spending the night elsewhere, away from our house. No matter how many times I told them that staying out without my permission was the most egregious of the broken rules, they kept it up and without concern, I guess, for any consequences I tried to dole out. Whatever they'd found out there on the streets was too good to miss, and the sound of my tinny and redundant proclamation that they had to come home at a decent hour—come home at all—was nothing but one more annoyance to ignore.

A few minutes after the Christmas rolls were in the oven, as I was leaning against the hot door until I felt my thigh turn red, the phone rang. Mary ran into the kitchen to answer, and I quickly realized it was Tom on the other end. After she spoke to him, Mary headed into the living room to hand the mobile to Amanda or Stephanie, and that's when I felt the flicker of temptation to intercept her. Maybe I'd gamble on asking the girls' father to back me up on this one. I'd ask for his support on the curfew I'd laid down for these children barely into their teens. But then an old, heavy dread filled my gut and I held my tongue. There was no way to predict what he'd do with what I asked of him, or with what I told him. He'd guffaw on the other end, for sure, reminding me of all the times he'd said that raising four kids alone was beyond me, that I'd never be able to make it right. Too often Amanda or Stephanie had shot back to me words I'd spoken to him in confidence—*Dad says that you said . . .* As if I'd been gossiping to him about our children instead of soliciting his advice and help. As if he were their pal and I sure wasn't, which gave him permission to rat on me to girls I lived and dealt with every day.

Since Amanda had returned from Tucson, Tom hadn't been in touch with her doctors or her counselors or her school, yet he'd become the one she went to if she needed to complain about me. Every few days, Amanda and then Stephanie put the phone to their mouths and made a case for my intolerance of their friends, for my need to control everything they did. They told him I wouldn't leave them alone about the way they dressed, where they went at night, how often they took a shower or washed their clothes and sheets. He listened, and, I'd later hear from one of the girls, he soothed, cajoled, and complained about me with them. "Dad says we don't have to put up with you," Amanda would say. "Dad says we can just leave if you start yelling. Dad says . . ."

If I asked him now to back me up on a curfew, I figured he'd turn my words against me with a couple of coolly delivered sentences. In fact, that's what I decided he'd absolutely do as I wandered back into the living room and knotted myself angry in my chair. I couldn't trust him. The coffee dripped into the glass pot in the kitchen and ornaments tinkled from Mollie's rustling under the tree, and I resolved not to say a word to Tom and then to despise him for our lack of conversation, for leaving me alone with this problem, even though he had no idea what I'd just parsed in my mind.

While Amanda and Stephanie talked on the phone from their musky-smelling bedroom, their giggles and hot whispers escaping from under the door, I thought about the exactly six presents each I'd bought for my daughters with money I'd saved all year—music I knew they wanted, and new sweatshirts and novels—and about the zero presents from their father under the tree. Another trip across the border when they went to Tucson for the second half of winter break was to be his gift, and the girls couldn't wait to head to their favorite Mexican beach, where they'd swim with porpoises and chase pelicans drifting across the water. During the weeks of Christmas planning, I'd let myself gloat again: I was the more thoughtful, the more careful parent—the one preserving tradition and ritual. But now I didn't know what I was. A fool. A fool for thinking that this was a game I could win—and an even bigger fool for making it a game in the first place.

I was back in the kitchen prying the brown, doughy rolls out of the pan when Stephanie came in, still in her sleep T-shirt hanging to her knees and now with a new dog collar around her skinny neck, sharp silver spikes punched through a leather band. Amanda's gift to her. Stephanie had garnished the punkness of the neck gear with a caterpillar's thickness of eyeliner across each lid. When she came closer, I saw that her tear ducts were full of fat sleepy-seeds and that her bottom lip was a little crusty from sleep—she hadn't quite succeeded in erasing the little girl who still lived under all that thick makeup and metal jewelry.

"Dad told us how much child support you get," she said, and she splayed her hands—chipped black nail polish and chewed cuticles—across the red counter. My own hand wrapped tight around the spatula.

"Did he?" I said without turning toward her voice. This cold block rising inside me was an early inkling that child support would be a main theme of our endless battles as the girls whipped themselves into the fevered belief that the money was theirs—that they'd been robbed because I used the monthly payment on food and mortgage and the heat that piped out of the vent in their room. Their dad's opinion, or so they reported, was that the funds came from his paycheck so he should be able to decide how it was spent, and he'd decided (the girls informed me) that they were old enough to use the dollars any way they wished, on whatever they wanted, and by God, Amanda said now as she came into the room, that's what they would do.

"If you get six hundred a month," Amanda said from behind Stephanie, "that's a hundred and fifty dollars each. We want it."

"It's our money," Stephanie added. She leaned into Amanda's side, clutching her sister around the waist and digging a couple of those silver spikes from the dog collar into Amanda's upper arm. Amanda pressed against her, ignoring the metal's prick to her flesh.

"Dad says," Amanda went on, "that we're not kids anymore. We can take care of ourselves."

I picked up a knife and scraped at the sides of the pan so that the hardened sugar would give way. I distracted myself with this noisy task for a second so my voice wouldn't shake with contempt, or with exhaustion, or with resignation—who knew what tone was about to come out of my mouth—when I answered them. I could have gone to my own bedroom right then to call Tom and get square with him about the advice he'd given, or not given, to these daughters, but I didn't even consider such an amicable move.

I don't remember why I couldn't take one of those deep breaths that helps put everything into perspective, why I didn't pull my daughters in close with a let's-talk-about-this calm. My blood was too close to boiling to be that easily cooled. I was embroiled in the fight, caught up in the dark thrill of polarization, ready to defend myself to the teeth.

"Tell it to the judge," I said to these girls, my head down so they couldn't see my trembling face. "He gave the money to me, not you."

"I knew she'd be that way," Amanda said to Stephanie, her arms crossed over her chest, her knobby ninth-grade knees sticking out from her pajama pants. They turned in a mutual huff. Amanda called backward as she stormed from the room: "Dad says it's pretty sick how you keep hanging on to us. He says you just can't stand to let us go."

I was a sophomore in high school the afternoon I tossed my books and leather-fringed purse onto my bed and heard Cindy, my eighth-grader sister, come into our basement bedroom behind me.

"What's that?" she said, pointing to our room's one small window, high on the exterior wall.

"I don't know," I said.

We both walked closer, climbed on her bed to get a better look. Cindy slid open the glass and I stuck my hand between two thick wires that blocked the passage to the outside world. It seemed that sometime that day while we were away at school someone had attached metal to our bedroom's window frame.

A while later, upstairs, I heard my mother telling a friend on the telephone that our father had put in this barrier because he suspected my sister and I were sneaking out at night. Sneaking out? I went back downstairs to find Cindy. I hadn't even thought of such a thing. Had she? She shook her head. "Where does he think we're going?" she said, and we hopped up on the bed again in our stocking feet. She slid open the window once more, and this time I wrapped my hands around a wire and shook it, its cold soaking into my palm.

My father was sixteen when I was born—barely finished with his sophomore year of high school—while my mother was seventeen. Maybe he believed I was certain to become a throbbing mass of raw hormones now that I was nearly that age myself. If temptation dangled juicily outside, he might have thought I couldn't help but pursue it—with Cindy not long after me, and our brother Ron, whose room was on the other side of the basement—also soon climbing out the narrow portal into the delights of the night.

Cindy and I didn't talk about the window after that afternoon's discovery; it was too strange for discussion. Sometimes at the dinner table Dad would chew us out over some undone chore or a less-than-great report card—our mother having filled him in about our transgressions—but otherwise I remember him mostly in the backyard throwing a baseball or football with Ron or in the front driveway shooting hoops with that brother, not all that much said to the girl members of the family (our dad once took us to a nearby park to teach us how to swing at baseballs, but I was lousy at it, and he never asked again). Many Saturday nights, my parents would go to a friend's house or out to a restaurant, but first Dad drove over to the nearby Big Bun or Red Steer to buy his four kids dinner. While my mother put on her lipstick and finished her hair, he went around the table to take one bite from everyone's hamburger —he stopped at Cindy's place at the table, at Ron's, at Becky's, and a quarter of my burger disappeared into his mouth when he finally got to me. I both fumed and marveled at this hunger, at his desire for this simple fare and not the meal that was ahead of him at whatever party or event they were attending. I wanted to give him my food while at the same time silently resenting the way he demanded it. If one of us moaned about how much he was taking, our father would grab the burger, dripping with ketchup and greasy cheese, and thrust it toward his mouth like he was going to gobble the whole thing. Then, laughing, he'd set it back on its crackly paper. "You can't spare your dad a lousy bite?"

Somewhere in our closet there was an 8mm movie of Cindy and me sitting on the Salmon High School bleachers—I was two and she a six-month-old in a baby chair—while our father strolled by us in cap and gown on his way to graduate. I don't remember him in those first years of my life beyond those brief images, and that's a movie-induced memory, not a real one. Shortly after he finished high school, we moved to another town so my parents could enroll in college. Dad got up at four A.M. to deliver milk, went to classes until late afternoon, and then worked in a service station down the street from our trailer park until after we were asleep. Sometimes our mother pulled us to the station in the red wagon, where we'd play with the windshield-wiper display, and then our father would set Cindy and me in whatever car he was fixing on the steel lift, yanking a lever that rode us up and down in the oil-scented garage bay.

At home, Cindy and I shared the bed in the trailer's small back bedroom; Ron soon joined us in that room, and, a year and a half after that, our sister Becky was in the crib against the opposite wall. My parents slept in the other bedroom, hardly any larger, their bed neatly made by the time we got up, not even an inch of sheet peeping from under the smooth spread. After we had our fill of dairy products in my mother's tidy kitchen—my dad got the outdated cream and cottage cheese and ice cream off his milk truck—Cindy and I went outside to play while our mom tended to babies.

I recall that on one of those play mornings, Cindy slung her three-year-old self into the loop of our one swing, its metal chains hanging from an ancient tube structure covered with chipping green paint, and began to pump, higher and higher—feet thrust straight out as she swung forward, then legs tucked tight as she flew back. I sat at the edge of the gravel drive and used a stick to swirl the sticky colors—deep reds and purples—in a small puddle of oil and water that had collected between the rocks. After a few minutes, one hollow side post of our old swing set started thumping—*bam, bam, bam* into the baked earth—and then the whole thing toppled, pitching Cindy into the air midswing. I watched her fly over me, a wingless bird, and fall hard on the sparse grass in our patch of yard. She picked herself up and wiped the dirt from her playsuit, and I went over to try to help her pull the set back in place, a futile effort, before my mother ran outside, anxious over the noise she'd just heard, worried about us, and before our tired father came home late that night to stand in the middle of the yard and yell at our mother about letting the goddamn kids have the run of the place.

During one of those shouting-match nights, I lay on the edge of the bed turned away from Ron's stinking diaper, my skin cool because of the fall air and the shouting outside—maybe it was a night when my parents were jamming the swing-set legs back into their holes and packing in more mud and concrete, which never seemed to work for long. I was maybe four and a half years old, and already was promising myself to avoid such voices whenever I could—to do what was necessary to make sure that whenever anger came out of my father, it wasn't directed at me.

A few days after the wires went up in our teenage-girl bedroom, they were suddenly gone. Without a word of explanation. Cindy and I figured that it had dawned on our parents that there would be no way for us to get out in case of a fire, so Dad must have cut the metal away and rebuilt the wood frame around the window. A window barely large enough to fit our long and narrow bodies.

Not too many weeks later, I found myself at that unbarred opening. Cindy was off to spend that Saturday with a friend, and I'd gotten up in the dead of the night to slip on jeans and a sweatshirt. I'd stood on my sister's bed in my bare feet and opened the window as wide as it would go. I squeezed the sides of the screen until it popped out. Late autumn air rushed in, as did the jangle of the leaves of the maple tree in our backyard and the clinks of metal chains against the poles of my three-year-old brother's (he was born when I was thirteen) swing set. With one good jump off the bed, I wormed my way out the hole, twisting my midsection across the hard metal lip and sliding my legs over its sharp edge. I scrambled into the ankle-deep grass, blades of it sticking between my toes. The yard was wet enough that moisture wicked up my jeans and made me shiver. I didn't have much of a plan except to follow my breathless crush on a boy who lived on the street behind ours; this, more than anything else, had driven me out into the dark. The intimacy of staring at his house, his window, in the middle of the night had charged my pulsing blood.

I could have snuck through our back-fence neighbor's hedges and hopped the canal and appeared out on the boy's road, but instead I made my way to the front of our house, hunching under my parents' window so they wouldn't spot my shadow, and started down the long, moonglowed sidewalk. Tiny pebbles got embedded in the balls of my feet and I had to stop and brush them off, the wind lifting the hair from my neck in a way that kept me stiff and scared. I didn't know what I was doing out here, but I kept padding down our block and then up the next street until I stood in the side yard of the boy who'd owned the territory of my thoughts over the past weeks. I'd guessed—without a single shred of evidence—that his bedroom was on this side of the house. I waited for a couple of minutes, sure that he'd hear my heart beating drumloud and come to the window to see me longing for him. He didn't, and then it occurred to me to be afraid of getting caught—my father's wrath, my mother's disappointment—and I turned to go home through the mysterious dark, past houses that, familiar as my own hands in the daytime, now loomed like prescient forces that sensed before I did my desire for freedom.

On the verge of Stephanie's thirteenth birthday and just after Amanda's fifteenth, my daughters' own bids for freedom were gaining terrible force. They had no qualms about doing anything—trying everything—they wanted. Two sisters united in risk and adventure. The drugs they were using, the boys they were involved with: I had only vague notions about these things, strictly not spoken of in my presence. I don't think it occurred to them to be afraid of me, as I'd been afraid of disobeying my mother and father; or to be concerned that they wouldn't be allowed back in our house, as I'd been concerned that I wouldn't be allowed back in mine. My threats were empty and the girls' sense of themselves was as invincible, daring. I'd realized by then too that one daughter's allegiance to me ended where the other's rebellion against me began.

Stephanie's loyalty to her sister hit me on the September day I stopped by the middle school to pick her up for a dentist appointment and was sent to the counselor, who told me my daughter was gone. She'd crawled out a back window in the middle of math class. The girl who'd been a straight-A student until that semester, the girl who'd been whisked off to the gifted-and-talented classes the year before and who was invited to the popular girls' slumber parties. The other kids watched that girl, my daughter, slip through the open window while the teacher was at the board explaining how to get x from one side of the equation to the other. Stephanie, the counselor told me, had run across the long green lawn to meet her sister, waiting on the other side.

"Oh," I said, sitting down on the spongy couch he kept in his office for kids who needed to talk out their troubles while missing science classes. He finished the tale of Stephanie's latest transgression, the most serious yet, and looked at me with a kind of pity I wanted to wipe off his face. I didn't need pity, I needed solutions about what to do here, for it was in this moment I realized that Stephanie had slipped away from me as well. From that day forward, Amanda and Stephanie would do what they wanted, go where they wanted.

"Who's going to stop us?" Amanda had said one night around this time when I told her she and her sister couldn't go downtown for a show by a group called the Detonators, a late-night concert where I pictured acid and ecstasy being handed out like candy. "You?"

I refused to ask for Tom's help. I'd not yet bothered to make the kinds of friends in Oregon who might round up the girls and get them to behave, as if there were any way to do that. So I dragged my girls to family counseling, where they sat with arms crossed, refusing to say a word; and I tried to find boarding schools I could afford (impossible); and mostly I yelled at my daughters with vacant threats of locking them out, of sending them away—and watched as they walked right by me to go where they wanted to go, to do what they wanted to do.

. . .

When I opened our front door to come inside one January night, I stumbled over the tent I still hadn't put away since we'd opened it on Christmas morning. It belonged with the lanterns and the sleeping bags and our old rusty Dutch oven in the back storage area, but this evening it was shoved in a corner of our front alcove. I shook the rain off my coat and so did Mary and Mollie behind me. I waited for them to run off to their room to start a game of rubber giraffes against rubber polar bears, wolves against pandas, like most every night, but they stuck close. They followed me to the kitchen, where I tossed the mail on the counter, picked up the power bill with URGENT stamped on the front, and set it down again.

When I leaned against the cupboard, Mary backed into me. She took my hands and crossed my arms over her chest, a big X. Across the room, Mollie opened the fridge and I smelled something—tuna, maybe, or cottage cheese—that should have been thrown out days before. "What's for dinner?" she said.

We were down to some canned vegetables, pasta, a few tubs of soup in the freezer, and whatever was stinking in the back of the refrigerator. Laundry was heaped in front of the washing machine, and I hadn't asked Mary and Mollie about their homework for a couple of days, which probably relieved and scared them at the same time.

I let go of Mary and reached for the phone to order a medium pizza for the three of us. Three of us, not five of us. For over a week, Amanda and Stephanie hadn't come home. It was raining the night they left and it had rained every day since they'd been gone, harder and wetter, it seemed to me, after darkness set in. For eight days, I'd picked up the little girls after work and come straight home, certain my gone-away daughters would get cold enough, tired enough, lonely and hungry enough to call me to get them off the streets of Eugene.

Eight days earlier, the attendance officer at the high school had phoned me at work to say that Amanda hadn't come back after

67

winter break. Neither had Stephanie, I found out from the middle school. They'd completely stopped going to classes and it had taken this long for anyone to say so out loud. Every morning, I dropped Stephanie at the front door of her school and Amanda at the front door of the high school and watched them walk in. I drove to my office pretending they weren't meeting each other five minutes after my car disappeared; weren't buying coffee at the drive-through hut on the corner and heading downtown to be with their punked-out friends, those homeless youth anguished over in the newspaper, those disaffected and disenfranchised young people dressed in black and metal.

Now the pretending was over, and I had no choice but to go home and confront my children.

Music throbbed through the walls of our house when I got inside, a bass beat pounding down the narrow hallway. It was Bikini Kill; I recognized the voice and the badass lyrics of Stephanie's new favorite, Kat Hanna. This was a CD Amanda and Stephanie had bought for themselves, tuned in as they now were to grrl bands and only grrl bands, their old Madonna albums tossed aside with embarrassed disdain. I was the one who'd bought them Hole's *Live Through This* a year or so earlier, along with Nirvana's *Nevermind*. I remember the puffed-up pleasure of being a with-it mother who carted the albums home and let her daughters hang a giant poster of a mascara-stained beauty queen on the wall of their bedroom. A few months later, I was blaming that same music for making my kids angrier than they already were and for leading my girls to this scene, this thing, that they apparently couldn't come back from. I hated Courtney Love and her pale, dead husband, hated the bands spawned from them and from which they were spawned, the Sex Pistols, the Ramones, the Pixies, the Dead Kennedys. Hated the thudding beat that ate its way toward me now down the dim back hall of our house.

I stopped at the open bathroom door, where the volume of the boom box balanced on the sink was loud enough to shake the light fixture and to tremble every pink and black droplet covering the porcelain. Amanda's hair was cut into chunks above her shoulders and dyed jet-black. Her ears and neck were black too, from the dye spread everywhere, on towels, floor, the shower curtain, and on her sister's hands. Stephanie's hair was halfway to becoming the color of cherry Kool-Aid. Both girls had makeup scrawled on their faces: black around their eyes, red on their lips.

Amanda saw me and nudged Stephanie, who lifted her head out of the sink. Amanda caught the back of the door with her foot and pushed it closed. I turned the knob and opened the door again. "You're not leaving the house," I said. There'd be no discussion of missed school and failing grades that night.

"Sure, Mom," Amanda said. She slammed the door again, and this time she clicked the lock.

I got Mary and Mollie out of their coats and sent them off to their room, then I went to the kitchen to call the police. The non-emergency number—I wanted help, not mayhem. I told the woman who answered that my daughters were trying to leave and that I couldn't stop them. She paused before answering. "What do you want us to do, ma'am? Have your daughters hurt you?"

I hung up and went to the front door. I made my body wide. My arms out, my feet spread. I waited there, a joke. If they wanted to go, they'd go. A part of me believed it might even be better just to get it over with and let them be gone. Except this night felt different than the other times they'd left. This time it seemed that what I'd stitched together in our little house was about to follow them out the door as a long, unraveled thread.

Amanda and Stephanie emerged from the bathroom and went into their bedroom next door. A few minutes later they were out again, their backs bent under the weight of loaded army packs, and their wet necks dribbling Manic Panic.

"Get out of the way, Mom," Amanda said. I reached past her and grabbed for Stephanie's skinny arm—that daughter wriggled away, and I pawed the air for a purchase on either of them, but then I stumbled over a chair that was heaped with Mary's and Mollie's schoolbooks and jackets, their wadded lunch bags and art projects. The chair and the stuff on the chair fell sideways and I fell with them, my hip smacking the floor with a thud. Amanda yanked open the door and she and Stephanie whirled into the night.

The younger girls held on to each other on the far side of the living room. I got off the floor and told them to sit on the sofa. "Stay right there," I said when they'd perched themselves on the couch and stared at me with big eyes. "I'll be right back."

"Mommy!" Mollie called, but I didn't turn around. She called me again, but I went on to the car. I wasn't sure why. Because I'd be a bad mother if I didn't at least try? Because I'd be a terrible mother if I didn't at least pretend to want my daughters to come back? I pulled out of our driveway and onto our street, scanning the sidewalks for a glimpse of my kids dressed in black, hoping to catch up with them but dreading what would happen if I did.

After about fifteen minutes of looking, I stopped at a pay phone to call home. I told Mary to make sure the doors were locked. "Brush your teeth and get in my bed with some books," I told her. It was only about seven in the evening. They hadn't had dinner, they hadn't watched the hour of television they were allowed, they hadn't practiced their times tables or cut current-events stories from the newspaper. But my bed was the safest place I could think of and where I wanted them to wait.

"Okay," Mary said.

Then I drove. Up and down the streets of downtown, checking at cafés and convenience stores. The bus station, the train. After a couple of hours, not willing to leave the little girls alone any longer, I quit.

The next morning I went to the police station to report my daughters missing. The officer I talked to stayed behind the Plexiglas window and spoke into a tiny microphone. I couldn't find a microphone on my side so I shouted my questions. I had to get to work and had only a few minutes on the meter outside, but I wasn't going to leave until I knew the police would start looking for Amanda and Stephanie that morning, that day.

But the cop told me it wasn't against the law in Oregon to run away from home. It wasn't against the law to skip school. My daughters couldn't be stopped or held unless they'd committed a crime. If they'd stolen from someone, which I knew they wouldn't do. If they'd sold or bought drugs, which I prayed they wouldn't do. Got in a fight, or broke the windows of a building to climb in out of the rain. Any of those things, the officer told me, would be cause to arrest them. But if they were picked up for any of those serious transgressions, they'd be turned over to child protective services, not to me.

"I have to go," I said then.

"One more thing," this officer said, slipping me a piece of paper. I picked up the note and unfolded it and saw that he'd scrawled a phone number there. "He used to be a cop in LA," he said with some measure of awe. "If you want him to, he'll find your kids."

I kept myself from wadding up the paper and throwing it at his face behind the plastic, to make sure he knew this wasn't my life. I stuck the note in my purse and turned to leave.

Eight days later, the Friday night I'd come home with Mary and Mollie to order a pizza and wait some more, I called the ex–LA cop. The seeker of runaways, the finder of bad girls. I didn't know what he did to get kids off the streets and I didn't want to know. All week I'd told myself I didn't need him, that we were minutes from see-ing Amanda and Stephanie walk up the sidewalk that led to our lit-tle house. They'd start laughing and tell me it was all a charade, a scam, or say that they'd come to their senses and of course wanted to be home with me, with us, and go to school and take a bath and just be normal kids.

Except earlier that afternoon, a friend had called to say that he'd seen them going into a Taco Time across from his office. A few min-utes later, I went into that restaurant too. There they were, my own two children, sitting side by side at a back table. Their clothes dull, their grimy hair sticking out from their heads, the pink not so pink anymore, the black more like gray. Amanda had on wool gloves with the fingers cut off, and Stephanie had a bandanna around her neck. Tiny cups of salsa were lined up between their plates of bur-ritos and Mexi-fries, and resting on the bench across from them were their fat water-stained backpacks with plastic mugs twined to the sides and rolled gray blankets attached to the tops. I'd never seen those blankets. Where'd they get those blankets? Who was giving them blankets?

Amanda looked up at me heading toward them. She yanked Stephanie's arm, and before I got any closer they were up and gone, squealing to each other, *Go! Go!,* as if this were some game of tag and I was It. They jumped in the women's room across the aisle from their table, and one of them threw the dead bolt on the main door. I leaned my back against that solid door and scanned the restaurant—5:15 in the evening and only a few people eating, the smell of grease and tortillas benignly drifting to this airless corner where I waited. Waited for what, I didn't know.

I rattled the doorknob. Stephanie squealed and Amanda giggled. I walked back to the table and picked up the backpacks. They were too heavy to lift easily, so I dragged them out the door, a filthy musk odor rising from the damp canvas as they scratched across the linoleum, and my work shoes clicking with that sound of an official, professional grownup.

It was raining outside and it was dark and I was standing in the dark rain with the packs at my feet when Amanda and Stephanie came out to huddle beneath the striped awning.

"Give us our stuff," Amanda said.

I scooted the packs behind me and hung tight to the straps. "We're going home," I said. "Come on."

"You want us to freeze?" Stephanie shouted, leaning out toward me. A few people at the public fountain behind us turned to look over the scene. "Give us our shit."

A woman stepped into the light cast by the street lamp. Her blond hair, done up in a neat beehive, shed delicate beads of water, and her face, held in a kind of practiced serenity, was hardly moist. I smeared the rain out of my own eyes while she started telling me about how she and some other women from her church often came down on the weekends to feed kids who had no other food and nowhere to turn. She'd brought sandwiches, she said, gesturing toward a box. Did we need sandwiches?

"No," I told her. I wanted to add that my daughters were not among those who had nobody to turn to and nowhere to go. My daughters had a home and people who wanted them in that home, but I only silently willed her to go away.

She didn't, though. She kept looking at me, boring in.

"Do you need help?" she asked.

"These are my daughters," I said. "And they're coming with me."

"Mom, get it through your head," Amanda shouted, "we are not going with you."

The woman moved in so she and I stood side by side, as if we were going to face these kids together. I felt the heat from her body, but I didn't know what I wanted from her. A year or two before, Amanda and Stephanie and I would have had a laugh over her self-righteousness, her certainty that she could provide easy answers with her Bible and her version of God. Now I would have given about anything for an easy answer. If I'd believed one was possible, I would have asked this stranger to bring it forth, to lay it on the street like a shining fish or sparkling wine so I could claim it.

"Let's get out of here," Stephanie said. She and Amanda started walking toward the corner of the building, toward the broad streets beyond.

"Hold on a minute," the woman called. The girls slowed down, stared back. The churchwoman put her hand on my wet shoulder. "Why don't you give them the packs?" she said.

Amanda linked her arm with Stephanie's. They waited to see what would happen next.

"They'll be cold," the woman went on. "You don't want this to be more intolerable, do you? They need their things."

Get lost were the words that formed in my throat. *Leave me alone and stop handing out food and money and understanding to my kids, and those damned blankets tied to their satchels.* That's what I wanted to say, but I only watched her pull her raincoat tighter while she gave me time to answer. And even though I didn't think I would, even up to the second of doing it, I opened my fingers and let go of the packs. They slumped to the ground. The woman took the straps into her own hands.

"I'm sure they love you," she said. "I'm just sure they do. And I'm going to pray for all of you."

A few hours later, at home, after our medium pizza was ordered and on its way, I sat at the kitchen table, numb. I'd given the skeletal version of my family's troubles to the ex–LA cop. He'd read off an address and told me to meet him there at the mysterious hour of midnight.

Mollie came into the kitchen and pulled my arms apart, wedging herself onto my lap. "What are we going to do tonight?" she asked me.

"I don't know," I said. Whatever we did, they had to be asleep by twelve so I could leave—leave my house and my daughters—to meet a stranger and ask him for help. "What do you want to do?"

Mary walked in then, carrying the box from Christmas. "Let's put up the tent," she said.

I stood up, moving Mollie off my lap, and took the box from Mary. "Why do you want to do that?" I said. "We'll get it out next summer."

My little girls stood in front of me, still and quiet. Mary's pants were too tight and too short, her long legs poking out the bottom, and Mollie's hair was in big need of a trim. Neither one of them had asked for anything for weeks, for months maybe, just kept skidding around as best they could on the ice rink we were living on in those days.

"Okay." I shrugged. "Let's put up the tent."

We shoved furniture to the edges of the room, and Mollie brought me a paring knife to slice open the box. I pulled out the folded canvas and handed it to Mary; it sent out a scent both chemical and earthy as we opened it wider and wider again. Mollie dumped poles and metal stakes from the bag; they clattered and rolled. Mary linked the rods, and we pushed them into loops, and a few minutes later, the three of us watched the structure rise to the ceiling like a hot-air balloon.

The pizza guy came to the door and I paid him, giving him a tip for not commenting on the camping gear in our living room.

74

While the girls got plates and napkins and sodas, I went to the storage closet for three sleeping bags. I laid them out inside the tent and moved the TV in too, setting it on a small table. I zipped up the flap, and Mary sat down on her bag with Mollie next to her, teetering pizza-filled plates on their laps. My girls watched Friday-night sitcoms, and I watched them. The rain beat against the roof of our house so hard it sounded as if it were falling right on our tent—waterproof, sturdy, roomy enough to sleep five.

At quarter to twelve, I put Mary's arm inside her covers and tucked her in tight. I moved Mollie's head back onto her pillow and gathered up the soda cans and the last of the dirty napkins and carried the garbage into the glaring light of the kitchen. I slipped out the front door, locked it behind me, and backed the car out of our driveway.

I pulled into the parking lot of a Carl's Jr. a few blocks away. The grill had stopped cooking, and the place smelled like cooling grease, like bread left too long under a warming light. My stomach flipped, queasy and shrunken. Sitting at the first orange table was a burly man with neat brown hair, cut short. He wore a white dress shirt, every single crease in place.

"Steve?" I said. He nodded.

I sat down and handed him Amanda's and Stephanie's school pictures, no dyed hair yet, no piercings in their faces, no hard lines around their eyes. I gave him a map drawn with Mary's marking pens of the girls' hangouts: the punk-music Icky's Teahouse, the IHOP that stayed open all night. I gave him two hundred dollars from my savings, which covered only the first day of searching.

When we walked outside, Steve took my hand in his, squeezing my fingers together. "I'll find your daughters," he said. I noticed then how his ears stuck out from the sides of his head. His neck was too thick to let him button the top of his shirt. Behind him, through his truck's windshield, I saw an air freshener hanging from his rearview mirror in the shape of naked woman, her bare breasts in a high salute. Before I could change my mind about what I'd set in motion here, he got in that truck and drove away, splashing puddles over the asphalt.

I watched the truck disappear toward the center of town and I let the rain run through my hair and down my neck. It soaked my coat and my sweater and wet my skin. It filled my shoes. I thought if I stood there long enough the rain would melt me into a different woman. The rain would shape me into a different mother. Maybe it would pound into me which of my choices had been wrong, which turns were misdirected. Maybe the rain would tell me how this had all gone so bad. Maybe, if I got cold enough and wet enough, I'd finally have a reason to go home.

4

BY THE SPRING OF 1995—A FEW MONTHS AFTER EX—LA COP Steve had snatched my daughters off a street in downtown Eugene—I was in the habit of driving 250 miles across the state of Oregon every other weekend to visit Amanda. Stephanie lived with friends in the deepest part of Montana now, in a remote forested valley not far below Glacier National Park—a long way from me, too far (this distance my oft-repeated excuse) for regular visits. But the five hours it took, exactly, from my own doorstep to the doorstep of the eastern Oregon ranch house where Amanda was staying was manageable. On alternate Fridays after work, Mary, Mollie, and I packed our things—pillows and blankets and animal families and juice boxes and apples and Disney tapes to sing along to and paper and markers to draw with—and headed through the shadowed Santiam Pass to wind over the Cascade Mountains. Past Hoodoo, around Sisters, and into the ski-resort town of Bend. After a quick dinner there, we drove through the last curve before entering the long, dark strip of asphalt—U.S. 20. Nothing but sagebrush and tumbleweeds and scavenging red-tailed hawks sitting on old fence posts on either side, a road that led through the dry and overgrazed part of our state to our destination of Burns, Oregon.

Burns. That's where Amanda lived now, with a bony rancher and his arthritic wife and their two cowboy-hatted boys. That's where I'd go to see my daughter who'd been given a title I couldn't bring myself to say aloud: foster child.

. . .

Earlier that year, I'd taken on a new job. I was editor of our town's alternative newspaper—*alternative* in that it came out weekly and was meant to dig up stories about subcultures in which the daily paper had little interest. Nearly every day I'd talk on the phone in my office with somebody pitching a story about the homeless, or I'd get a pile of pamphlets about legalizing marijuana, or I'd hear about how some cop had abused a kid at a Nike protest. I sat down with the paper's lone reporter to go over his latest story on the anarchists who'd become a fixture in our town—some of whom lived in trees, others of whom squatted in abandoned houses or on the streets, and all of whom dressed and talked and acted like Amanda and Stephanie. I couldn't quite make sense of the fact that in my job I was supposed to recognize the plight of the downtrodden while in my personal life I was doing everything I could to keep my daughters apart from these same people, who I believed had pretty much ruined my family.

The disingenuousness of the job occurs to me now—to write a story deploring the lack of programs for high-school dropouts, for instance, while forcing my own kids to stay in school. I sat at the paper's ratty conference table listening to punked-out protesters complain about arrests while suspecting these were the same guys who'd given my daughters drugs and booze and a place to sleep at night, and hating them for it. The separation between editor and mother was nearly impossible for me to maintain, but I showed up at work every morning to play the journalist. I went home at night to take care of Mary and Mollie, the three of us alone in our house—they hardly ever invited friends over or got invited to their friends' homes, and I kept almost entirely to myself as well. And twice a month, I appeared with my younger daughters at the Burns home of people I called, uncharitably, Rancher Bill and Rancher Wife Donna. Ready to defend my position as Amanda's mother.

After he left me at the restaurant, Steve the ex-cop had gone to his hotel to pick up his clone of a son, who would help him search for my daughters. They found the girls the next morning. An easy catch.

Amanda and Stephanie were sitting on the curb in downtown Eugene, feet planted in the wet and grimy leaf-clogged gutter. Steve walked up behind them; his son approached from the front. Amanda looked up, her hand straight over her brow to block out the sun. "Do I know you?" she said to the boy.

"You're Stephanie, right?" he asked her.

"No," she said.

"You're Amanda," he said, pointing to Stephanie.

The girls got up, glancing around for a quick escape, and then felt Steve sidle up behind. He clamped a hand on each of their shoulders. "I work for your mother," he said.

Steve told them that the police had called our house to inform me that a warrant had been issued for my daughters' arrests. "She doesn't want you to go to jail, so she asked me to hide you for a few days until she can sort this out with the cops."

Stephanie shook his hand off. "Leave me alone," she said. "We don't want her help."

"Can't we talk this over?" Steve said, getting even closer. "Come on, let my boy and me take you to breakfast."

"No way," Stephanie said, pulling on Amanda's arm. "Let's go."

But Amanda hesitated. For a reason she's never been able to explain, she decided she'd go with them to a restaurant; she chose to hear about the plan I'd supposedly made for them, and she coaxed Stephanie into coming along.

A few minutes after they were in the back seat of Steve's truck, the girls knew they'd been duped. Stephanie tried to open her door and jump, but Steve had set the childproof lock. Amanda started shouting, calling this man and his son every foul name she could pull out of herself, and continued to blast profanities the one hundred or so miles to Steve's house, located in a small and touristy mountain town called Sisters, Stephanie joining in the verbal battering of Steve and his sidekick. As if volatile and earsplitting words could break them loose, could put them back on their own road. The boy turned around halfway through their trip, when the girls had momentarily quieted down, spent and furious. Joan Osborne had come on the radio: "What If God Was One of Us." They ought to listen to the message in these lyrics, the buzzcut son said. "It's a really good song," he instructed in what Stephanie later called a soft preacher's tone. "It could help you." The girls huddled into each other, slouched in the narrow back seat, and tried to think of any means of escape.

When they arrived at the house in Sisters, Steve's wife stripped them, lathered their bodies and flea-packed hair with Lava soap, and hid their clothes. That night, Amanda and Stephanie sat at a picnic table set up in the living room—a glorious view of the mountain peaks of the Three Sisters glowing in the pink sunset out the window—with four other girls in the same lot, all of them barefoot in sweatpants and T-shirts. Amanda asked how she might get hold of a cigarette. "Yeah, good luck," one girl said. Steve's wife brought out hamburgers and cottage cheese. Stephanie told her she was a vegan—no meat, no cheese, no dairy products at all. So she got a bowl of corn flakes, without milk. For the next twelve days, she ate cereal, dry toast, white rice, and canned vegetables cooked into mush.

A week and more than a thousand dollars to Steve and his wife later, I'd settled on the next thing for my kids. Next was to be a wilderness-therapy program that hauled teenagers like mine deep into the Oregon woods for three weeks of counseling and hiking and bushwhacking and fire building and bone-tiredness and forgiveness and redemption. I wasn't sure where the money for this nature cure was going to come from—insurance would pay for part but a hefty balance would remain. I had to count on my father's pitching in. I also called Tom with the plan, telling him that the family therapist we three were seeing thought the trek was nearly the only choice left, short of lockup. To get into a state lockup, a kid had to be a major criminal or a heroin addict, and that, at least, wasn't our daughters' plight. I talked fast, trying to convince Tom to go along with this treatment even when I wasn't so sure about the whole wilderness thing myself—the better part of a month in the outdoors in the middle of winter? I wanted to believe it was going to bring about a cure, a new beginning, but I wasn't confident. Still, at least the trek would get them off the streets.

First it would cost a lot of money.

"Maybe they could come down here and live with us for a while," Tom said when I gave him the figure. "Maybe they just need their dad."

"You can keep them from running?" I said, picturing their two-bedroom home with their new baby, Ellen's two kids from her earlier marriage, and the thirty seconds or less it would take the household to explode when willful teenagers moved in. As tempting as it was to make them his problem instead of mine, I wasn't falling for it. Within days or maybe weeks the girls would be on my doorstep and I'd be in charge once again of figuring out how to manage. "What are you going to do when they're back on the streets?" I asked Tom. "What are you going to do if Amanda tries to hurt herself?"

I heard him put down the phone and mumble something to Ellen. Then he got back on, agreeing to pay his half and also agreeing to appear at the final family gatherings in the woods, three and then four weeks hence, when each girl came out of her separate frosty wilderness.

The Sunday following the phone call to Tom, I drove to Albany, Oregon, and down the cold empty streets of that small downtown, finally locating the headquarters of the wilderness-therapy program—a tall and narrow building between a bank and a coffee shop, both closed. Mary and Mollie were with me; the three of us climbed the stairs to the main office's door. A big man answered—a huge man—his beard full of golden doughnut crumbs, and a styrofoam cup of coffee looking dainty in his mittlike hands. He told us to help ourselves to the food on the table and then to take a seat. I walked to the far side of the circle of metal chairs and lowered myself into one of them—rigid and chilled, just like metal chairs are supposed to be—with Mary and Mollie on either side. The girls had picked out their own doughnuts. Mollie had one covered with whiskery sprinkles, and Mary had one covered with chocolate; the pastries sat on their laps, barely picked at. I counted seven other sets of parents in the room, all of whom had arrived before us, and was surprised that I seemed to be the only single mom. Married couples had this kind of trouble too? It hadn't occurred to me that such a thing was possible—I had so long placed the blame for our misery on the divorce and, in part, on the fact that I had no other adult in the house to back me up.

The other parents had their teenagers with them, each one hemmed in between the mom and the dad. The kids—about to be launched on a grueling trek together, they knew by now—were so different from one another, or so it seemed to me, that they could have been randomly snatched from suburban high-school cafeterias from one end of the country to the other. The New York preppy girl with straight blond hair wearing a bright red miniskirt and expensive boots, who I'd later find out was addicted to her mother's sleeping pills and other prescription drugs and who'd run her parents' credit cards to their big fat limits; the sullen skater boy, a day-and-night marijuana user, who was flunking high school and had wrecked his dad's car; the child of migrant farm workers who'd been sent to the program by the juvenile court after one too many arrests. His parents spoke only a little English and mostly looked confused and lost about why their boy was bound for jail if he didn't make this work.

I was confused and lost too. What was I doing here? At that moment I couldn't believe that my beautiful, bright daughters belonged with these other kids. These children were beaten down, common even in how they made trouble or rebelled against their parents. Amanda and Stephanie were never going to be ordinary, and I was never going to accept that this was our real life. I expected my daughters to peek around the corner, to jump in the middle of the room saying never mind, this was all a big joke, or at least offering a contrite plea to go home and start over. I almost stood up and started laughing myself: no way could this be happening to us. I hadn't yet realized that sending my daughters out to the snowy woods was supposed to startle me awake too—that nothing was going to get better until I stopped pretending that we weren't in terrible trouble or that it was all going to end nicely, neatly, in a cheerful reconciliation that took not a scratch from my hide.

I scanned the room. What had these trek people done with Amanda? I knew the ex–LA cop Steve had driven her to Albany the night before—he'd called to tell me she'd been "safely delivered." The following Sunday he'd do the same with Stephanie, transport her here for the wilderness folks to deal with until I arrived and we all sent her out to the cold mountains. The psychologist who ran the program had told me he was opposed to the girls going on a trek together. He'd ship them out a week apart and would make sure their groups were separated in the woods. "One of the main goals," he'd told me on the phone, "is to get Amanda and Stephanie to see themselves as individuals instead of extensions of each other."

That seemed to be a theme with counselors lately: my oldest daughters had become two halves of the same person.

"Where's Amanda?" Mary asked me, pieces of her pastry breaking off and falling to the floor, chocolate pieces scattered around her feet.

"I don't know," I said, although just as I whispered the response, there she was at the door, my oldest child. I stood up partway to see her: clean, faintly pink, wearing new jeans and sweatshirt, and on her feet a new pair of leather hiking boots I'd sent money for; they covered her ankles and would endure weeks of snowpack without rotting her toes. Her back was straight, her shoulders square.

"Amanda!" Mollie cried out, throwing her arms, her open hands, out toward her sister. Amanda turned in our direction. I waited for a sign of happiness, one tiny indication of pleasure at having us there, but her look was solid ice. The man who had his hand around the top of my daughter's arm—another huge person whose flannel shirt stretched nearly to the splitting point across his shoulders—led her to me and asked Mary to shift over one chair. He wanted Amanda to sit next to me.

For the hour that followed, Amanda did everything she could to avoid touching me, or even looking at me. Each of the parents was asked to describe what had brought the family here—one broken-down story after the other. Each child was asked if he or she was ready to turn things around—one version of *you can fuck yourself* after another.

During the hour of the meeting, I couldn't grasp what I'd gotten us into. My daughter's rage burned next to me bright as one of those flares shot into a night sky after a fisherman falls out of his boat, and the intensity of this so-called wilderness repair made my head hurt. Couldn't we just go home and be normal? I couldn't remember why I was dumping my kids into the frozen mountains. For what? What could be fixed out there that a good and dedicated and stern mother couldn't fix herself?

Before I could forge any kind of peace with this decision to send Amanda away, to woods where she'd be alone and lonely and cold and probably in pain a lot of the time, I was standing on the sidewalk watching her get loaded into a big green van. Mollie held one of my hands and Mary stood in front of us waving, waving goodbye to her big sister.

During the meeting, we'd been told there'd be eleven or twelve feet of snow for the kids to hike through and camp in during the next twenty-one days. "Nature is the best teacher," the lead psychologist told us. Burly men and a couple of equally muscular women stood at every doorway, making sure that no one left the room. The teenagers didn't stop thinking about getting away, though. Their eyes darted around for a way out—seeking any chance to dash down the street and get back to a predictable life, a drug life, a life of thieving or lying that each one had negotiated quite well until he or she got caught. "Let nature do its work and issue its consequences," the psychologist told us. The kids would do all their own cooking—lentils and beans—on fires they would build themselves, sparked with flint and steel instead of matches. If they wanted a bowl, they'd have to carve one. If they wanted a spoon, they'd whittle one from a tree branch. If they wanted a shelter to sleep in, they'd have to build one out of snow. "This is bullshit," Amanda said under her breath. I agreed. It was bullshit, though I didn't lean over to admit to her just how crazy it felt. Just how from-some-other-planet. I closed my eyes and hoped that by agreeing to this outrageous therapy, by convincing Tom and my father to pay big portions of the cost, I hadn't screwed everything up beyond repair.

Once she was in the van and about to leave, I tried to catch my daughter's eye. She glanced out the window, moving her hand slightly in response to Mary's wave, but Amanda refused to turn toward me. The bus started up, its diesel engine rumbling against the still air, and the driver pulled out onto the empty street. I'd been promised a phone call from one of the counselors in one week—the following Sunday. The same day Mary and Mollie and I would return to this building, to the room upstairs, to the same pastries, fake orange juice, and weeping mothers, to send Stephanie off to the same woods with different leaders. Amanda's bus was gone now and this wilderness plan set in unstoppable motion. I stared into the last of my hot coffee, waiting for an answer—any answer—to come rising out of the steam.

When I'd asked my father, who lived in Idaho, if he'd do it—pay a share of the treks—he'd said that this woodsy therapy was the most overinflated, self-satisfied, New Age thing he'd heard of yet. "I'll kick their asses for a few weeks. It won't cost you a penny." These were smart girls who knew the difference between right and wrong, he went on. They knew their way home—right? And they knew the rules for enjoying the privileges of a house to live in and food to eat. If they didn't want what I offered, my dad told me, to hell with them. Yet a few days later he sent the check, while also stirring a profound concern in me that my being afraid to say no, afraid to be tough with my children, was the very source of our disaster.

The bill was paid in full, and the girls were gone—Stephanie's family meeting and her departure in the same green van as full of despair and confusion as Amanda's—and I had to figure out how we'd start over as a family in less than a month. But instead of mapping out our future, instead of forcing myself to account for the ways in which I'd failed myself and my daughters, I lived for Sundays. For that one day, the counselor hiked to a satellite phone area to report in. The calls were mostly about how each girl was "opening up," "coming clean," "facing her issues." I knocked away the therapy talk since none of it applied to our real lives, our days in the same house that were coming up frighteningly fast. One counselor told me that although the idea was that the girls would never run into each other, they had—their two groups had been called into the same large wall tent when a ferocious snowstorm hit, and Stephanie, realizing her sister had to be nearby, began singing Blondie songs at the tiptop of her voice with a Deborah Harry squeak until Amanda heard her. They each pitched a fit until they were allowed fifteen minutes together. Fifteen fleeting minutes: What did they talk about? How to run again? Where to go next? The counselor couldn't tell me—the girls had been left alone. Nor could he tell me if Amanda and Stephanie still thought of themselves as my daughters, or if they wanted to rejoin this family, their family. I needed to know if they were ready to get back to school; to step into our household again with whatever version of ease we could manage; to let me figure out how to know them, care for them. To remember how much I loved them. "Does she miss me?" I asked the counselor on the other end of the phone one Sunday afternoon.

"Yeah, sure," he said. "She talks about you. I think she wants to come home." But he gave me not one clue as to how to make that work.

Near the end of Amanda's three weeks, the psychologist called to say he'd gone out to visit the girls' encampments, had interviewed both daughters, and had decided that neither one was ready to live in Eugene. He predicted it would take six months to cure them of the street, to rid them of the high of sleeping in abandoned buildings and spare-changing on street corners, of drifting off at night in a blur of some drug I'd never heard of. It would take half a year at least, he thought, to get them to let go of each other.

What came over me like a warm burst of wind as he said these things was unexpected relief. Sitting there at my kitchen table, I could finally admit how much I didn't want to be in charge of my own children again. To be the house police again, the enforcer. I was afraid of my daughters—and I'll bet they were afraid too. The trek was entirely about changing them, altering them, and nothing about changing me. The original plan of wilderness therapy was for them to come home caked with three weeks of dirt and sweat, carrying a new resolve, embracing the same house with the same rules and entrenched patterns they'd left. Now, the trek's head psychologist told me on the phone, they wouldn't do that. Neither of my daughters was going to return to me. And I could blame the decision to keep them apart from each other, and from me, at least for a while longer, on the experts.

But where would they go? Our friends in Montana, who'd loved the girls since they were little, had already offered to let Stephanie live with them if that would ever help. I called Richard and Jane and took them up on it. But I couldn't think of any family or other friends who lived in an area remote enough to keep Amanda from running. The psychologist suggested a family in Burns, fourth-generation ranchers, who needed someone to help cook for the hired hands and to pitch in on household duties for Donna, the arthritic ranch wife, whose fingers had curled like talons and whose knobbed knees wouldn't allow her to stand quite straight. Their house sat at the top of a sheer cliff with a face as wide and pale as a drive-in movie screen. Getting to the road from the house required hardscrabble travel; even if Amanda managed to make it that far, no locals would pick up this waif of a girl obviously out of place. And so it happened. At the end of her wilderness trek, and without a chance to say goodbye to Stephanie, who'd be shipped to Montana a week later within hours of emerging from the woods, Amanda was driven to Burns.

They didn't see each other again for half a year. And for that, they would not forgive me.

Donna and Bill had long been in their beds (they'd gotten up before dawn) when I drove the car across the dark parking space behind their house. It was late April. A shadow flitted beside my window: Amanda. She'd been waiting under the eaves even though the clear night was biting cold. I slowed down so she could open the passenger door and climb in. Without a word she sighed and reached for my hand.

"You're freezing," I said, squeezing her long, thin fingers. She laughed and looked back at her sleeping sisters in the rear seat.

"I'm glad you're here, Mom," she said, pressing my fingers in return.

I pulled in at the guest cottage, a remodeled outbuilding at the edge of the pasture, that Donna called her bed-and-breakfast nook and for which she charged me sixty-five dollars a night. This on top of the thousand dollars a month we paid—Tom's mother contributing the majority—for Amanda to live there and help her with ranch duties. Most of the time the nook was rented to the just-married-and-just-graduated from Burns High School, young couples who didn't have money enough even to get to Bend for a night's honeymoon and who couldn't leave the chores at their ranches for that long anyway. The morning after they stayed, the newlyweds would join Donna and Bill and the boys for bacon, eggs, and French toast with whipped cream and frozen strawberries before getting back to their lifetimes of togetherness.

Under the twinkling stars of eastern Oregon's big sky, Amanda helped me unload the bags from the back of the car. We carried them into the cottage as quickly and quietly as we could; neither of us wanted Donna to appear on the house's front porch and start up a chatty conversation.

Though I barely knew this woman who'd taken in my daughter, I'd already let myself form an intense dislike toward her. Everything from Donna's living room decorated with Hummel figurines and elk antlers to her folksy syntax gave me more reason to hold her in disdain. She didn't think much of me, either. I'd caught her giving me the once-over enough that I figured she was gathering goods for the following week's gossip—my worn jeans and sweatshirts and my long, straight, undone hair; how I was divorced and full of ideas about books and writing and social causes; and how I'd tromped my daughters straight into the lower regions of hell.

It was hard to justify despising someone for taking over my role as Amanda's mother, especially when I'd asked her to do it, even more especially since I was secretly relieved to hand over my troubled child to someone else, but I did despise her. Once Amanda landed in Burns, the thought of another woman holding sway over my child drove me to madness—I stewed over it endlessly when I was back home. Jealousy was part of it, no doubt. Some of what I longed for was embodied in what Donna and Bill and their kids seemed to come by so easily: loyalty to one another. No matter what, I could tell every time I was there, the four of them were going to stick it out as a family.

Amanda and I got Mary and Mollie roused enough to move from car to bed. Once we were all inside, I dead-bolted the cottage door. For at least this night, Donna would have nothing to do with us, and I'd have nothing to do with her.

I changed into my nightgown and got onto the folded-out couch. Amanda stretched out next to me on top of the covers. She was still dressed but shoeless. She started talking to me about things she wouldn't have if we'd been home, if Stephanie had been anywhere near and they could have sneaked off to meet their friends on a dark street. Amanda told me she'd written an essay on *A Separate Peace*, and the teacher said it was the best paper she'd ever read at Burns High School. She told me about some boys who'd caught her outside one day during lunch and dunked her head in a bucket of muddy water and how the principal said it was just one of those things boys do. There were the girls in the bathroom who called her a slut and told her to keep her slutty hands off their boyfriends, who Amanda wouldn't have gone near anyway; the ranchers' wives who came up to visit Donna but didn't want this girl, with her tattooed arms and frizzed hair, in the same room with their kids. Donna and Bill's sons had been hard on her too. They ignored her most of the time and convinced their dad to assign her the worst jobs—shoveling cow shit or cleaning the hen house. The boys had given Amanda a feral kitten when she first arrived, but they neglected to tell her not to let it outside. Coyotes got it on her third day there.

She rolled closer to me on the bed and put her head on the edge of my pillow. With her warm breath against my face, she begged me to take her home. It would be different now, she said. She'd mind my rules. She'd go to school. "I want to go to school. I like school," she said. She swore: no more drugs, no more running off for days, no wild boys or booze or hair dye or cigarettes. No cutting open her arms and legs with paper clips or her Swiss army knife. "I promise, Mom. Really, I promise."

I sighed and pulled her closer—closer to me than she'd been for many years, since she'd left, an angry and confused girl, to go live with her father in Tucson. I didn't say anything—every bit of me wanted to accept her promises and whisk her on home, but I was too frightened of what that might break open. More I couldn't handle. We teetered there on a moment too fragile for words. It felt like all the reconciliation in the world was available if we'd just reach out and snatch it from the air—but wasn't that too simple? Yes, it was too simple. Both of us knew we were ignoring the one glaring part of this that hadn't been sorted out: Stephanie. Amanda hadn't mentioned Stephanie, not once, nor had I. Stephanie was in Montana, two states away, inaccessible, separate, while Amanda and I were right there with each other, pretending we were on the very cusp of change.

I hadn't seen Stephanie since January. I didn't phone her often enough and I knew it. I meant to call—like, I suppose, all those times Tom had meant to call the girls on their birthdays or after band concerts at school—but didn't. I'd wake up first thing on the Saturdays we weren't in Burns promising myself to have a long conversation with Stephanie over the weekend, a resolve that would nag at me until Sunday night and it was too late. I had a lot to do—the laundry, groceries, bill paying, catching up on work tasks, getting Mary and Mollie to lessons and activities—things that distracted me from the telephone. That was the excuse. That was my justification for not doing what needed to be done for my daughter.

When I did call, Stephanie and I talked for a couple of minutes—too cool and often monosyllabic—then I'd ask her to put Jane on. Jane was the one who gave me the real news on how my child was faring, how she spent most afternoons sitting under an apple tree at the far end of their meadow writing Amanda letters that were dozens of pages long. Letters that would be read first—and censored—by Amanda's ranchers, who picked up the mail every day and who'd been given permission by the trek's leaders to "scan for trouble."

Richard, Jane's husband, sent me copies of the book reports he'd urged Stephanie to write, and she sent me postcards from the cities he took her to on his travels around the country—*Mama,* those small notes would begin, or, once, *Mi Madre.* I left the cards on the counter, stared at them as if they'd arrived at the wrong address, mail from a stranger to a stranger. At the time I didn't consider myself to be neglectful of her—I can't remember quite how I saw it then, though I recall my indignant burn and surprise when Richard called me at work one day to ask what was I doing by not checking in with Stephanie more often. "Don't you know how much she needs to hear from you? She's going crazy without Amanda. We can only help so much. She *needs* you."

Was that right? Did she need me? Or was she counting on me to be the one who'd eventually spring her from her cage, nice as that cage was? I couldn't tell. I felt dead on my feet every day, and I wanted that to be enough of an excuse to justify being withdrawn from this one daughter. I wanted someone to give me permission to stay clear of one powder keg of problems until I'd rested up again. I created shallow reason after shallow reason for my step back from Stephanie. She wrote postcards and letters with simple sentences about going here, doing that, learning how to cook from Jane, spotting a mountain lion in the hills while hiking with Richard, reading to their baby, who'd just started to walk. I wrote her back about a play Mary and Mollie had put on in the backyard and about the endless rain of winter. Stephanie reached out to me in small, calculated ways—and I reached out to her in small, calculated ways. But I couldn't find enough strength in myself to make something big or important happen between us. Amanda was closer, and, stuck as she was with the ranchers, I was convinced she needed me more than her sister did—an opt-out that would haunt me for years.

Every day Stephanie waited for me to make things right with her was another day I let her down.

"Mom, please," Amanda said in that Burns cottage as she pressed herself under my arm. "Get me out of this place."

It didn't matter if I believed all of Amanda's promises to change—I had a fueled desire to head into the house the next morning and be her champion. I'd tell Donna that Amanda's bags were packed and that she was going home, where she could read poetry in her room if she wanted, or the Sunday *New York Times* piled on the coffee table. At home, she could speak certain names aloud—Bill Clinton and, worse, Hillary—without getting lectured and scolded. In Eugene, she could argue that cattle shouldn't have the run of public lands and streams without becoming the town's pariah. And when Stephanie did return to us in Eugene, that daughter would see that Amanda and I were on the same side, and then she would soon fall into place too.

I imagined how Donna introduced Amanda to the people at church, and at their weekly 4-H meetings, and at the Sears where she went to buy jeans and shoes and her plain cotton blouses. "This is Amanda, our foster child." It was that word *foster* that stirred up judgment and pity in strangers, and I loathed both sentiments. Every day at home I was consumed with an the urge to drive to Burns and demand my daughter back, but I couldn't. I'd made a deal with the psychologist to see it through until July. Amanda's compulsion to return to the streets and to drugs wouldn't be broken in her otherwise, he was sure of it. The minute she and Stephanie saw each other they'd be back with their friends, and maybe even do what they'd long threatened: jump on a freight train to another town, where I'd never find them. Even without Stephanie, Amanda could be drawn out by old pals—substance ones and human ones—and I'd be the enemy again. And wasn't that one reason to keep her in Burns as long as possible? The ranchers got the isolated Amanda, polite and mostly obedient but not alive the way a girl should be alive, and I got to sweep in every fourteen days to be cherished. I could hardly stand what Donna and Bill and their sons, as well as everyone in town, assumed about Amanda's bad home life. So what. I'd weather it all. I'd swallow Donna's tsk-tsk-ing about my lax and liberal ways if I got the other part of the deal: right now, my daughter adored me.

When I was a girl, whenever there was a NASA rocket launch on television my mother made sure to wake my siblings and me in the early hours so we could watch it. Sitting there in our living room, bleary, dry-mouthed, and wrapped in blankets, my sisters and brother—and later, another brother—and I looked on as our mother celebrated the country's voyages into space, her hand pressed flat to her pink-robed chest. Before we got to trick-or-treat on Halloween, she had us walk around the neighborhood with UNICEF boxes shaped like pumpkins, asking for donations for kids in countries I'd never heard of. Down at some drafty warehouse on the edge of town, we loaded boxes for the needy on Christmas Eve. My parents regularly left us with babysitters to attend Jaycees or YMCA meetings or some philanthropist's ball. When I was in the upper grades of elementary school, my mother took a clerical job with the Idaho state affairs committee—within a couple of years she was administrative director for the legislature's most powerful committee and sometimes stayed at the capitol building until late, hammering out the details of a bill proposal or a hearing. During the months the legislature wasn't in session—and when my father was traveling for work—my mom would often get up on a Saturday and call her neighborhood friends for a come-as-you-are breakfast, the women soon gathering in pajamas and slippers with blue curlers stuck in their tinted hair. She held bridge tournaments in our living room, with borrowed folding tables and chairs from one wall to the other and icy bloody marys lined up on a tray. She volunteered at our schools and with our Girl Scout troops and drove us to our lessons and activities and over to friends' houses. She jammed every one of her suburban-life minutes to the hilt. And I could tell it was not enough for her.

What would have been enough, I had no idea back then. But her longing for the nebulous something was obvious. Obvious in the way she *plink-plink*ed two Alka-Seltzer tablets in a glass of water at night and settled down to watch *Marcus Welby, M.D.*, and fold and iron clothes. Obvious in the way she might suddenly fly into our bedroom and shout about the messes we made, which she couldn't put up with anymore. Her laugh on the phone, full of longing.

I didn't really comprehend the extent of yearning in my mother until she starred as one of the molls in a Boise community theater production of *Guys and Dolls*. On opening night I sat in a worn black velvet seat in the second row next to Cindy, Ron on the other side—Becky was off at the babysitter's, and my dad out of town again. My mother was beautiful. She had on a short lime green dress that swayed with black fringe from top to bottom, and high-heeled black tap shoes that made her calves and thighs taut and shapely under fishnet stockings. Her dark brown hair was piled in curls, dotted with sequins, and she—with the long line of other women on either side of her—kicked her legs sky high, singing, "Take back your mink, take back your poils . . ." Cindy leaned over to me and whispered, "What's a poil?" I shook my head because I didn't know and also because I didn't want to be distracted from the sight up there on the stage—what I read as a full-on display of my mother's desire for something more than she had.

It didn't surprise me when I came in the door one day—a few years after *Guys and Dolls*—from Fairmont Junior High to hear the mewling of a newborn in the back of our house. No shock. I simply wondered what sort of project my mother had gotten involved with this time.

It had been an uneasy few months between us. I was thirteen by then and awkward in every way that applies to a girl that age—gangly limbed and stumbling in front of other kids at the bus stop and dropping dishes in the kitchen for no other reason than my hands just didn't work sometimes, and ranging, constantly, through the spaces of my mind for some sense of myself. Something in me had turned temporarily sour toward my mother, turned like a river that suddenly cuts across its meander to become straighter and faster. There was an iciness I neither liked nor recognized, but that seemed out of my control as it coursed through my body. My suddenly oversensitive and indignant teenage self didn't like how she smelled—though she'd smelled fine just a month earlier. The noises she made when she ate made me run to the other side of the house. She seemed so old—thirty that year I was thirteen—and, I had recently determined, her presence was stifling to me.

It was when we were in the car together—just the two of us on our way to my piano lesson or to the grocery store—that I would get especially sulky while she went on about someone else's child who'd brought home terrific grades or who'd won a 4-H ribbon at the fair or a prize at church. I wouldn't say anything out loud, though I had plenty of silent opinions: 4-H? I'd sink into my seat even further until she was asking me what was wrong and I was muttering, "Nothing."

What felt wrong to me at the time was that I was my mother's average daughter. Not especially pretty, and not talented. My grades were fair but, until I reached college, unremarkable. I didn't come up on parent-teacher night as the student who'd written the paper most worth noting; my artwork wasn't featured on the bulletin board. I couldn't sew or play volleyball or swim with the splashless strokes of the adept and poised girls from my school. My beautiful and multitalented mother—the most social of the mothers and the most vivacious—was, I worried back then, heartbroken over my blandness. She had suffered her parents' bitter disappointment—the town's disappointment—by getting pregnant and having a baby in high school. She'd not been able to finish college because of the pressures of young motherhood. And for all that trouble, she got me? Not too many years later she and I forged a new friendship, and I felt cherished by my mother again. But the year I reached thirteen I spent a lot of teenage energy suspecting she'd replace me in a second if she could.

That day after school I followed the sounds of an infant crying to the back of our house, stepping just past the threshold into the sun-drenched room meant for guests and projects. A crib was set up in the corner. My mom was sitting in the rocking chair that she'd moved up from the downstairs den, where it had been when I left that morning. In her arms was a baby, wrapped in a pale pink blanket.

"Look how small she is," she said when she saw me. She pulled back a corner of the blanket so I could peer down at an even pinker, and wrinkled, face.

I set my book bag and wadded sweater on the floor and moved closer to the chair. "Who is she?" I said, putting both hands on the armrest and dipping my face near the baby's. A clean smell of spring and cloying baby powder filled my nose.

"She doesn't have a name yet," my mother said. "What name do you think we should give her?" She looked at me expectantly, offering me this piece of engagement in her new project. But I shook my head—why was it up to us to name someone else's child?

My mother's gaze returned to the infant in her arms. "She's going to be with us until they find someone to adopt her." Mom didn't clarify the *they,* and I didn't think to ask who would thrust a strange baby on our family on what should have been an ordinary Wednesday, with chores and meat loaf for dinner and my dad arriving late from New York.

"How long will that take?" I said.

"A few days, or a week maybe," my mother said, sliding the back of one curled index finger across the baby's cheek. The infant opened her eyes and blinked, looking out, though not at either of us. "She'll find a mommy pretty soon," my mother said.

I don't remember how much time went by before someone came to get that baby, a day or two maybe. But it didn't take me long—that child's stay and maybe the next one's—to understand that this was going to be my mother's mission for a while. She would be a foster parent to foster babies. Our house would be a way station between birth and the rest of life. That's the way it happened, and indeed that's the way it stayed—while my father's work took him farther and farther from us and for longer periods of time—until my mother had taken care of over fifty children and, in the middle of the foster-child flow, we all decided we should adopt one of the babies ourselves, a brother. Then we were a family of five children instead of four.

My mother happened to drive through Burns on her way to a business conference in the spring of 1995, and she arranged to stop and see Amanda and meet the foster family she lived with. At breakfast the morning after I'd arrived with Mary and Mollie in late April—Donna serving us hamburger-and-egg casserole, bacon from their own pigs, and white toast—Donna gave me her version of meeting my mom. She talked about what a wonderful woman she was, about what a great conversation they'd had.

My mother hadn't given me too many details about the couple of hours she'd spent in Burns—realizing the soreness of the subject with me—but she had slipped in a few nice compliments about Donna. "She's one of those down-to-earth women who's perfectly happy with her life," my mother said. "Isn't that refreshing?"

Once Donna was finished with the conversation about my mother and had finished her plate of eggs and bacon, she asked Amanda to clear the table. "Just wipe them off and set them in the sink, then you can take a walk with your mom."

The sound of her voice grated—a dull knife blade across ceramic—on me. Why did she think she could order my daughter around like this, as if she were the parent and I were the guest? But of course she had every right. This was her house, her rules, and Amanda was under her watch. I got up to help my daughter clear, crimping my lips together to keep myself from telling this woman to leave us alone. If Amanda noticed my anger or a tone of derision aimed at Donna, she didn't show it. It was as if she knew I couldn't defend her here in someone else's territory, nor could she defend me.

Outside, the boys waited for Mary and Mollie to climb in the back of a small hay-filled wagon hitched to one of the family's several four-wheelers. The eleven-year-old son was about to drive this one out to a distant pasture where there were baby goats to pet. I went out to push Mollie to the far end of the trailer and to pack a bale of hay up at her side, then did the same with Mary, ensuring they wouldn't bounce out if the boy hit a bump going too fast. The other child, the ten-year-old brother, was already revving the engine of his own four-wheeler, and I had little doubt there'd be a race as soon as they were out of our view.

"Hold on tight," I told Mollie.

"Mom, they're fine," Amanda said, taking my hand and tugging at me. "Let them go."

She and I stood next to a fence watching the ATVs tear over the rolling hills—Mary's hair flying backward like a flag—until they were out of sight.

"I want to show you something," Amanda said. She led me around the other side of the gate and away from the house, where, I guessed, Donna stood watching us through the window. A breeze stirred a fine skiff of dirt and dead grass around our ankles as we wandered toward the ranch's gray outbuildings—small sheds in which Bill stored his tools and equipment, larger buildings to house tractor and combine, and low-roofed pens for livestock. Amanda took me to one of those pens. A few cows glanced up from the fenced pasture to see what we were doing. Pulling my cardigan tight across my chest against a wind scented with cowpie and cow skin, I followed my daughter into a dim interior, sunlight streaming through the cracks between slats of wood and dashing the floor in long, fluid lines.

A cow stood in the middle of one pen, her udders bulging between her back legs, with two calves bawling at her side. Amanda leaned against the railing, reaching her hand over and clicking with both her fingers and her tongue at the babies. One stopped crying and blinked at her, moving his feet a few steps as if considering her request to come closer. This one was big-eyed, with long black lashes, and his smooth coat was brown with a few spots. But the other calf, hunkered behind the cud-chewing mother cow, was sickly, with a rough coat that looked as if it had been combed in the wrong direction. His legs were skinny and not quite straight.

"What's wrong with it?" I asked Amanda. I draped my own arms over the wood pole barrier, overwhelmed by the animal smell in the closed-up room—the smell of rotting flesh. I lifted the edge of my sweater and held it over my face like a veil.

Amanda, who seemed to have no such discomfort with the stench, pulled her arm back to her side. "His mother's sick," she said without looking at me. She explained how the cow in front of us had given birth to twins a few days earlier, and how one of those babies was stillborn, wet and sticky and lifeless. Amanda had helped Bill dry it off and wrap it up, placing the body behind the shed. A few hours later, Bill happened upon a newborn calf out in the field—the sick one now in the pen—trying to suckle from a milkless mother. He'd brought the half-starved one in and, fast as he could, skinned the dead calf's coat from its body, then grafted it onto the live calf's back—a quick stitch or two to hold it in place.

The decomposing skin, the source of the odor of death, hung on the sickly baby like a bad toupee.

"Bill's going to give it another couple of days," Amanda said. "He's hoping the cow will still recognize the smell enough to take this one on as her own." She reached her hand out again, this time calling to the sick calf. He stayed in place, head low and a breathy, mucousy bawl coming from his open mouth, while the large cow next to him continued her chewing and tail swishing, her nonchalance. Amanda watched for a second, then put her foot up on the rail in a cowgirl stance I hadn't seen from her before.

"But I don't know," she said. "It doesn't look to me like it's working."

That afternoon I drove Amanda, with Mary and Mollie in the back seat, to the small shopping center in downtown Burns to buy her new socks and makeup and a couple of fashion magazines that she could put under her bed and keep for herself only. We walked from shop to shop nearly out of things to say, all of us beat. No one had brought up Stephanie's name, and I had a feeling if I did, the goodwill that quivered so tenuously between Amanda and me would be ended too soon. In the hour or so since we'd left Bill and Donna's, a new impatience over this foster-care plan had bubbled up in me. It seemed as if Amanda was at an end with it too. She'd tamped

99

down her anger for over three months, but I knew rage was still in her—if anything, her time in Burns had added to the heat. And if anger came blasting out of her one day, what would happen then?

My intolerance of the deal with the ranchers had kicked up when Donna pulled me aside before we left on our shopping trip to tell me she'd intercepted several "disturbing" letters from Stephanie. Some of Stephanie's notes proposed a getaway plan—she'd hitch a ride to some small town in Montana, she'd wait for Amanda to get there, and then the two of them would disappear where we couldn't find them.

"What?" I said to Donna. "May I see those letters?" Richard and Jane didn't read Stephanie's mail, coming or going—they found the idea ridiculous. Steph had been mostly happy in their family, sullen and difficult sometimes, but even during her bad times these friends treated her as if she were their own loved child rather than a ward or a prisoner. So Donna's claim confused me. Stephanie might have had no problem running from me, but I couldn't believe she'd run away from Richard and Jane. These were people she adored, and she had to know that they'd probably saved her from her own set of ranchers.

Donna shook her head, refusing my request to see the letters. She'd already sent them to the psychologist at the wilderness-therapy program. "I had to show him how serious this is. These girls aren't even close to getting over this thing," she said. Along with that packet of mail, Donna had penned a note of her own proposing to the psychologist that July was too soon—that she was going to need the summer at least to turn Amanda around.

"No," I said as she described this plan to extend Amanda's stay. "This is over in July."

Donna opened her mouth, as if she were about to tell me to mind my own business—that she and the experts had this figured out, and I was only getting in the way. But I stared her down and she didn't say another word.

Now, as I watched my daughter pick through baskets of on-sale lipsticks and try on cheaply made earrings—the only junk available in these junky stores—I wondered how much of Stephanie's plan for escape, if it was true, Amanda was in on despite the intercepted mail and the monitored phone calls. How had I let myself become so blind, and so dumb? I got it now: Stephanie wasn't waiting patiently in Montana for the day she could rejoin her happy family. She was champing at the bit to go, to vanish, and she was going to make sure Amanda was with her.

By the time we got back to the car, I'd made up my mind. Amanda couldn't be a foster child any longer. I wouldn't let her. This experiment with a remedy had gone on too long and had divided us too much, and I wanted Amanda home and settled and happy and unified with me before Stephanie saw her again. My oldest daughter needed to fit somewhere, to make friends and find companionship, to do some kind of work that satisfied and fulfilled her. As soon as I could, I was getting Amanda out of Burns.

In the middle of May, I found a youth corps in Eugene, a professional company that hired kids from sixteen to nineteen years old to work in the woods as trail builders and tree planters. The crews packed up and drove to the wilderness one early morning and stayed out for six weeks. I called Amanda on a Monday afternoon after I'd talked to the corps office and had found out there was a spot left on one crew—the group of twelve kids and two leaders would leave for the Ochoco Mountains on Saturday. Could I get my daughter there, geared up and ready to go by then?

"Can you get to Bend tomorrow night?" I asked her. "Do you know anybody who's going that way?"

"I'll find a ride, Mom, don't worry," she said, breathless. "I'll be there."

I didn't speak to Donna or Bill or the wilderness-therapy psychologist—I didn't even think to speak to them, or consider for a moment that their feelings about this change in the plan for Amanda mattered or counted. I had one goal only, and that was to get my daughter back onto my turf and off theirs.

On the last Tuesday of her foster-home stay, while Donna was taking the boys to a doctor's appointment, Amanda left a note on the kitchen counter saying that she'd hitched a ride with her

English teacher who was off to Bend on an errand and that she wouldn't be back. That evening she walked into the parking lot of the Buffalo Drive-In, where we'd planned to meet, and opened the front passenger door of our car. "Shotgun!" she called, just like she used to in the old days. Mary climbed into the back with only a little complaint, and Amanda slipped into the seat and buckled in. I opened my window to let the evening's cool air blow on my face and hair—I hadn't felt this much freedom in a long time. I turned the car out of the drive-in parking lot and we went home.

Five months after Amanda left the ranchers' house, after she'd spent some good months with the youth corps far out in the Northwest wilderness, and not long after Stephanie returned to us from Montana, they were gone again. This time they went as far away as Stephanie's letters had promised they would. They went farther than Steve the ex–LA cop could look. They shed the wilderness treks like so much bad skin; the long separation from each other and from their sisters and from me proved to be useless.

That summer, when both girls were home again and we were trying to start over as a family, I was fixed on my bond with Amanda, made in Burns. I figured that bond would hold for a long time. I relied on Amanda to convince Stephanie to give up the idea of running, even though Stephanie talked constantly of her aim to become a traveler, one of those street kids who wandered from town to town by freight train. She often egged Amanda on for an adventure with all the money earned from trail building, stream cleaning, tree planting. I dismissed these ridiculous threats of leaving; the thought of Stephanie jumping a train was outrageous, too audacious even for this audacious girl. I had to believe my daughters would get back into school and settle down. What couldn't happen was that things would get bad again, as bad as they were before. None of us could survive that.

But it took only a week, maybe two, for Amanda to start staying out all night with her sister. She stumbled in with Stephanie after being gone for days, reeking of alcohol and cigarettes, a new tattoo on her arm, her hip, her belly, and a thick silver stud pierced through her tongue. They slept all day while I was at work, took off again before I got home, leaving filthy clothes and empty red packs of Pall Malls behind on their bedroom floor. The husband of one of my friends, a lawyer, called me with advice—it was time to put an end to this. He said I had the legal option of typing up a letter stating that they weren't allowed in the house any longer. I should post it on the front door. Change the locks. Then go to court and start emancipation proceedings. Cut my daughters away from the family before they once again cut away from us. But I couldn't go through with such a plan. I was desperate for Amanda and Stephanie to stay home and be the girls they'd been a few years before, or even the girls they'd been when Amanda was in Burns and Stephanie in Montana. Yet at the same time part of me wanted them to go away—as far as they could go—and leave their sisters and me alone.

In other words, my daughters had to act, one way or another and fast, so I didn't have to.

5

ONE EVENING, NOT LONG BEFORE MY DAUGHTERS JUMPED a train that would take them to San Francisco and, later, down the coast and east to Tucson, Stephanie showed up at our house. Without my knowing it, my fourteen-year-old daughter, who hadn't been around for several days, slipped through the front door and made her way to the bedroom to gather clean underwear and T-shirts, cramming them into a bag while she whispered to Mary to wrap up some of the cookies—their smell gave them away—I'd just baked.

A few minutes later, Mary sidled up next to me at the stove and whispered, "Mom," in such a way I knew one of my disappeared children was in our home.

"What's she doing?" I asked Mary, who simply moved closer. I don't know why I asked. It was obviously Stephanie's turn to show up for restocking: her turn to dump dirty clothes in the middle of their floor and get clean ones; to grab whatever food she could and maybe a few things to sell on the street; to come and go as fast as possible.

I walked down the hall to the bedroom with the barest flicker of hope that she'd come during the evening hours for a reason—that maybe she wanted to talk to me, wanted me to urge her to stay home.

"What's going on?" I asked her as she hunched over to jam more stuff into the canvas bag. Instantly I knew this was another useless question in a string of useless questions aimed at these girls. I held a spatula in my right hand, held it like a flag, its flat rubber surface glistening. I was making pork chops for dinner, with apples fried in butter and cinnamon. This seemed the moment to remind her that she liked that meal, and also that she'd once been glad for my food and my comfort, happy to sit at the table like a normal child to eat the food on her plate and to talk about her day and, after dinner, to help with the dishes and get ready for school, to do her homework and straighten her room. Not this bullshit of showing up to take what she wanted, our house her loading dock. Our house and the people in it her department store.

"I'm not getting into this with you," she said without looking up. "Amanda's waiting for me. I've got to go."

"You have to do everything Amanda tells you?"

Stephanie laughed at this, shaking her head as if I couldn't possibly understand her or them. "Amanda wouldn't let me down and I'm not going to let her down." She buckled the last strap of her pack and heaved it onto her back.

She walked past me just as a drip of butter rolled down my arm. The smell of cigarettes and sour beer and dusty alleyways wafted from Stephanie's threadbare clothes, mixing with the scent of cooking coming from me. Her oily hair stuck to her head, flat on one side where she'd slept on it in some concrete corner of an abandoned building, some patch of grass under a grove of trees in the park. The dirt packed under her fingernails also ringed her cuticles. I followed her as she scuffed through the living room.

Nearly gone now, her hand pulling on the doorknob and the wrapped cookies tucked under her arm, Stephanie turned back to look at me. That's when I blurted out what I'd been hesitant to say out loud: that my mother had called. She'd be in Portland on business that weekend and had invited us up to swim and go to dinner and stay the night at her hotel. "She wants to see you and Amanda," I said. "Can you do that? Can you go see your grandmother?"

Stephanie's face froze. Her chewed-raw lips twitched and she looked out the open door. She shrugged and pulled herself in tight. "I don't know, Mom. I'll ask Amanda."

She closed the door behind her. I stood in our dusk-washed

front room for a few seconds with, I noticed, Mary a few feet from me, trying to decipher once again this position I was in with my daughters. I put up with their showing up and leaving because I didn't know what not putting up with it would look like. If I told Amanda and Stephanie they absolutely weren't allowed back in the house unless they came home to stay, I'd give up the last shred of contact with my own children. I wasn't about to do that.

This was a quandary I couldn't quite explain to my mother. When I'd spoken with her on the phone earlier that day, she'd said she wanted to see all four girls when she came to Oregon for the weekend—she hadn't been around them for quite a long time. I'd already told her Mary and Mollie and I would be up in time for a late dinner, but that there was no use bringing the older ones.

"You wouldn't recognize them," I said.

She was quiet for a second. "I thought things were better," she said. She was referring to the wilderness therapy and to the foster care, both of which were supposed to have straightened out my teenagers. "How bad could they be?"

"Bad," I told her.

But in the end my mother convinced me that it would do us good to get out of Eugene and into a place where civilized behavior was expected. Maybe if we got on the road, even a short trip, the girls would come around in ways they had refused to—or couldn't—at home.

What I didn't tell my mom was that I had no idea where Amanda and Stephanie were staying at night or that days passed without my hearing a word from either of them. I didn't bother to describe the hopelessness that had found a permanent perch on the bony surface of my sternum. Nor did I talk about the chasm between my world and the one my daughters had chosen, the impossibility of a bridge spanning from them to me. I wanted my mom to believe that this was a teenage phase that would sort itself out any time. That the girls would soon enough return home to be cooperative, cheerful, loving, as they used to be when she took them to Disneyland, or to Washington, D.C., to see the sights; when she took them shopping for school clothes each fall. Or when she'd show off her polite and sparkling-clean granddaughters to her friends.

Or did I have another motive when I said yes to Portland? Sure. Part of my desire was to pull my daughters off the street and into the car and up the hundred-mile stretch of road so someone else could witness the misery we'd fallen into, and for that someone else to please, please notice that I was down to my last inch of ability to cope. I dreamed about—I plotted and fantasized about—another person taking over. Someone who'd call the cops, deal with counselors, soothe Mary and Mollie, and face these girls who showed up for clothes and food when they felt like it. So far, no one had come around volunteering to pick up where I so very much wanted to leave off. Hillary Clinton was quoted again in the newspaper saying it took a village to raise a child, but so far my village seemed empty, doors locked and shutters sealed tight.

Amanda called me, as promised, the night following Stephanie's drop-in. "I heard you wanted to talk to me," she said, her voice flat and distant.

I told her about visiting my mother in Portland. "Can you manage that?"

There was a long pause on the phone. "This better not be another trick," she said. "I'm not falling for any more of your tricks."

"Amanda," I said, a little surprised that she'd believe I had the inclination or the energy or even the money to have them picked up and hauled off to the woods or anywhere else. I was tapped out, and everyone around me was tapped out too. "It's a visit with my mother. You want to call her and check it out?"

Another silence. "I'm only coming if Riki comes."

Riki. A squatty girl Amanda had hooked up with along the way; a girl who went about everywhere Amanda and Stephanie went, the three of them a triangle rarely parted. I didn't know much of Riki's story except that her parents had supposedly released her to a street life, telling her that she could come home if it didn't work out. Amanda loved to throw that one at me—how there were parents who let their kids try what they needed to try, who were enlightened and understanding beyond anything I could dredge out of my miserly self. Riki. The last person I wanted in my car was this girl with her wool hat covering every bit of her SOS-pad hair, and her squinty little eyes darting around while she plunged her hands into the deep interior of her overstuffed coat.

"What's Riki going to do? Nana's not going to want a strange kid around, she wants to see you."

"Fine. We won't go then."

"Okay, all right," I said before she could hang up. "She can go." I asked Amanda to be at our house on Friday by the time I got off work, and to bring Stephanie too.

"We'll be there. And so will Riki," Amanda said. "And I'd better warn you: she has a knife."

I laughed, one of those laughs with no joy in it. "What are you talking about? She has a knife. Why would you say something like that?"

But Amanda had already hung up.

The drive up I-5 was too quiet, Mary and Mollie uttering no more than a few soft-spoken words and avoiding sisters who'd become mean and strange. Estranged. The teenagers in the back seat reeked —their clothes, their feet, their hair. I rolled down the windows to let the odor out and fresh air in. I called to Mary to see if she was okay and she sent back one barely audible *yes.* Against my better judgment, to make room for Riki, I'd let Mary, who'd recently turned eleven, climb in the back of our station wagon with the luggage. She'd hunkered down in a nest she'd made with her blanket and pillow and slept most of the way to Portland, while Mollie sat beside me, staring ahead, sometimes holding my hand. The teenagers whispered and giggled to one another and took off their half-damp boots, upping the volume on the sweaty-feet, no-bath-for-a-month stench. Amanda spoke directly to me only once during the trip—she leaned between the two front seats to say she wanted to stop for a cigarette. When I didn't respond, thinking as I tended to then that it was better to say nothing instead of something, she muttered to Riki, "See what I mean?"

Finally we stood in front of my mother, who'd changed out of her business suit and into an equally spotless outfit, a pale yellow pair of sweatpants and a matching zip-up top. Her hair was done, her makeup right. The look on her face the second she answered the hotel room door let me know that it — *it* being the shape my family was in — was worse than she'd let herself imagine. Up to this moment, my mother hadn't yet seen her granddaughters' full street regalia: ragged canvas pants, Doc Martens boots, black sweatshirts covered with patches, face piercings, the chopped and dyed hair. No one in my mother's Idaho looked quite like this, like neglected, motherless children.

Though we'd talked on the phone about dinner downtown and a walk in the riverfront park, my mom suggested we stay at the hotel; when we got to the restaurant on the first floor, she asked for a table at the back, near the windows. The hostess did one better — she hurried the seven of us around the corner to the closed section and told us this way we'd have plenty of privacy. She reached across to hand out plastic menus and said someone would be along to set our table. Then, trying not to shift her eyes to stare at the girls but staring nonetheless, she rushed away.

I lowered myself into a chair, heavy with a mix of emotion. Exhaustion, bitterness, embarrassment. But defensiveness too. A feeling that hadn't burned in my chest for a long time. No matter how they looked, these were my daughters, and still just kids. Not criminals, not deviants, just girls out there on some messy and confounding edge. Without expecting to, I resented the hostess for running off to the kitchen to gossip about the unsightly teenagers at the back table, even though I thought and even talked about my girls in those terms all the time.

Putting the menu in front of my face, I searched for the cheapest glass of red wine, as I planned to have several. I'd plunked my daughters into the middle of my mother's world, which was unfair to her and unfair to them, and now I writhed under the results of that decision. My mom had told me on the phone that she could handle the kids no matter what, but I'd known she'd be uncomfortable once they were around her; I'd known this visit would prove disastrous. Yet I'd brought them anyway. And now that we were in the middle of our evening together, I didn't feel any more understood by my alarmed mother, who sat at the other end of the table asking Mary and Mollie about school, nor could this brief visit allow her to peer deep into the layers of mess we were in. And the three older girls, lined up opposite me, waving knives around and sucking the cream out of the small plastic containers, didn't seem to care what any of us thought of them. They were too invested in being punk and homeless, unpredictable, frightening, and rank.

By ten o'clock I was in one bed with Mary, and my mom was in the other with Mollie. Amanda and Stephanie and Riki had spread their ripe sleeping bags on the floor. They'd taken off their boots but slept in rumpled clothes: old Carhartt's and thin cotton shirts, bought secondhand or rummaged from a free box. I listened to their soft breathing from the far side of the room and felt the warm bundle of heat that was Mary next to me. I lay awake, figuring my mother wasn't sleeping either. She was probably wondering how to help me with these girls who'd become alien. And like me, she was probably counting the hours until we would leave, until we could all go to our own homes and stop pretending that this wasn't a disaster.

The next day we went downtown. As soon as I parked, Amanda and Stephanie were out and gone, Riki running after them. Scattered. I had no idea if they'd meet us at the car at the appointed time and in fact expected they wouldn't. Every corner here in Portland had its requisite allotment of street kids, begging for change, digging through garbage for five-cent returnable cans and bottles, sharing cigarettes that passed from one set of lips to another. Amanda and Stephanie would fit right in. Maybe I'd unwittingly — or willfully — given my kids a two-hour boost on their ultimate trip out of town, the one that had been long fomenting.

"What are you going to do?" my mother asked once Mary and Mollie were far enough away not to hear her question, looking at clothes or music in a shop or just staying apart from what they knew would be a rag on their sisters. "You can't let this go on."

I couldn't give her an answer then, nor could I give her an answer when she asked again at the airport later that afternoon. "What are you going to do?" I didn't know what I was going to do, except just drive home. All five girls were in the car, ready to head to Eugene, where the older ones would hit the streets and the younger ones would follow me into our house. I watched my mother pull her suitcases into the wide revolving airport door so a plane could take her back to her own life and I got back into my car and drove away.

Mary was in front this time, Mollie tucked in between our bags in the back. Another reason to hate Riki, and I did hate her, aiming my wrath at her small, squat body and unable to admit how over-easy it was to use her as this day's central target. I'd made no effort to get to know her, instead behaving like the closed-down, hyper-judgmental woman that I'm sure my kids had portrayed me to be. I twisted to glare in Riki's direction just because I could.

It had started to rain. Pour, in fact, the streaking water keeping me from seeing the green highway signs over our heads. I was searching for the first exit to a populated area where I could find gas. I'd hoped I wouldn't have to fill up, stretched as my finances had become that weekend, even though my mother had paid for about everything—I wanted to think I could sputter the hundred miles to Eugene on the last few gallons, but we'd been on E for too long, and now I was worried.

"What's that one say, Mary?" I asked her.

The wiper dashed the rain out of her line of sight for just a second. "Stafford," she called out.

"Stafford," I repeated. I didn't know if it was a place with gas stations or one of those exits that led to wide acres of farmland, but I couldn't take a chance: the arrow on my fuel gauge had sunk even deeper below empty. I turned off on the exit. Within five minutes I realized I'd blown it—we were driving away from buildings and people and toward wet emptiness. There were no turnoffs, no opportunities to flip around on this highway. And there were no gas stations. The engine faltered, the last of the fuel gone, the car jerking and coughing before it died.

I turned the wheel toward the shoulder and rolled as far as I could onto the gravel-and-weed bed and then shut off the ignition. I laid my face in my hands.

"What the fuck?" Amanda said.

What the fuck was right. What the fuck was I doing in this car with three girls I could hardly tolerate—one of whom I trusted not at all. What the fuck was I doing one hundred miles from my house—the only place I felt even the slightest bit safe anymore. What the fuck was I going to do to get us out of this.

Though the rain wasn't letting up, we still had three hours of daylight left, and that was a good thing. But not a single car had passed us on the highway. I told Amanda she had to stay with the little girls; Stephanie and I would go over the berm to see if we could find help.

"No way," Stephanie said, glaring at Amanda as if waiting for her big sister to bail her out of this one. But Amanda was worried about herself.

"You're not leaving me here," she said, sticking her head between the seats so her breath mingled with mine. "Forget it."

"What do you suggest?" I said. "Do you have a better plan?"

I knew it was a stupid question the second I asked it—of course she had a better plan: the three of them would get out of the car, thrust out their thumbs, and be on their way. But she didn't say that. She shrugged instead. "Just hurry up," she muttered.

Stephanie, sighing, climbed out of the car and up the steep roadside hill with me behind her, both of us clawing at the soaked ground to stay on our feet and pulling on the vegetation for leverage. Most of those bushes were blackberry vines, loaded with thorns that tore into my hands and raked my arms. Halfway up the incline, Stephanie shouted at me that she was stuck—tangled—and I rushed over to work the thorny vines from her short crop of hair, but not before the stickers had split red lines across her cheeks and forehead. She wiped the blood away and kept climbing until we reached the top—muddy, scratched, wet. Dogs barked at us from a yard not too far in the distance, and I saw a man come out the sliding door to see what the ruckus was about. "Hey!" I shouted, making my voice loud enough to compete with the pounding rain. "Can you help us?" He slammed the door shut and turned out his lights.

"What's wrong with him?" Stephanie asked as she slipped and slid across the muddy ground to the fence. "Hey, mister! Come back out here!" She turned to me. "Mom, make him help us!"

I looked at her through the rain and let myself believe, for the first time since we'd left the car, that Stephanie might be in this with me. That we were going to do what we had to do together. That feeling alone, slightly warm and almost delicious, pushed me on up the hill.

For an hour or so, we wandered across farmland and through thickets of wild brush until we finally came out on a small rural road. I dreaded the moment Stephanie would ask if we were lost, because we were. If I'd absolutely had to get back from here to my daughters left in the car, I wouldn't be able to. What if Amanda had grown sick of waiting? What if she was getting high in front of her sisters? What if she and Riki had jumped out and waved down a passing car, leaving her little sisters?

"She has a knife." That's the line that wouldn't leave me alone. "I'd better warn you, Riki has a knife."

Stephanie and I walked along the side of the road in silence, both of us shielding our eyes from the rain so we could catch any hint of an approaching car in the late-afternoon light. Finally, we did see one. A station wagon came right at us—a shiny Volvo, its wipers sweeping rain from the windshield. I waved my arms and shouted while Stephanie stayed back on the lower part of the road's shoulder. "Please stop!" she yelled from there. "Please help us!"

The car slowed, then pulled over, and I ran around to the driver-side window, my heart leaping at the first chance of getting out of this. The woman at the wheel rolled down her window a couple of inches, peering at my drowned-rat face and hair, while I explained that my car had broken down on a highway back there somewhere, and that I'd left children alone over an hour earlier. "Could you get us to a gas station?" I asked.

She, a neatly dressed woman in her forties wearing a soft sweater and a flashy wedding ring, glanced over at a girl in the passenger seat. Her daughter, I guessed. The girl, whose long white neck was adorned with a simple silver chain, was silent as she stared back at her mother, advocating neither for us nor against us. Two silver thermos mugs sat in the dashboard cup holders. The girl picked one up and held it tight in her hand.

"Okay," the mother said, turning back toward me. "I suppose. There's a place not far from here."

"Steph, hop in!" I called, and opened the back door. I slipped onto the leather seat, slopping mud and water into their spotless interior. Stephanie brought in more detritus on the other side. "I'm sorry about the dirt," I said, but stopped speaking when I registered the shock on both faces from the front—the mother-daughter pair who'd twisted around to look at us hadn't really seen Stephanie until now. They took in the eyeliner running in thick black streaks down her face; the quarter-size medallions wedged in her stretched earlobes; the spiked dog collar around her neck; at the Harley-Davidson tank top that had been her father's in college, under an open hoodie that was plastered onto her. I could tell the woman was about to chase us back out into the dusky afternoon. "Please. I've got to get to my little girls," I insisted, I begged. "I'm sure they're scared out of their minds." I didn't stop talking until she'd turned around, put the car in gear, and drove on. Then I sat against the warm seat. I closed my eyes and let my head fall forward, bowling-ball heavy, my sinuses aching from physical exertion and wet air, and my soaked legs and back hot and itchy against the upholstery. Trickles of acid stung my throat and I was about to open a window for fresh air to keep myself from going a little nuts when I felt Stephanie slip her hand into mine. She wrapped her cold fingers around my cold fingers. I looked over at my daughter in the dim light. Rivulets of black ran from her eyes to her chin. I felt her warm breath on my face in the warm, muggy car. I dared not scoot toward her or even relax in her direction; I dared not move lest she pull the hand back into her lap. I wanted to make a show of this, let the mother glancing in the rearview mirror know that my daughter was as worthy of love as her own, but I stayed still. Until we reached the gas station, Stephanie didn't let me go.

I called a tow truck from the Chevron station where the woman dropped us, and when that driver arrived, Stephanie and I traveled back out to the Stafford highway with him. As soon as we pulled behind my car, Riki and Amanda leaped out. "Where the fuck have you been?" Amanda yelled. "Do you know how long we've been sitting here?"

The tow-truck driver—an older man with a potbelly and black suspenders, gray whiskers, and bad breath—stood up straighter. His fist clenched and he shot me a quick look. *If this were my kid,* that look said, *I'd knock the teeth out of that sass-mouth.* He went around to the front of the car. I pushed past Amanda and climbed in; Mollie reached over to wrap her arms around my neck. Her face was red and puffy, and Mary's chin trembled. They'd burrowed into the back of the car, Mary said, and stayed there while Amanda and Riki stood outside and smoked, threatening to leave as soon as they found a ride. But Amanda hadn't left. Maybe she'd had the chance to go, but she had stayed to watch over Mary and Mollie. I'd let myself lose faith in her, sure she'd ditched her sisters, but she hadn't. I embraced Mollie and thanked Amanda, though silently. I still regret not stirring enough generosity in myself to tell her how grateful I was to find her there.

The driver poured gas in the tank, and I tried the engine. No matter how I fiddled, the engine wouldn't start. The fuel-injection system had seized, and there was no fixing it out there in the dark. Just as the tow-truck driver had warned me when I first got him on the phone—it's a bad idea, he'd said, a very bad idea, to let a car like mine run out of gas.

He packed our luggage and all of us into his truck, hooked up the car, complaining to himself and dragging chains back and forth, and hauled us to the nearest settlement, which was nothing more than that same Chevron and a motel. He left my car in a bay to be attended to the next day, a time-and-a-half Sunday. While I wrote him a check, leaning over his hood, the teenagers, all three, ran away—gone before I could see them leave. I looked up, and they were no longer there. "Where'd they go?" I asked Mary, who shook her head. I shook my own head and cursed them, then lugged our bags and Mary and Mollie across the highway to the hotel. My mother was long home in Idaho by now. Once I checked in to a room, I phoned to tell her what had happened with the car. And to tell her that the three girls had jumped from the tow truck and disappeared. After I hung up, I settled into the pillows, though my back felt like a pile of bricks rather than soft flesh and warm blood. Mary and Mollie, already in their pajamas with the TV on and the covers of the other bed pulled up tight, seemed glad to be somewhere calm and safe.

"I'm hungry, Mom," Mary said out of that relative calm.

"Me too," Mollie said.

Of course they were hungry; we hadn't eaten since we'd grabbed sandwiches in downtown Portland that afternoon. The hotel had vending machines with bags of crap; the only other place within walking distance was the Chevron across the street, out here in the middle of nowhere. I put on my shoes and jacket and headed for the gas station. I had no idea how much money was in my account, but it wasn't much. If the attendant wouldn't take a credit card for food, we were out of luck. I'd put the motel room bill on that same card. I couldn't imagine how much the repairs would cost—more than I could manage. I scurried across the highway, remembering how Mollie had once asked me why when you're worried, your stomach gets so small. That's how mine felt now, tight and small.

When I got to the edge of the parking lot, I saw Stephanie leaning into the driver-side window of a souped-up sports car, a low, red, throbbing car. Stephanie was giggling, her hip cocked, and the boy in the driver's seat was grinning at her—she reached out her hand and he put something in her palm. I ran to the car, pushing my daughter aside and sticking my own face close to the boy's. "Do you know how old she is?" I shouted at him.

The kid, maybe seventeen or eighteen, leaned away from me and stomped on the gas pedal to make his car roar. "What's your problem, lady?" he said.

"My problem is that my daughter is fourteen years old. I saw you give her something. What did you give her?"

He looked over his right shoulder and sped his car backward out of the parking spot, forcing me to jump out of the way. Then he peeled forward across the asphalt and was gone.

Stephanie stood on the sidewalk, hands on her hips, with Amanda and Riki behind her. "Why did you just do that?" she said. "What is with you? Why can't you leave me alone?" She turned to look at the other two girls, as if waiting for them to join in the castigation. I stood with my hands on my hips also, the very picture of the irate mother, in front of the three of them. Stephanie took a step toward me. "Why don't you go back to the hell you came from?" she shouted in one last burst. A line she'd apparently been waiting to use on me at just the right moment, and the moment had arrived.

"Let's get out of here," Amanda said, tugging on Stephanie's arm. Then the three of them bolted. Like a startled flock of dull, gray pigeons, they were off all at once, leaving me to stand between two yellow lines. They melted into the night, hooting and shouting.

I plodded in the other direction, into the overlit gas station. The weary clerk nodded, as tired of me as I was of him. Shaking with anger and fear, I bought wrinkled hot dogs and chips and milk and the last sad apple in the place. And one ice-cold microbrewed ale.

When I got back in the room, the phone was ringing. It was my mother, who'd told her husband, who happened to be a state police officer, about what was going on. "We think you should go home tomorrow," she said. "If the girls are gone, they're gone. You can't stay there and look for them. If you leave them behind, it's because they've asked for it." She was frantic, I knew, to help me.

I didn't admit that I'd just seen them. I didn't tell her they'd taken off again. I just thanked her for her support and her ideas, which were both correct and impossible for me to imagine acting on, and hung up to go in search of any metal thing that would get the top off my bottle of beer. Mary suggested the buckle on her shoe and brought it over to me. I sat on the end of the bed and worked the thin silver buckle around the crimped cap, prying against it until my arm muscles were about to pop and my upper molars ground into the lower ones. Finally the lid flew across the room like a miniature Frisbee, pinging off the cheap wood dresser and flipping to the floor. I left it on the carpet and drank the beer in a series of long cold pulls while staring at an old episode of *The Simpsons*. Homer was beating Bart; Lisa was trying to calm everyone down. Mollie laughed. Mary asked if I was okay. I stood up to latch the chain on our door and to close the curtains over the windows. I shut us in for the long night ahead.

Eleven thirty was the hour shining from the bedside clock when I opened my eyes in the dark. Mary was shaking my shoulder. "Somebody's at the door," she whispered. Mollie sat up in the other bed, clutching her blankets to her chin. "Mommy, I'm scared," she said, her hair sticking out as if electrified.

I'd heard the pounding on the door, dull thuds, but had tried to convince myself the noise was coming from the next room and had nothing to do with us. But the sound was ours, and now the worst possibilities pushed into my mind: It was the police telling me one of the girls was dead. A county deputy informing me that they'd been arrested, raped, maimed, run over on the black strip of highway in front of the hotel. I wondered how to protect Mary and Mollie from the news on the other side of the door, and how to protect myself. I threw the bedspread around my shoulders and made my way toward the steady banging, not at all prepared to face whatever this was, many miles from home in a place where I had no transportation, no money. I peered through the peephole. It was Stephanie's face on the other side.

"What happened?" I asked her after I'd unlocked the door and yanked it open. Stephanie stood on the motel breezeway, cold air rushing around her and into the room, the lights of the Chevron station glaring in the background. I was face to face with her, cooled adrenaline pooling in my hands and feet. "Where's Amanda?" I said.

"She's sick," Stephanie said. "She needs help."

I peered down the breezeway for some glimpse of what was going on, then turned back to tell Mary and Mollie to climb in bed. I followed Stephanie, the concrete walk chilling the bottoms of my bare feet and the motel bedspread dragging behind me like a train. Around the corner, along another corridor of doors that led to rooms just like ours, Amanda was lying on the ground, her eyes closed. Riki squatted next to her.

I stopped just before we got to her to glare at trembling Stephanie, who hadn't quit gnawing on her fingernails since I'd opened the door.

"What did she take?" I said, kneeling down. Amanda twitched; she moaned. I stared at Riki, sure she was the one who'd suggested they get drugs, which obviously they'd managed to do even way out here in Podunk. I put my hand on Amanda's face; it burned hot.

"Mom, she's not on anything," Stephanie said. "She's just sick."

"Jesus, come on, Stephanie," I whispered so we wouldn't wake the people in the room behind us, so they wouldn't call the front-desk clerk, who'd send someone up to kick us out. "Don't give me that bullshit. What's she on?"

I got Amanda to her feet and wrapped the bedspread around her body. Stephanie held her on one side while I propped her up on the other, and we began shuffling her toward the room I'd rented. "You have to tell me what happened," I said again. "Where'd you go? What did you take?"

"We didn't go anywhere, Mom. Why can't you believe me?" Stephanie's face drooped with fatigue and exasperation. She rubbed her eyes with her free fist. "We just walked around and she said her ears hurt. She has that bad cold."

That statement caught me short. I hadn't noticed Amanda had a cold. Wind gusted over the hotel railing, chilling me, embarrassing me. Even though I'd spent the past thirty-six hours with her, I'd failed to notice my own daughter's illness.

Mary let us into the room, and Riki stood Boo Radley–like in the corner while I rolled Amanda onto one of the beds and told

Stephanie to get a warm washcloth. I called the front desk, and the clerk—the same guy Stephanie had badgered into giving out my room number while Amanda slumped across the lobby sofa—agreed to call a cab. "Could you make sure they'll take a card?" I said. "I don't have cash."

The guy sighed. "I'll do what I can," he said. "Be downstairs in ten minutes."

Ten minutes later, we were in a taxi, Amanda and I. She rested her hot face against my shoulder, and the cabdriver, a shock of red hair and a face full of freckles, chatted long strings of words. I ignored his banter and watched the meter click ahead, dollar to dollar to another dollar, while pretending the physical tenderness between my daughter and me—her head bouncing against my shoulder, my arm around her, squeezing her toward me—was part of our normal way of being with each other. The driver took us to a hospital on the outskirts of Portland, the closest emergency room, and agreed to wait until we were finished. "I won't get any calls," he said, stretching his arms. "I'll just take a nap."

Alone in the emergency room, we were ushered by a silent nurse into a cubicle. Chilled, too bright, jammed with medical equipment. Amanda sat at the edge of the examination table, revived halfway, her eyes pried open and drool glistening on her cheeks. I stood next to the table, holding her still while the tired doctor listened to her lungs and looked in her ears. He didn't mention her filthy clothes, her smell, the crust of dirt on her neck, and for that I was grateful—if he'd said something, I'd have had to try to explain or to defend myself as her mother, and I was incapable of doing that.

"That's a doozy," he said with a whistle when he put an eye against the scope he'd pressed into her right ear. "No wonder you passed out."

Her temperature was 104 degrees. She had walking pneumonia, and both ears were infected. One of the eardrums had burst, causing the pain and the blackout. When the doctor asked me how long she'd been sick, I couldn't tell him because I had no idea.

While I signed the insurance papers, a nurse packed Amanda's pockets with samples of antibiotics and prescription painkillers, and then she sent us on our way. It was nearly two in the morning. In another few hours the repairman at the station would come on duty and I'd plead with him to fix our car so we could all go home.

In the taxi, riding back to the motel where Stephanie and Riki were probably asleep on the floor, Mary and Mollie in the bed, I popped three pills from the cellophane package and laid them in my palm. Amanda took them, one at a time, dropping each on her tongue and swallowing it with a sip of the water I'd bought with my last quarters on the way out of the hospital. She handed me the bottle, then laid her head on my lap. She curled next to me like a kitten. I put my hand on her caked hair and searched in myself for a sense of possibility. But no matter how I tried to create a swell of hope, I couldn't. The past twenty-four hours outweighed the last two. The months and years of struggle outpaced and overcame any glimpse of reconciliation. The drive back to the hotel with Amanda didn't feel like the beginning of anything. The air between my daughter and me smelled and tasted and felt like goodbye.

The next day, a Sunday, they left for good. We'd been home only an hour or so when my oldest daughters came out on the patio with army packs stuffed full and tied to their backs.

I stood up from the flower bed, where I'd been pulling weeds and dead Shasta daisies, to face them. Amanda, remarkably improved after a day of antibiotics and ten hours of sleep, said they were going out for coffee. A pair of dirty Chuck Taylors dangled from the strap of her pack. "You need an extra pair of shoes for coffee?" I said. Amanda, a hand-rolled cigarette between her lips, turned and walked through the gate, Stephanie following. I went out the gate too, but waited on the sidewalk as I watched my children move far down the street. I didn't do anything to stop them. I didn't run ahead, jump in the car, call out their names as I had before. I didn't phone the police, who'd have ignored me anyway; I didn't say a word. I didn't tell them they could come home if things got too tough or that I'd love them always, no matter what. I didn't speak and I didn't move. This time, I let my daughters go.

6

WHEN AMANDA WAS A TODDLER, SHE PRETTY MUCH skipped baby talk, the usual burblings that meant *blanket* and *dog* and *juice* and *cookie*. The first words she spoke after *mommy* and *daddy* made a clean and clear sentence: "Stay out of the street." Of all that I'd said to her since she was born, this is what stuck. On warm afternoons, I'd sit on the front porch—soon into Amanda's second year I was swollen and pregnant with Stephanie—while my little girl puttered around the yard. Lumbering on legs that had just figured out walking, Amanda went after a ball or squatted to pick up a stray leaf from the grass. *Don't go far,* I'd call to her from a few feet away. *Stay right where I can see you.*

And stay out of the street.

In November 1996, the month Amanda turned seventeen, I'd gone three months without seeing her. Without putting my eyes on either her or on Stephanie. This marker in time came at the end of Thanksgiving break, after the two little girls and I had returned to Eugene from a long weekend that was supposed to get us *away from it all.* Mary, Mollie, and I had flown to Spokane, where we rented a car and drove through the snow to north Idaho. We turned east into Montana and made our way nearly to the Canadian border before stopping in a little town where we cooked up a holiday feast with Richard and Jane in their log cabin, all in an effort to blur what had been going on in our house, in our family. Except it hadn't helped: I'd come back as limp as the girls' jackets soaked with Oregon rain, which now hung over our dining room chairs and dripped puddles on the oak floor.

This time my oldest daughters were truly gone; this time they were among the missing—but was that the right word? The missing depart without their own volition. Amanda and Stephanie, especially with the boldness of this last departure—leaving no single clue as to where they were—had disappeared because they wanted to. They'd planned to go where they couldn't be located by me or by anyone I might hire to find them. The girls had swung their army packs onto their backs that early September afternoon when they should have been chatting on the phone with friends or worrying about a math test, when Amanda should have been in bed sipping hot chicken soup, curled up next to a heating pad with Stephanie beside her, both of them flopped on the bed to watch *The Princess Bride* for about the hundredth time. But instead, they'd sauntered down the street and didn't turn back. I've heard people say that the absence of a loved one is like living without an arm or a leg, but that description doesn't quite cut it for me. This time, with no sense of where my daughters were or when they'd be home again, I felt like I was being cleaned out one thin layer at a time, like the edge of spoon scraping away against the insides of a pumpkin. Like those late October evenings when I'd help my girls make a Halloween jack-o'-lantern, pulling away the seeds and the stringy guts and gouging at the orange meat until I was biting way too close to the skin, or until the skin was split.

Now, having been gone for a long weekend without checking the machine, I set down the pizza I'd picked up coming in from the airport and hurried to the phone to listen to voice mail, just in case. But the tape was blank. There was nothing, no word, no message, from my oldest daughters.

Mollie, cranky and yawning from hours of travel, moved the pizza box to the lip of the table to peek under the lid while Mary went off in search of the cat—under a bed, in the linen closet, or curled next to the water heater. I walked into the dark hallway, near the older girls' bedroom door, which we kept shut, to switch on the furnace I'd turned down for the trip. I stood over the same vent Mollie huddled on every winter morning to tent her nightgown and warm up her legs and tummy until breakfast was ready. The air streaming through the grill now was bitter, freezing, and I was restless—itchy almost—as if I knew bad news was coming. As if I knew that in a few minutes I'd once again be forced to wrap my mind around the unthinkable concerning my two oldest children.

The front door opened, and Barry, along with a bite of winter and more of its rain, pushed into the house. This man I'd become close to had driven in from his place in the country, nearly fifty miles away, to retrieve us at the airport. The girls and I had walked out of the terminal, and Barry, fairly new in their lives and not so long in mine, had stacked our luggage on top of the shovels, chains, handsaws, and axes that he kept in the back of his dirt-encrusted truck while we squeezed into seats that smelled like the fir trees near his house and something like the river he lived by. He'd brought us home through the rain, and now he moved back and forth from his truck, hauling suitcases and plastic bags, pillows and blankets, into the chilly living room.

During the past summer, when Mary and Mollie were gone for a two-month visit with their father, while Stephanie was still in Montana and Amanda working with the youth corps, I'd ventured into what would soon become the most stable adult relationship in my life. But at first it was new, and it was tentative: Barry and I made trips to the coast and had late-night dinners and swims in the river in July and in August, but over the fall months and with this new crop of trouble, I'd been waiting for him to fade away and wouldn't have blamed him if he had. Even that afternoon at the airport, I'd half expected to find a taxi driver holding a placard with our names on it and then handing me a note from Barry saying he'd had the Thanksgiving weekend to think about all this family complication and couldn't do it anymore. But here he was, steady as always and once again belying my fears, dropping a suitcase next to a pile of rumpled pants and muddy boots and plastic bags of bones and Montana moss. "One more load," he told me, water dripping from the square shoulders of his coat, beading on the edges of his trimmed and graying beard.

When I turned the corner into the kitchen again, Mollie reached out to pluck the edge of my sweater. "Can we eat?" she said, tugging. I looked down at her face. Of course I wanted her to eat, but I was slow to pull a stack of plates from the cupboard, hoping for I didn't know what—maybe some elusive homecoming relief. But calm didn't wash over me no matter how much I wanted it to. My body remained as tense and irritated as it had been at a bumpy thirty thousand feet in the airplane. On the ground, in my own kitchen, the knots should have loosened, but they didn't. Wrapped in my own hurt those days, I was pretty much blind to everyone else's—even Mary's and Mollie's sometimes. I got easily fed up when anyone or anything failed to tend to my pain. Even my old, frozen house.

With Misty stretched in the scoop of her arms, Mary sat down at the table. Barry came in with the last load, winter wind whooshing as he shut the door against the night. I put my hand on Mollie's head, smoothing bumps of sand-colored hair, sticky from several days of playing in the woods and no bath. She leaned in to clasp her arms around my waist and to press her face into my chest. I soaked up my youngest daughter, her wood-smoke smell and her warmth, even as I realized it wasn't good to need a child this much, to paw at her for comfort as often as I did. Barry moved past me, rolling his knuckles across my back, and I tried to believe it was possible to give in to this night and finally be home.

"Grab the napkins," I said to Mollie, releasing her from my hug. I moved things off the table, the small deer skull and the rocks the kids had hauled back, my own satchel of unread *New Yorkers*. Barry opened the refrigerator door, looking for drinks. "Milk for the girls," I said, peering past his shoulder for the icy ale on the bottom shelf. I'd saved it for this first night home. I planned to let it run down my throat and swirl into my arms, the muscles of my shoulders unclenching with each swallow. A ten-minute escape from everything.

After pouring glasses of milk and delivering them to the table for the others, I'd just opened that beer and sent the cap skittering across the counter when the phone rang. The voice at the other end made me still, my hand clammy on the receiver. I heard a woman repeat my name and was sure this was someone I didn't want to speak to.

"That's me," I said anyway.

"We have your daughter in custody," she said. The woman explained that she worked for the police in Tucson. She said an officer from her station had arrested Amanda the day before.

"Wait," I said, "wait a second." I shot Barry a look—*please keep the girls busy*—and then slipped into their room, painted the shade of a ripe tomato, a color Mary and Mollie had taken weeks to settle on. My knees were already jelly as I lowered myself to the end of Mary's twin bed. Her pink quilt wasn't warm, but I picked up the edge and wrapped it around my thighs, as if my child's comforter could stave off the worst of the woman's statements. I held the phone to my ear with one hand while the fingers of my other hand twisted the blanket in my lap. I heard Barry finish setting the table; I heard Mollie ask where I'd gone.

The woman said *drugs* and then she said *heroin,* and my mind stopped working, like a cassette tape stuck in a player, whirring and screeching but going neither forward nor back. "Are you all right?" she asked me when I didn't respond. Before I could answer, she repeated what she'd apparently already said: Amanda had been found on the streets a day earlier, on her seventeenth birthday, overdosed. She was lying on a sidewalk when the paramedics reached her and strapped her to a stretcher. The EMT gave her a shot that shocked her heart back to a normal rhythm—the kids around her, this woman said to me, told the paramedics that Amanda's heart had stopped twice in the hour before help arrived; one of them had breathed into her mouth and pumped on her chest.

My mother will want to come over to help and she'll see how dirty my refrigerator is, I was already thinking. I let any meandering thought keep away the news being delivered by this indifferent stranger. I wasn't going to let myself imagine Amanda nearly dead on the street or wonder yet about these "other kids" the woman referred to and whether Stephanie was one of them. I only pulled the quilt to my neck and pressed the phone to my pulsing ear while I let my mind go where it wanted. *Mary and Mollie won't want to go to school tomorrow. Barry will think he should stay the night, but maybe I need to be by myself. My father's going to ask why he sends money to help these kids if none of it does any good.*

I stood up, pacing the room, realizing I hadn't turned on the light. The stuffed animals on Mollie's bed, a javelina her father had sent her from Arizona and a soft-antlered moose from Barry, stared at me with black marble eyes. I studied their gray outlines for a second and wondered why the dark made stuffed animals look so mean. I did everything I could not to think about the heart in Amanda's chest. How unprotected it was now, and how unpredictable.

"Where is she? Can I talk to her?" I finally blurted out, though when I said the words aloud I surprised myself. They didn't sound tender. They sounded reluctant, hesitant. I was strangely apart from what I'd just requested, not sure I wanted to speak to my own daughter. What would I say to her? That even though I'd been furious at her and at Stephanie and about out of my mind with concern over their safety, I'd whisk her back into our home, all forgiven? I wasn't ready to go that far. I couldn't release the fear and the fervor that had built in me for months, for years, just like that. And what would Amanda say to me? That running away and living on the streets and shoving heroin into her veins was no big deal and that she was over it this fast? I doubted we were going there either.

"She doesn't want to come to the phone," the woman said. *Thank God*, I muttered under my breath. "She gave us your number but doesn't want to talk."

I didn't want to talk either. To anyone. I only wanted my life and the girls' lives to rewind two years so I'd get a second chance to stop all of this. But it wouldn't be stopped, so I turned my focus to making a plan, to bringing the gumption and fortitude of motherhood to bear—as if I had even one clue how to do that. I wasn't sure anymore what it even meant to be a mother. A real mother would know what to do next. A real mother would never have let this happen in the first place. A real mother would be thinking about her daughter as the police dispatcher went on and on about the condition that child was in. But my mind, seized and scared, was full of one ricocheting thought after another as I groped for any story other than the one coming from this phone.

What I thought about was the dark space under Mary's bed and the mouse we once found there.

The girls and I—five of us together, no dog collars or tattoos or pink hair yet; no *Sid and Nancy* weekend marathons; no bad acid trips in the field behind the too-expensive private high school where Amanda had lasted maybe two weeks; no threats to run away; no running away—didn't know it was dead or that it was a mouse until it started to reek. A decomposition stench that kept us from that end of the fixer-upper house I'd bought, with Mary and Mollie sleeping in my room once the stink got bad. One evening after work, I convinced Amanda and Stephanie to help me move the bed from the wall. When we exposed that area of the floor, we found a brown mass about the size of one of Mollie's socks splayed out, maggots throbbing from its mouth and squirming on its pointy teeth. I leaped back while Amanda and Stephanie screamed at the perfect pitch of adolescence, squealing and hopping from one foot to the other as if the mouse was about to jump up alive and skitter up their pants legs. In the hallway, Mary and Mollie started shouting too, all four of them running in a football huddle to the living room. Over the din, I called to Amanda to bring me a broom and the dustpan. She thrust those at me a few seconds later, making me walk to the bedroom door because she refused to come in again. I returned to the mouse and held my breath, squinting so I had to see only a blurry apparition of death, its little legs stuck out like dry twigs. With one sweep, I got most of it on the pan, though it took a couple more flicks of the broom to dislodge the last gooey chunks. I held the dustpan as far from me as I could and dashed down the hallway, out the door, and straight to the back fence with my four chattering daughters trailing behind. I tossed the mess into the strip of city-owned bushes. Gone that fast, peace reclaimed that quickly.

Now I opened the door of Mary and Mollie's room and let a thin line of yellow light penetrate the dusky interior where I stood. I watched the three at the table sticking triangles of pizza in their mouths. Barry looked over at me and held his hands palms up as if to ask what the heck was going on, his face a knot of confusion. I could tell he was concerned at my long time away, at being left out of the news, whatever it was, of this phone call. He wanted to help. I could see that. I could have gestured at him to come in, but I shut the door instead. I couldn't take anyone else's questions at that moment; I couldn't begin to explain what was going on. The woman was talking and talking, telling me that she'd called Amanda's father before she'd phoned me because Tom lived only a few miles from the youth center where our daughter was being held.

"He said it wasn't a good time for him, that things were difficult with his wife right now," she said. "So what do you want to do?"

Crawl into bed, stick cotton in my ears, fill my gut with a sleeping potion, pretend none of this was real. "I'll get her a plane ticket tomorrow," I managed to say, knowing I'd do just that but already scared about what it meant—of course, what it meant was that Amanda was coming home. A return that now terrified me, wished for though it was. "I'm sure her dad will put her on the plane to get her here."

Before she hung up, the question I'd been holding, too afraid too ask, had to make its way out. "What about Amanda's sister?" I asked the woman. "Is she there?"

"What's her name?"

"Stephanie."

Fourteen years old, disappeared with Amanda, the two of them deciding they'd rather hop on a freight train in the middle of the night and live on the streets than be with me.

I heard the sound of shuffling papers. "No Stephanie," she said after a few seconds. "There's nothing here about a sister."

· · ·

The therapist who crammed us into her little office once a week had suggested that Mary, Mollie, and I talk about the gone-away girls—how it felt to have been left by the gone-away daughters. We didn't go home and practice as she'd instructed, however. To speak about the way they had left us again made it too real, too in-our-faces. So I'd closed the door of Amanda and Stephanie's bedroom and let dust build in the darkness. In the rest of the house, Mary, Mollie, and I fell into distractions; or I should say, I encouraged distractions, because I liked thinking that being distracted was healthier than sitting around fretting about where they were and when they'd be back.

The weekend after Amanda and Stephanie had left, Mary, Mollie, and I packed up our swimsuits and towels and snacks and bottles of water for a day at our favorite swimming hole. We went without the girls who loved the small tributary deep in private timberland, called Mosby Creek, even more than the rest of us. It would have been easy to stay home and stare out the window wondering how we'd come to this and wishing they'd show up to squirrel themselves away in their room and turn their music up to blaring levels and paint new anarchist *A*'s on the walls and complain about how they were misunderstood, slogging out to the backyard to sneak a smoke and to chip the black polish off their fingernails. But I took my youngest girls to Mosby Creek because I thought it worthwhile to prove to myself, and to them, that Amanda and Stephanie's absence wasn't going to rule every minute of our days.

The three of us crunched our flip-flops over the gravel road that led to the swimming hole, heat waves rising from the bed of crushed rock laden with the stink of oil and tire rubber, and at least a dozen times I glanced behind us, still waiting for—hoping for—my scowling teenagers. Two miles into the hike, I scrambled down a hill behind Mary, tossing her our basket of food before I slid down the hard slope. The girls hopped over round chunks of granite and upthrust tree roots until they reached the creek's bank. When I got there, I spread out a towel at the edge of the slate blue water and pulled a novel from my bag, which I would finish in that one warm afternoon, a distraction, while Mollie ran to the highest point on the rock cliff and took her first long leap into the creek. She landed in a dark pool that my kids, summer after summer, had yet to find the bottom of. Mary followed her a second later, hooting as she jettisoned off the rock, scissoring her legs and flapping her arms. I stayed at the shallow end of the hole, wandering into the water until I was in waist deep and nearly numb from the cold. I watched, rather than felt, little trout nibble at my toes while I buried myself in the book, the sun hot on my shoulders and the top of my head. From my middle down, I felt practically nothing. A strange and comforting sensation, that half-aliveness. I listened to my squealing daughters in the background, the ripples of water over downstream rocks, and a screaming hawk overhead and didn't let myself remember a single thing in my life that had gone wrong. I couldn't bear to start adding up the mistakes I'd made as my daughters' mother—the wrong turns that had somehow led to this incomprehensible end.

When I think back on that woman in the creek, I see how I was equal parts wounded and defensive by then. When Amanda and Stephanie had come home from wilderness therapy and foster families, my efforts to heal us—that period when they went in and out of our home at will, gone for days then back for food, sleep, and another fight with me—I'd been re-contorted by my spun-out daughters. I was depleted by girls who'd long refused to do what I demanded, what I couldn't stop demanding: Go to school, come home. Stay home. At least when they were gone I could turn my full attention to Mary and Mollie, making sure the younger girls were being fed right and getting to their dance and music lessons and paying attention to schoolwork. But wait; could I so easily forget that two of the people I loved most in the world were nowhere I could find them? Each of the thousand times a day Amanda and Stephanie rose in my mind was another hole drilled through my sense of what was right—of what was wrong.

I wonder what that woman in the creek—what I—wanted. I hardly remember now any specific desires, any specific goals. For my children to return, to gather around me like the towheaded ducklings they were when they were little? Maybe. But I must have realized that if they'd returned, Amanda and Stephanie wouldn't suddenly have clean clothes and smooth hair or become girls who went to class and helped with the dishes after dinner. It would take them about five minutes to get back into the scene that made me crazy and kept me breathless—the booze, the drugs, the piercings and tattoos, the boys who offered endless adventure and pleasure. Days and days and too many nights without hearing from them. Absolutely I wanted them to come back—or did I? Returning to the same old crap, the same old tired patterns, would do us all in.

Best to stay in Mosby Creek, book up against my face, and let the cold sap me of all feeling.

When it became more obvious every day that Amanda and Stephanie were gone, gone, and not coming back anytime soon, Mary started listening to her tall collection of Billy Joel tapes for hours after dinner every night, wrapped in the pink quilt with her big cat curled devotedly in her lap. Mollie lost herself in skipping rope —pounding her way down the hallway and back up again until I thought the floor would fall through to the damp crawlspace below, where possums sometimes holed up for the winter and scratched away at our blankets of insulation. In their small room at the back of the house, the girls played with their families of plastic animals. They watched TV in the living room, memorizing nearly every line of every Adam Sandler movie we could rent, bantering back and forth with their favorite quips from *Saturday Night Live,* a show I let them stay up for once a week while I dozed on the couch. We ate dinner and talked about how our days had gone. We coped. We got by. We waited. And at night, just before bed, we fell into reading other people's stories—one more distraction before sleep to keep us from talking about the sisters who weren't there anymore.

On an evening a few weeks before our Montana Thanksgiving trip, Mary and Mollie settled on either side of Barry on our couch. He'd started to come by the house often, and though I had trouble trusting that such a person could happen to me, I slowly gave in to him and let myself notice that he was there when I needed him, and even when I hadn't realized I needed him. He didn't push

ideas of parenting, of how I might deal with or solve this particular parenting crisis of mine, but he listened while I complained
about social service agencies that hung up on me or a school counselor's threat to have me charged with negligence because my kids
hadn't shown up to classes for months. He let me show him photo
albums of Amanda and Stephanie as babies. Even better, he teased
Mary and Mollie—he got them to be light, to laugh and play, when
so much else felt ponderous. This night, Barry set his boots atop
our scratched coffee table, his wire-rimmed reading glasses halfway down his nose. Mollie tipped in toward him, her head against
his shoulder, while more cautious Mary stayed curled up at the
other end of the couch. Taking over our custom of reading a few
chapters of a novel before bed, he opened a worn copy of *Water-
ship Down* at the place I'd marked the night before, picking up the
action near the ultimate battle between Hazel and Woundwort.
Though I headed back into the kitchen to finish the dishes, I tuned
in to his voice. It was hard not to let him go on forever, so melodi-
ous was that voice, but I needed Barry to stop before the book's cli-
max. At just the right point, I handed him foil-wrapped leftovers
and walked with him out to his truck, sliding in close to get a kiss; I
watched him drive up the road toward his own home, where he felt
safe. I'd wait for his call in the late hours of night, when the girls
were asleep and I could talk to him from the soft warmth of my
bed, where I felt safe, the phone sunk into my pillow and my ear
sunk into the phone.

Barry left, and the last pages of the book were saved for the three
of us alone.

As they had at the end of *Where the Red Fern Grows, The Old
Man and the Sea, To Kill a Mockingbird, Island of the Blue Dolphins,*
and *Rascal,* Mary and Mollie climbed on my bed in their soft night-
gowns and we promptly choked up. This time, it was over the rab-
bits' close calls and their deaths and their cruelties and friendship.
I propped my head on a stack of pillows while Mollie scrunched
up under one of my arms, her bare toes digging into the side of
my leg. Mary sat on the other side, Misty in her lap. At the right
moment she ran to the bathroom to get toilet paper, handing out

strips for the toughest passages. I began reading again when she got back, Mollie's shoulder quaking against mine, and I told myself that I was, after all, finding a way to let my girls cry.

Other nights when Barry was at his own house or gone on his long weeks of travel for his work as a writer, I came home to sit motionless on our juice- and jam-stained couch and stared at the television, too beat to get up and change the channel or turn it off, the remote long ago misplaced. The fat husband kidding the skinny beautiful wife, while their just-this-side-of-rotten-but-ultimately-redeemable kids tried to get away with something. Mary's low voice drifted in from her bedroom, where she and Mollie made islands out of brown and green towels and populated these lands with dozens of animals: elephants and wolves, hippos and polar bears. On their door hung a piece of typing paper listing their latest requests for birthday or Christmas presents: a baby walrus, a mother turtle, a father grizzly.

On one of those evenings, credits ran on the small screen across the room from me, and I felt full of quick-dry cement. It pinned my thighs to the cushions. I had to get up or I'd be sunk there forever. I moaned, bent my legs, and stood.

"What's wrong, Mom?" Mary called. In recent weeks, the least strain in my voice caught her attention.

"Nothing," I said. "Time for homework."

"No, not yet!" Mollie said.

But within minutes, Mary sat at the dining room table surrounded by sharpened pencils and open textbooks, her long white-blond hair twisted down her back. "Which states border Colorado?" she asked.

"I'll bet you can figure that out," I said from the kitchen. "You go to one every summer and I miss you when you're gone."

She flinched at that comment, as if trying to figure out how she was supposed to both spend time with Tom and make me feel okay about it. She got up, her way of escaping the subject, and carried the map into the kitchen, holding it in front of me as I moved bricks of frozen hamburger and bags of corn around in my freezer, searching for my last bag of blueberries from the summer. "What's this river?" she asked me, pointing to a squiggly line that ran through the square that was New Mexico.

"Look that state up in your book and read me the names of rivers," I said. "We'll sort it out."

I locked the beaters into the mixer while Mary went back to the table to shuffle through pages. Mollie tossed her jump rope into the hallway. Temporarily. In the middle of dinner, I knew, she'd stand up and grab the plastic handles into her calloused palms, still chewing a hunk of bread or a leaf of lettuce, as if she couldn't sit still another second. She'd swing the rope over her head and start jumping again, our plates and glasses and silverware shuddering each time her stocking feet hit the floor.

Now she climbed onto the blue chair and began to unwrap the butter I'd set next to the stainless steel bowl. Her arm above the mixer, Mollie let the cube fall off the paper in a heavy glob. I gave her a plastic cup filled to the lip with white sugar; we both watched as she tipped her wrist and the grains cascaded in, smoothing the butter to creamy ridges.

"Rio Grande, Pecos, San Juan, Gila?" Mary said from the table.

"You're getting close," I said without turning toward her. "Keep going."

I watched Mollie crack eggs, sprinkle in vanilla. I poured in the flour, baking powder, salt, and crackling fruit. Mary was behind me now, asking for the beater, homework abandoned on the table. "If she gets the beater, I get the bowl," Mollie said in the growly voice she'd been born with, reaching down to give her sister a push.

"Mom!" Mary shouted, tugging at my shirt to make sure I'd noticed.

I spooned purplish dough into rattling paper cups, relaxed for the first time that day. Even the girls' bickering proved we were doing it: faking a normal life. Getting through whatever this was with Amanda and Stephanie, this inexplicable thing they'd entered that had left Mary and Mollie raw and fearful and me wondering if the muscles in my neck would ever again unclench. Tonight a few items in my kitchen had come together into a sweet, warm whole, soothing the helplessness I felt most of the time and muting the remorse that lived in the shallow caves under my shoulder blades. For a few minutes anyway. When the muffins were out of the oven, I focused only on the way steam rose when I broke one in half, and the way the soft insides soaked up a dab of butter until every crumb was yellow and glistening. The softness in my mouth and in my daughters' mouths. The sweet softness.

What I didn't think about was how to live with the fact that other daughters were gone. Or how to get past my fortress of defensiveness over their leaving. How to live with being a failure. How to live with the whiffs of relief that would sometimes come upon me about their absence. Or how I missed them with a ferocity that was turning me inside out.

Amanda has a wrinkled scar across the apex of her left shoulder. When she was thirteen months old she'd yanked the crock pot's electric cord, which was dangling off our kitchen counter, tipping the container on its side and spilling broth and chicken and vegetables that had been simmering all afternoon. I was only a few feet away when I saw it happen. I jumped to reach her, soup splashing my shirt, the yellow hot greasiness of it trapped against me — I knew then the scalding temperature of the liquid that had just hit my child, and that scared me — but more terrifying was Amanda washed in it, her trunk and neck and the side of her face. A dead flesh and chicken odor steamed from her skin. I scooped her up and peered down at her bleached-white face.

At first I couldn't say more than her name, "Amanda, Amanda." As I slid her into the kitchen sink, I realized she'd hardly breathed since the soup had covered her. I nudged the spigot with my elbows, unclipped the hooks on her overalls, whispering, "Breathe, breathe, please breathe." She stared at me and sucked in air, then she howled — her hands slapping at my face and yanking my hair. She battered her socked feet against the metal edge of the sink, clubbing me with her fists. She stared at me as if she couldn't understand why I kept hurting her, why I wasn't taking the hurt away. My fingers slid over globules of fat on her skin, chicken broth congealed by the cold water that drenched her body and my arms; I unsnapped the neck of her red and white cotton shirt, pulled it over her head, the skin peeling from her body and sticking in white patches to the fabric of her clothes, as if I'd drawn plastic wrap off pudding. Her exposed shoulder was a hunk of raw meat.

We had only one car then, which Tom took to work. I called him to come get us, the phone stuck between my chin and shoulder as I garbled out what had happened and rocked Amanda at the same time. By then, I'd wrapped her in a towel grabbed from the laundry basket into which I'd packed ice cubes cracked from a tin tray. Amanda was sleepy now, sobbing lightly, her breath flickering in the back of her throat. I hung up the phone and sat down in our old orange chair and pulled up my shirt, moving my sticky and heavy breast to her mouth. She fell into a frantic nursing while I stared out the window, adding up all the ways I was unfit to be a mother. I did little all day but keep my eyes on this child; the one moment I'd looked away, she'd been hurt. In my own kitchen. Hurt. I soon enough realized that the accident, Amanda's burn—and the scar she'd carry on her shoulder for the rest of her life—was evidence that I'd failed to do what I desperately wanted: keep my daughter from harm.

When it was time to get Amanda at the Portland airport, I went alone. It had been a little over two weeks since I received the call from the woman at the Tucson police station. The following morning, I'd screwed up the nerve to phone Tom. He spoke in a low voice, as if he'd slunk off to the far recesses of his house for our discussion. "It's not a good time here for this," he said, repeating what the policewoman had already told me he'd said. When would be a good time to find out your child is using heroin and has nearly died from it? That's what I wanted to ask, but didn't, afraid that once I got insulting with him the nastiness wouldn't stop. Besides, I didn't feel any different: it wasn't a good time for me either. Definitely not a good time.

Tom obviously wanted to hurry off the phone. He laid out his ideas in a few words, and there was no recrimination from either side for once: his insurance would cover at least some days in a recovery unit in Tucson, that same one Amanda had been in two years before, at fifteen, when she'd swallowed all that Tylenol, a time only vaguely remembered for its relative innocence. He'd check her in there again, he told me, so she could get off these new drugs, these street drugs. Then he'd put her on a plane home.

That's what he did: picked her up at the police station and then signed her in at the clinic for a two-week stay. Now her time there was over, and she was on her way to me. After Christmas, maybe after New Year's, she'd move to an Oregon State drug treatment center for women, which I had yet to tell her about, where she would live until someone in charge deemed her improved—or at least able to get on with whatever her future was going to be.

In the airport waiting room—all dark furniture and garish light—I leaned against the row of vinyl chairs in front of the jetway as passengers stumbled out, one by one. Mary and Mollie had asked me to let them come; they wanted to see Amanda, to figure out what had become of her in these months away. But I'd left them with a friend. The last time Mary had seen her sisters, months before, it was by mistake—she was home with a sore throat one September day not long after Amanda and Stephanie had taken off. I'd loaded her with juice and lozenges and a couple of movies and, in the afternoon, had gone to work for a couple of hours. I should have stayed home, but missing even one paycheck would have jeopardized everything, and I'd become overcautious after taking so many hours and days off work because of my children. I couldn't give anyone an excuse to call me a less-than-devoted employee: a frazzled anxiety that had propelled me to the office.

Mary was dozing in front of our small TV—I'd put in the movie she most liked to watch when she was sick, *Big* (a movie she loathed for its sappiness when she wasn't ill). She heard broken glass—later she told me how she slunk out of her bed and tiptoed down the dim hallway to peek. Shadows shot past the crack under the laundry room door. She heard voices and hid in a dark space in the hall until she realized those voices belonged to her sisters. Mary remembered what they were wearing when they came around the corner. Stephanie: black jeans with patches, torn and dirty hoodie that she'd sewn back together with dental floss, leather bracelet with silver studs, chain-mail necklace. Amanda: torn jeans and a *Clockwork Orange* T-shirt from which she'd cut the collar band and the sleeves, her hair dyed black, and a green devil tattoo glaring from her forearm.

When I got home with Mollie that day I found Mary curled in her bed, silent, her quilt tight around her like a pink cocoon, and Misty curved around the top of her head. Having chased the cat away, I laid my hand on her damp forehead. "What is it?" I said. "Are you worse?" Mollie went off for water, and Mary unpinched her body enough so that I could at least see her blank face.

It took her a long time to say it — that Amanda and Stephanie had broken a window to get into our house. (As soon as she mentioned broken glass I felt cold air that shouldn't have been there.) They had rifled through drawers for money, packed up canned food, and taken sleeping bags and camping dishes from our stash in the storage closet. Mary had followed them through the house begging them to stop, until Stephanie led her back to her room and said, "Get back in bed. You're sick," and closed the door. Mary stayed put, listening to the sounds of her sisters, who, minutes later, left for the train yard and for the train that would take them out of town.

As passengers from Amanda's flight began to appear in the room, I did my best to keep my expression flat, holding back the heat building inside me, my internal daughter-related furnace turned to High. I was both relieved beyond measure that she was alive and full of dread at having her in my house again. That day in the airport, I was also stuck fast on the idea that my daughters had done me wrong, and many of my thoughts were centered on that particular nugget of pain. *What had I done to deserve this?* How could my children walk away from me, from what we had together? The daughter soon to step out of the airplane was broken — broken by rage, by drugs, by rebellion gone terribly wrong. Every time I asked her why, her answer was the same: *This isn't about you, Mom.* It felt like it was about me. And looking for reasons why things kept getting worse between us was like crawling down a dark cistern looking for fresh water and finding only mud.

I recognized Amanda as soon as she stepped from the doorway, but it took me a few seconds to accept that we were in the same state, the same town, the same room. I hadn't seen her for nearly four months. Her head was shaved except for a patch of straggle on top, jet-black. She had on new black jeans and black Doc Martens, bought by her father. A black long-sleeved cotton shirt and no coat. She carried nothing. Not a book or a bag. Her arms hung straight beside her lanky body. I didn't call out. I waited for her to spot me across the room; when she did, she walked toward me without a gesture of greeting or even a shift in her straight, chapped lips. The winter light cast across her pale face made her even more pale: the color of old soap left in the cupboard under the sink; the color of the fog we'd drive through on our way home. I didn't move until she was in front of me, until I could see the edge of her shoulder scar peeking from the neckline of her T-shirt. I pulled my daughter toward me. Her arms stayed at her sides. Her jutted shoulders, once a sign of about-to-erupt anger, had become permanent points. She was, I guessed, about fifteen pounds lighter than when she'd left. Five feet eight and maybe a hundred pounds, a wisp of a girl. She smelled salty, earthy, like the faint rot of old compost. When she stepped back from my hug I touched one of the furious red bumps on her neck and she said her first word: "Scabies." I pulled away fast, and a small grin flashed over her mouth. "Don't worry," she said, "they're not contagious anymore."

She had a screw in one earlobe. A zipper pull in the other.

Downstairs, Amanda moved to the edge of the rubber track that rumbled by carrying strangers' luggage. She pressed her knees against the metal frame and scanned the suitcases for her one bag. I wanted to walk up behind her so she'd feel me against her back, but I stood apart from her and waited, trying to imagine how to bring up Stephanie's name, how to find a way to plot with Amanda —whose every signal was for me to keep my distance—how to get her sister home. I had to believe Amanda had some clue as to where Stephanie was and why she hadn't called. I needed to believe Stephanie was safe.

Her suitcase in one hand, Amanda headed for the revolving door; I followed. The door dumped us outside. She pulled a pack of cigarettes from her back pocket and, with a pinch of finger and thumb, slid one Pall Mall from the middle. She flipped it to her lips, lit it, took a long drag, and blew out strings of gray from between her teeth. "This is hard," she said, picking a fleck of tobacco off her tongue.

I nodded. "It's hard for me too . . ." But I didn't finish because she was swatting that comment away along with her smoke, refusing to take it on, worried, I suppose—and she was right—that I wouldn't be able to keep from telling her how much she'd hurt me, how much I'd been wounded and saddened by her running away and the decisions she'd made while she was out there, whatever those were.

"But I'm glad to be home," she finished. She looked straight at me for the first time. "I want to be home."

Later I'd understand how difficult it was for her to say such words—how impossibly hard it had been to choose to return to our house, as coming back to me required that she drive a wedge between herself and Stephanie. But she wasn't ready to fill me in on that part yet. She was years from filling me in on that part.

On our hundred-mile drive to Eugene, Amanda rifled through the tape box in the car looking for music she could stand to listen to, and I finally said Stephanie's name. That's when I got Amanda to tell me—as much as she was willing to reveal, anyway, as much as I was willing to hear—about their last night together. The girls had appeared at their father's house, but when Ellen saw how dirty they were (and likely how stoned), she refused to let them in. Tom came out on the porch and handed Amanda a twenty and told them to get something to eat. They had to stay away awhile; maybe come back in a few days, he told them. "Dad," Amanda said, but he shook his head and put his hand on the doorknob. Ellen called his name. Their toddler began crying. Amanda and Stephanie walked across the grass and down the street, where they caught a bus. A few hours later, they spent the money on a batch of heroin.

Tom had given them dollars to buy drugs—this part of the story both infuriated me and, in a typical reaction to his perceived wrongdoings, inflated me with self-righteousness. I gave Amanda a sidelong glance, firing the same old thoughts in her direction: *Why do you keep going back to him? Why can't you realize that he'll do you no good?* In that moment in the car, I let myself believe I would have done marvelously well if Amanda and Stephanie had landed on my doorstep, that I would have brought them into the house and worked out some kind of agreement, even a fury-filled tentative pact, which would at least have kept them safe. But that was a story to make me feel better, better about Amanda's heroin use and better about Stephanie's disappearance. I was every bit as wrung out by these kids as Tom was, and in truth I probably would have done the same—some equivalent of thrusting cash out and shooing these troublesome girls away.

Amanda's story of that night continued: After the shot of bad heroin, after the overdose, Stephanie went with her sister to the hospital by ambulance. Hours later, Amanda was conscious and cleared by the emergency room doctor. No insurance, no names or phone numbers for them to call on her behalf; once she was coherent, she had to get out. A cop took them to a state-run group home, which the girls promptly ran away from. They slept on the streets that night, and the next morning they were separated—Amanda hauled away by another police officer, and Stephanie gone. Gone where? Gone how?

"Where's my stuff?" Amanda asked me. She stood in the opening between the living room and the dining room with her arms crossed high on her chest, skinny elbows shot out like arrows. Behind her, the door to the room she shared with Stephanie was open, the overhead light switched off. The day before, I'd cleaned that room, mopping the oak floors, pounding dirt out of the rug, washing her sheets and blankets.

"What stuff?" I asked her, though of course I knew exactly what she was talking about. Mary and Mollie stepped closer at the suggestion of argument in this tense exchange. They'd hovered near me ever since we got home, whispering as if a sick person or baby was in the next room, while I made tuna fish sandwiches and tomato soup for lunch. The three of us now stared at Amanda.

"What do you mean, what stuff? My records. My clothes. My posters," she said, fists clenched. "All my shit. What did you do with it?"

I opened my mouth, then shut it again. She whipped around and returned to her room, muttering under her breath and snapping the door closed.

It was true: the Sunday they'd left on this longest of runaway ventures, I'd barged into the girls' bedroom. I'd claimed everything I wanted to claim. If they were going to walk out on us again, I decided, I was going to take what I wanted. The filthy piles of shirts and pants and single Converse tennis shoes and Hamm's beer cans in the closet and endless oblongs of flattened red Pall Mall packages taped to the walls. Tattered Nirvana and Hole posters from when Amanda was in the seventh grade. Records by the Subhumans, Bikini Kill, the Dead Kennedys, Dystopia. I scrubbed the anarchist letters off the wall; I painted over the slogan I'd never understood, which Stephanie had scrawled huge above the closet: *Sell out, shell out.* With an extra-wide garage broom, I swept everything to the middle of the room and shoved it in plastic bags. My fury at these daughters poured from me and into the broom handle, into the bent straw bristles that swept hard across the floor, and into the scraped-up piles of crap. From one corner to the other, I made clean surfaces in a room that had, for too long, been the dark, dank secret edge of our house.

When Amanda and Stephanie were little girls, I'd get fed up with the clutter of their bedroom—an earlier bedroom in an old rambling house—and would give them one hour to clean it up. Whatever was left out after the hour went into a plastic bag, and the bag went into the basement for two weeks. I soon figured out they secretly loved the idea of the disappeared toys. Two weeks after the bag had been taken from them, they'd bump it up the stairs to their room to rediscover its treasures, Stephanie reaching into its maw while Amanda waited, holding her breath, to see what nearly forgotten thing would come out first: a Barbie dress, a smelly marker, a Strawberry Shortcake doll. But there were no bags stored away now, waiting for their return. I had dragged the sack out to the curb and propped it next to the green trash bin. I paid the extra ten dollars for the garbage service to haul everything away, determined not to see every day or live in the same house with the symbols of what my daughters had become—what they believed in now.

On Christmas Eve 1996, eight days after Amanda's return from Tucson, I knocked on the door of that room, which she'd reclaimed and begun to re-clutter with her drawings of skinny, bald punk rockers and her wads of dirty clothes that I could smell from halfway down the hall, and I asked her to come out and join us. Mary and Mollie were reorganizing piles of presents for the tenth time that day and drinking mugs of eggnog topped with freshly grated nutmeg; Nat King Cole crooned from the stereo about baby Jesus. Barry would come first thing in the morning, for the present-opening and the homemade cinnamon rolls, but for now it was just us. Amanda had hardly left the room since she'd gotten back, and I didn't know if she would now. She listened to Tom Waits: *Frank's Wild Years* mostly. She read Adrienne Rich poetry and Denis Johnson stories. She wouldn't watch television or movies with us—she'd come to hate television, and refused even when Mary had invited her to "cogitate in front of the tube" when *cogitate* was on Mary's English class spelling list. Amanda emerged from the room to eat and then went back in. She slept. For over a week, she'd been sleeping day and night.

She did come out from the dim interior after my knock, the scent of sour milk trailing after, a red scarf tied around her head making the nubbin of hair there stand forest straight. Amanda had the mobile phone in her hand; she'd been clutching it since breakfast that morning, and I knew why. She was sure Stephanie wouldn't let Christmas pass without a phone call. The holiday had always been a big deal with the five of us, with Stephanie watching the closest to make sure we performed each of our rituals the same way as the year before—hanging the fake-candy train ornament, digging out the stockings, setting out a hot toddy for Santa, making the old family cinnamon roll recipe for breakfast. If Stephanie was going to call, it would be on Christmas.

"Do you want to find the Santa candle?" I asked Amanda. She rubbed the crust from her eyes and shrugged. I'd purposely left the candle in the cardboard box after pulling out the ornaments and tinsel. It, too, was seventeen years old, bought at a garage sale a few months before she was born. As soon as she could hold a match, Amanda had the job of lighting it. Every Christmas Eve, this old Santa burned while I read *The Night before Christmas*, then she alone blew out the flame. The head was gone now, except for a few white curls at the chin. We had his red-clad body left to melt down, his belly and stubby legs and black-booted feet.

Amanda unwrapped the candle from tissue paper and set it on a pile of magazines, pulled her Bic from her pocket, flashing the flame, and leaned toward the stunted wick. Mary handed me the worn book that waited on our shelves, and, the little girls on either side of me, I began to read about the thrown-open shutters and the moon on the snow. Amanda didn't leave the room, but I could tell she wasn't listening. She lost herself in one of our tattered wing chairs, knees to her chin, and stared at the phone, willing it to ring. I raised my eyes between pages to look at her and noticed Mary and Mollie too were more intent on their sister than the story.

"Can we open a present now?" Mollie said, jumping to her feet.

"Sure," I told her, relieved to be setting in motion another Christmas Eve tradition, a single gift before bed. It was one of the last things we had to do to put this night behind us.

On her hands and knees, Mary dug under the tree and pulled a small box from Amanda's pile. "Here's one," she said, holding it out.

Amanda swung her feet over the arm of the chair, kicking toward Mary in a bored rather than angry way. "I don't want to," she said. "You guys go ahead."

Mary's face fell, defeated, and I felt the whole room teeter on the verge of coming apart, each of us about to fly to another area of the house to avoid the others.

"Let's do presents later," I said, standing up, shaking myself out, scrambling for what to say next so that no one started crying, so that Amanda wouldn't retreat behind her closed door for more long days.

"Why don't we write Stephanie some letters?" I said. It came out in a spurt—a kind of on-the-spot suggestion that actually frightened me a little. Once we started writing, I realized in the stark moment after I spoke, I'd have even less control over what was said and what emotions might be in our house, my jangled emotions included.

Amanda didn't answer. She watched me piggyback Mollie into my small office, where I gathered typing paper and a handful of pens while my youngest daughter knifed her chin into my shoulder. Back in the living room, Mollie slid down my legs and took a seat at one end of the coffee table; Mary was at the other. I gave the little girls the letter-writing accouterments then held out the same toward Amanda. She rose from her chair, blue sweatpants sagging low on her narrow hips, her gray wool socks flopping a couple of inches beyond her toes. She took paper and pen and headed into the dining room.

I sat on the sofa, laid a book in my lap, and smoothed a clean piece of paper in front of me. *Stephanie,* I wrote at the top of the page. Nat King Cole finished "Silent Night," and the tape clicked off. The only sounds now were the hum of lights from the tree and rain falling on our roof.

Since the letter idea was mine, I had to write one to my daughter, who'd be fourteen for only another week. I began by picturing her—tall and thin and fine boned, brown eyed, with a long neck and a perfectly shaped nose. But what to say? I love you? I hate you—or at least, I hate what you're doing? I remember you? I don't remember you? I want you to come home? I didn't know what I wanted anymore—dealing with Amanda felt like as much as I could handle. I wondered if I could endure these two together if

Stephanie did show up on our porch. Yet how could I go on, even another day, not knowing where she was?

I re-smoothed the paper with Stephanie's name written across the top. I wrote it again, *Stephanie,* the second name beneath the first, remembering the day she was born—blasting into the world, screaming and red faced. I recalled again how adults had always loved her quirks, which I could guarantee went mostly untolerated in their own kids—the way she wore the same dress every single day of kindergarten along with a floppy straw hat and a pair of pink jelly shoes; the way she would drink milk only if it was food-color-dyed a deep-sea blue. And from the time she was a toddler, that part of her that wanted to hide, wanted to *run.*

One night when Stephanie was not quite three, Amanda found me in the produce aisle of the grocery store. "I can't find Stephy," she said.

"Doesn't Daddy have her?" I looked toward the magazine rack. Tom was leaning against the end, engrossed in the latest issue of *Omni.*

"She went somewhere," Amanda said.

I hurried toward my husband, my basketball belly bouncing against my thighs—Mary was a month away from being born. "Where's Stephanie?" I asked him.

He looked up from the magazine. "I don't know. Didn't she go with you?"

I walked the length of the store, calling Stephanie's name up and down each aisle, Amanda next to me and calling too. We met Tom in the middle and started over again. After the second search of the store, legs prickling and jaw clenched, I went to find the store manager and stood beside him as he made the announcement over the loudspeaker. Two-and-a-half-year-old girl. Blue pants, cats on her shirt, hot pink parka. Sneakers on her feet. "Her parents are pretty scared up here," he said. "Can everyone stop and have a look around?"

I walked to the front door of the grocery and watched the automatic doors slide open every time someone put weight on the black rubber mat. If we didn't find Stephanie within a few minutes, we'd have to search outside, call the police, get crowds of people involved, and real confusion would start. The parking lot was huge, slick, and dark. If she had wandered out there, no one was going to see her past the narrow light cones of the high fluorescent lamps.

What was it going to mean if Stephanie was gone? I felt myself start to die at the thought of it until the baby inside me kicked, an elbow or knee stuck out in a lump under my rib, advocating life. I pressed my hands against the chilled store window as cars went in and out of this lot without a thought or a care.

"Here she is!" A woman's voice. I ran toward the sound, following Tom who now had Amanda in his arms. Turning the corner I saw Stephanie bathed in the grocery-store-blue light, holding the stranger's hand, smiling when she spotted us. "She was behind the toilet paper," the woman said, trembling a little over her discovery. I reached in to gather up my daughter, who laid her head on my shoulder, who nuzzled her mouth into my neck and fluttered her soft eyelashes against my skin.

I could have written in my letter about the times, the dozens of times, we had to stop everything to search for Stephanie. The afternoons she claimed she was going to live forever on the strip of grass in the middle of our boulevard. The clothes-shopping trips where she'd plant herself in the middle of a circular rack and refuse to come out. What would she care about those memories? Now she was gone. Now there was no coaxing her back. I held the paper flat, the pen poised. I wrote simply, *Please stop this,* not even knowing what exactly I meant by that—if she stopped, then what would we do next? How would I get her home, keep her home?—and signed it *Mom.*

My letter finished and folded, I gathered Mary's and Mollie's and waited for the last one.

A few minutes later I peeked into the dining room where Amanda was still writing, her head down on one folded arm, stubby black hair on white skin. I went to the living room, pulled Mollie onto my lap. Mary stretched out at the other end of the sofa. When Amanda stepped through the opening between rooms, maybe a quarter of an hour later, I was wondering what we should do with the letters. She was holding hers in one hand and had a stock pan in the other, as if she'd read my mind.

"Let's burn them," she said.

Mary, Mollie, and I followed her outside to our concrete patio. A misty rain fell on our bare heads and our shoulders—none of us had grabbed a coat. We tore our letters to bits and let the flakes fall into the pan, the four of us huddled together so the rain wouldn't soak our fuel. Amanda knelt to light the jagged pieces on the top, blowing with pursed lips until orange flame licked at the metal rim. The paper burned fast—within a minute or two it was smoldering at the bottom of the pan, our letters turned to ash while we looked on. Amanda picked up a wet stick from the patio and stirred the orange glow, and a few tiny firebugs danced around until the rain snuffed them out. Soaked and shivering, I tugged on Mary and Mollie, and the three of us dashed inside. The girls hurried to their rooms to change into dry pajamas while I watched Amanda through the window.

The flames in the pan were extinguished but a trail of smoke drifted through the damp air and over our fence toward the road. Amanda sat with her back against the cedar slats, wet and alone, moving only her hand up to her mouth to puff on a cigarette. I lingered at the window, keeping an eye on her while she waited. For what, I wasn't sure. But waiting. She didn't want me to comfort her or talk to her, and I knew it. She'd never believe that what she feared most was what I feared most. So we stayed in our places, each of us, until every bit of smoke disappeared.

7

AFTER THE HOLIDAYS, AFTER THE CHRISTMAS EVE LETTERS to Stephanie were burned, and the gritty ash released to who-knows-where, and after I'd scrubbed the char from the bottom of the pan and placed it back on the shelf, I checked Amanda into a women's group-home clinic that was supposed to make her better by ridding her of the desire for a dark drug. But one February morning, a Saturday and less than two months after she'd arrived back in Eugene, I was on my way to move her out of that concrete shell of a building pitched on a barren stretch of ground. She couldn't wait to get away from the group sessions and the twelve-step cheerleaders, to break apart from the other women who'd bet their last chance to stay clean, or at least to stay out of jail, on this state facility. She couldn't wait for me to arrive and to set her free.

Seven weeks she'd stuck it out. A whole seven weeks. Only seven weeks. I couldn't weigh out this choice of hers to quit. Had anything sunk in? Would she make her way downtown that very night to buy a needle and drugs on some seedy street corner from some sleazy guy? Would she jump on a train to some distant city to try to reconnect with, to find, her sister? I hadn't the slightest idea what was ahead, and yet I kept driving toward Amanda as if a positive future for her were a sure thing, as easy to put together as a Lincoln Log house, this slot snapped into that slot and done. I couldn't let myself indulge in the doubts I felt about whatever was going to happen next.

The only thing I was sure of was how pleased Amanda would

be to leave the institution I'd stuck her in. I felt a small stir of triumph over saving her from a place she despised, even while the truth twisted in the bottom of my gut—here was our old, familiar pattern revisited, the one I ruefully kept alive: she got in trouble and I rescued her (since there was no possibility of rescuing Stephanie from whatever was happening to her wherever she was, what a comfort it was now to leap to Amanda's defense). Amanda needed me. She needed me, and that was the last thin reed I could hold on to.

She'd no doubt risen early to pack her small piles of clothes into her duffle, to strip the worn white sheets off the twin bed with its plastic-covered mattress, and to sweep the pale linoleum floor between her dresser and the one next to it. She'd probably skipped breakfast in the cafeteria—food as bland as every wall and floor and wan face in the place—and was waiting for me in the chair next to the locked front door, bag in her lap and knitted cap pulled down to her eyes, and glibly satisfied that she'd once again talked me into getting her out of a situation she couldn't abide.

Amanda had proclaimed the treatment center a waste, and she told me a hundred times that being there only made her want to die ("If you force me to stay here I'll kill myself"). Peggy, the center's head counselor, insisted during our clipped hallway conversations that Amanda still needed a lot more time to reach a breakthrough. I shrugged; my eyes glazed over. If there was a clear line between right and wrong, between what helped Amanda and what hurt her, between what ultimately would succeed and what surely would not, I'd long ago lost sight of it. These days, I worried only about the putting of one foot in front of the other, no longer believing in anything but managing to live through this until it was over. Stephanie was gone and Amanda was locked in a place that made my blood freeze every time I went in—every time I met with bleached blond, overly skinny Peggy, who'd try again to get me to admit that I was equally addicted to drugs or booze, just hiding it better. "Your daughter can't come clean about her history until you come clean about yours," she'd say, her tobacco-laden breath in my face. I'd never admitted to her that, yes, I often had a beer or glass of wine in the evening—I didn't even think to mention it—and instead fumed about her assumption that I was somehow the one who'd taught Amanda to stick a needle in her arm.

It didn't matter what I thought about Peggy or the center or Amanda in it, anyway. The institution wasn't a lockup, Amanda couldn't be kept there against her will even at age seventeen, and, with or without my blessing, she was finished. She planned to move in with a boy she'd met before she'd last left Eugene—an arrangement that terrified me, that nearly buried me with the possibility of more chaos—and she promised to find a job and stay off the drugs. She announced these plans during our last meeting with Peggy, and she said that no one was going to stop her from carrying them out. Not me, not her dad, and not the staff at the center. Amanda, a high-school dropout whose only real job had been building trails in the temptation-free wilderness, thought she had everything solved.

It had been five and a half months since Amanda and Stephanie left Eugene together—since they'd done what I'd dreaded and jumped on a freight train. Five months, and we still hadn't heard from Stephanie. Her January birthday had gone by with barely a mention from Mary and Mollie. The whole house—everything in it, the cats, the furniture, the paintings on the walls, the unwatered plants—seemed an unsettling combination of dull and tense that day, too dead and yet too alive. The day Stephanie turned one decade plus five. When I called Amanda at the center to see how she was faring on a birthday we'd celebrated in past years with home-made pesto and fresh-tomato pizza, Stephanie's favorite meal, and a lit-up white cake with butter-cream frosting, she declined to speak to me. All I heard was the emptiness of the hollow hallway on the other end of the receiver until the receptionist came back to say that my daughter would call some other time, when she wasn't so busy.

While Amanda was a resident of this clinic where I saw women wandering the halls with their heads down as if the worries crammed in were too much to bear, I convinced the director to let

me take my daughter out once a week. I planned outings to poetry readings, to ballets, to new Vietnamese restaurants, and to
coffee shops. Amanda tolerated the meals and shows every Thursday without saying much of anything, not ungrateful but not all
that interested either. She told me about the high-school GED lessons she'd been taking, how she finished the worksheets a minute
or two after they'd been set on her desk and then sat bored and impatient while the rest of the girls worked through their own problems and quizzes. Amanda was nearly as bored on her nights out
with me. It started to get obvious that she might have loved the
art, the performances, the food—but each week's event became tedious for her because I was the only one doing the choosing, where
we should go, what we should see. She wasn't discovering what she
wanted to do because no one was letting her try, not even me, the
one pushing her to figure things out. I'd drive her back to the center by ten P.M., our curfew, and watch her walk through the door,
troubled by the wind-bent shape of her, so forlorn, so lost.

On this Saturday moving-out day, as I pulled into the treatment
center's parking lot for the last time and spotted Amanda through
the window, I was still trying to sort out what I should do from this
point on. Should I step away, let her determine the what-next by
herself?

It would have been best to let her wriggle out of her own dead
skin the way bees somehow slip from constricting exoskeletons and
leave paper-thin ghosts of themselves behind on some porch railing or tree branch. But come on. I was too stuck on the idea that
Amanda couldn't possibly transform without me. And some part
of me believed that if I had Amanda to fuss over, I wouldn't fall
into even more despair about Stephanie. During this time when
my second daughter was still missing, there was no keeping me
from the center of Amanda's business: I wanted to plan where she
should live, what she should do with her time, what kind of food
she should eat, and where she might work. I decided I should be
charged with her future, or at least I should hand out heavy doses
of advice. Back then, I couldn't understand why my goodwill, my
insistence, so often made her furious.

And then there was the problem of Amanda without Stephanie. During these months, I'd picked up on something bitter and maybe even irreparable that had happened between the girls during their last days on the road together. One had ditched the other. One had made a choice that the other, finally, couldn't stand. Amanda hadn't told me the particulars of what had occurred, but it was an obvious source of pain in her. *The* source of pain. Whatever the split between them, the deep resentment of it lived in Amanda's body and darkened her face every time Stephanie's name was mentioned. Why hadn't Stephanie called her? I know that was the burning question on Amanda's mind every day. For a long time, Amanda had existed at the center of only one life—her sister's—and had a bond of safety with only one person—Stephanie. It was a horrible break. The most horrible break.

As I climbed out of the car and walked toward the clinic's front door, Amanda saw me and waved with a slight movement of a hand that quickly became a closed, tight fist, which she used to knock on the glass door until the receptionist released the electronic lock. This time the stern woman at the desk wasn't buzzing me in. She was buzzing Amanda out for good.

My daughter stepped into the cool, cloudy day, her bag swinging from one hand. We met on the sidewalk without touching, the roar of the river behind us, and the wind off that rushing water working its way under our jackets.

"Is that everything?" I asked her, pointing to her duffle.

"Yes," she said with a smile. A rare smile. "I've got it all."

Several weeks after Amanda left the treatment center at the edge of the river and moved in with a boy named Billy, he all gangly limbs, narrow teeth, and scraggly hair, I went to the tiny apartment they shared and knocked on the door. I'd come by earlier that day—a Saturday—but no one had answered. Now, grocery shopping done and errands finished, I'd stopped by again. They didn't have a telephone; sometimes Amanda walked down to use one on the corner to check in with me, but I hadn't heard from her for days. That worried me, especially after her supervisor from work phoned to say Amanda hadn't shown up for a few shifts. The nag inside me wouldn't ease up—I had to find out what was wrong. That meant going to an apartment that, by its mere existence, left me feeling soiled and defeated.

I knocked on the warped door, once white but now chipped and grimy. I tried to look through the front window, but the curtains were pulled shut. I went back to the door and knocked again. My rap wasn't angry or loud but it was insistent. I stopped when I heard noises inside, and maybe a minute later the door opened a crack, Amanda's shadowed face appearing in the airy gap behind the drooping links of a security chain.

"What?" she said.

"Can you come out here?" I asked. "I want to talk to you." The one-room place was dark, but I could see a few shapes in the background—the brown swoop of beer bottles covering the countertops and a lump in the bed. Billy, I assumed.

"About what?" she said.

"Amanda, please," I said.

Amanda rubbed her barely open eyes and then pushed a hand through her puffball of hair. "Mom, I'm still sleeping," she said. "We had a late night."

"It's two thirty in the afternoon," I told her, as if this would matter, as if her mood allowed her to comprehend time or assign any significance to the numbers on the clock face.

"I'll call you later, when I'm awake," she said, and shut the door.

I went home long enough to put the groceries away and to take Mary and Mollie to a store for art supplies and wrapping paper and then on to a slumber party for a school friend's birthday. I wouldn't have to pick them up until the next morning. By four that afternoon, I'd returned to Amanda's door. I knocked sharply, my fist tight enough that the skin stretched thin and white over my knuckles, and kept it up until she opened the door.

"Come on," I said to her bleary face, which was as pale and droopy, as yanked into consciousness, as it had been earlier. "We need to talk."

She sighed and dropped her shoulders in one dramatic slump.

She unhooked the chain from the door, reaching backward to grab her pack of cigarettes off a table before making her way outside. In the light of day, even this last golden light, my daughter looked like hell. She still couldn't open her fat pillowed lids all the way and her lips were parched and bluish. She wore wrinkled brown cords and an even more wrinkled long-sleeved cotton shirt ripped open across the back, a stained T-shirt underneath (the kind she called a wife beater). Bare feet. When she lifted her hands — one to hold a cigarette, the other to light it — the sleeves of the shirt sagged down her arms, and her wrists popped out, looking like chewed corn-cobs.

Her right arm and the cuff of that sleeve were covered with splotches of dried blood.

I grabbed her hand and pulled it toward me. "What's this? What happened?"

She shook me off and cradled the arm across her chest. "Nothing," she said. "Forget it."

"Get in the car," I said, walking toward my station wagon. For some reason she didn't fight me and she didn't argue. She made her way around the car and climbed in the front seat and slammed the door shut. In the close quarters, windows up, I got my first whiff of her. Amanda — if odor was telling the truth — was rotting.

An hour later, at home, she'd had a shower and put on some of my old sweatpants and a soft blue sweater. She'd brushed the rats' nests out of her hair, and now her shoulder-length strands — dyed a Mad Dog 20/20 shade of purple — hung around her face like wet curtains. Amanda had hopped on the counter while I made coffee, and up there, more relaxed than she'd been for a long time, she let me draw close enough to have a look at her arm. What I found under the rolled-up sweater sleeve was a jagged line running down the inside of her forearm from the wrist to the bend of her elbow, red and oozing, with a Frankenstein set of stitches holding the two raw sides together. I looked up at her, my mouth gaping, and Amanda quickly told a story about a fight the night before and how Billy had locked her out of the apartment. She was drunk enough, she said, that she'd thrown a hunk of rock at the side window, shattering it into a hundred pieces. "I tried to climb through but stopped when I realized I was getting cut," she said, lifting her wound for me to see again. "I just started screaming until he came out and took me to the hospital."

The story was bullshit and we both knew it. But was I ready to talk about what she'd really done and the state she was really in? She'd picked up a knife—a paring knife, a butcher knife, an X-Acto knife, something close by—and sliced open her arm. In pain or frustration or drunkenness, or hit by a combination of every dark force bombarding her, she'd splayed open her flesh and watched herself bleed.

This episode, which Amanda and I couldn't speak of frankly— or even hint at the truth of—had to be her low point, her scrape of the barrel's bottom. It couldn't get worse than this, could it? I wondered if she suspected the same, felt it in her guts and her slashed-up limbs: either turn back for the surface or die. While these wounds on her arm healed with fresh cells and newly knitted skin, she was consciously going to have to pull herself out of this dark hole.

That change would occur, but I had no hope of it—not yet—and so it was with utter despair that there, in my kitchen, I rolled her sleeve down and turned to pour coffee into two mugs. I didn't ask the obvious questions about her version of what had happened—she'd climbed in the window arm-first? Nothing else got cut, her face, her neck? Instead, I handed her a hot cup laced with half-and-half, which she sipped gratefully. "Ow," she said, blowing on the surface.

I considered calling her old therapist, or even calling the treatment center she'd checked out of too soon. I'd likely have to eat a couple of big crows in front of Peggy—who'd remind me again how wrong I was not to force Amanda to stay in the square concrete room of the sprawling concrete building until a new resolve came upon her—and I'd have to plead with Peggy to give Amanda another chance. That is, if Amanda would consider going near the place.

I couldn't see how or why to try. My daughter wouldn't let me transport her to within a mile of the treatment center, nor would counseling do any good if she refused to go to the appointments I made and had to pay for whether she showed up for them or not. The thing to do here was to get professional help—one more type of aid that I'd add to the endless string of possible solutions tried over these years. Except none of it, it seemed to me, all these dollars and hours later, had made much of a difference. Despite counseling session after counseling session, Amanda was a little kid riding a screaming sled aiming for a tree; a stunned driver in a car headed for a cliff; a woman on the top floor of a burning building about to jump. My daughter embodied the cliché of out-of-control.

That day, I took the coward's way out. Instead of suggesting even more therapy or another hospital or new drugs for her depression, I suggested dinner. Not at my house, where there was too much history, and where I might say too much about how she was living now or about how she was in danger of losing a job she'd just gotten or about a boyfriend too much in the thick of drugging and boozing with her. We drove to a restaurant. A Chinese restaurant near the University of Oregon campus, a place as benign as the blunt, blond-wood chopsticks that soon wagged in our fingers. I ordered chicken, and Amanda ordered shrimp. Her dish arrived glistening with color, green peppers and pea pods, yellow bamboo shoots and baby corn, the hues shining in startling contrast to her pasty face. Sitting across from me at the narrow table, Amanda shoved her fingers and dirty fingernails into the food to load it on the chopsticks. I asked her not to, unable to hold back my mother talk. She dug her fingers in deeper.

Since she'd been living in the apartment, I'd tried to drop by every few days—although I hardly ever let her know I was around. Sometimes I left a small sack of groceries or a bag of secondhand sweaters and socks. If I had to speak to her, I preferred to talk to this daughter on the phone. A little distance—a little façade of accommodation. If I had her voice only to deal with, I could sometimes pretend that things weren't as awful as they clearly were.

I'd also tried to pretend over that same period of weeks that Stephanie's seven-month absence hadn't wormed its way into me.

But the piling on of days and weeks without a word from her had begun to eat at the marrow of my bones. I ached in a deep place in my body that I'd not known existed. An old problem of sleeplessness was now firmly entrenched; I ate only when I felt like my body was going to give out on me; I rarely kept myself from exploding when a store clerk annoyed me or when I was left too long on hold by the phone company. Or when I sat on the other side of a desk to stare down Mary's teacher or Mollie's while she explained to me again that whichever daughter under discussion had grown distracted and tearful and that her grades were suffering. Of course the girls were distracted; of course they were suffering. There were many ways Mary and Mollie might have reacted to this situation, and none of them were good. One of them could get sick—really sick. They could run away too, like their sisters. They could do scary things that I'd have to react to. If my younger daughters were merely distracted, I told the teachers, then that was a relief. The possibility of a C in math (which never happened) was the least of my concerns. Other signs in them were more disturbing: once again I'd been called to the elementary school because the playground attendant on fourth-grade recess duty found Mollie crossing the concrete bridge, the one built to get children safely over the busy roadway. She'd been halfway across, head down and blue coat buttoned tight, when the attendant caught up with her. Mollie cried as she was being carted back to the school building, saying that she had to set out to find her sister as soon as possible. Stephanie had to be found.

The problem was, Stephanie wasn't going to be found until she wanted to be. The cops wouldn't watch for her, and the youth shelters that dotted the country either ignored or returned my packet of posters—they weren't in business to help the parents, their notes told me, their job was to take in and take care of the homeless kids. I could have hired another seeker of runaways, another ex-cop to search the entire country. But there was no money for such an endeavor. So I went nowhere, looked nowhere, and waited for Stephanie to decide it was time to contact one of us.

This night in the Chinese restaurant, as Amanda ate, I tried to find subjects that didn't include her sister. I couldn't open up both of us to bereavement after months of nothing from Stephanie. Though I didn't want to—didn't want to inquire so I wouldn't have to be disappointed—I asked Amanda about school. Didn't she want to finish high school? Might she want to take classes at the community college? Could I set up a meeting with a counselor? I asked if I could help her make a plan, but she looked away. "I'm not like you," she said. "I'm not a planner."

What she wanted, she said, was to be free. I assumed at the time that she meant she wanted to be free of me, and released from family life. She wanted to be able to drink if she felt like it. To do drugs if she wanted. To leave town any time she got the hankering, nothing holding her down. And certainly without my looking over her shoulder, scolding. These years later, though, I'm not so sure that's what she meant. Freedom could have been finding her own way through her own confusion without me there, implementing the Plan for Amanda's Future.

That night at the restaurant, I hoped that this food, and this neutral setting one story above the city street, would allow the hidden Amanda, the calmer girl who'd started to peek out in our kitchen an hour earlier, to emerge even more. But the longer we were together, exchanging sharp, tense sentences, the more apparent the lack of resolution between us. Finally, we stopped talking and concentrated on our food. Pearls of rice stuck to my teeth while the earthy saltiness of soy sauce coated the back of my throat. I could hardly swallow. I couldn't imagine pushing on. The turning point—giving up on my daughter—was in the room with us. I felt it. The very moment I would give up was right there, breathing down my neck, even while I had no idea what truly resigning might look like, how it would change my days or my life.

The plates emptied of their colors, leaving only smears on white ceramic. The teapot was dry. I got up to pay the bill, and Amanda said she'd meet me on the sidewalk. She wanted to go for a smoke.

I stepped to the counter and took out my credit card. Inside my wallet was a twenty-dollar bill I'd been thinking about giving her. Once she disappeared down the stairs and left me alone at the counter, I drew out the bill and held it. I folded it in half and half again and closed my palm around it, the sharp edges biting my skin, still not sure whether to hand it over. If I did, the money could be transformed into beer and cigarettes within a couple of hours. Or, worse, drugs. But maybe there was a chance she'd save some for a good breakfast. I didn't know; I couldn't know. Maybe it was best to give her no money but instead invite her to our house more often for meals, but she probably wouldn't agree to come. I was lost about how to help.

A few minutes later, down the stairs myself and into the chilly, starless night, I looked around for Amanda. She wasn't waiting in front of the restaurant or down the block. I didn't see her any-where. Had she left? Had she gone without telling me, found a ride home, or made her way to a pay phone to call Billy to come retrieve her? I couldn't stand to think that she'd done that—had just taken off—so I stared at the surface of the road, which, for some reason, was spider-cracked from one end to the other. Long cracks splayed into short cracks, from this corner to that corner. I'd never seen a street fractured like that, a forked and reforked jag of lines trail-ing off into the darkness. I walked a few feet onto the asphalt and leaned down to get a closer look, to touch the breaks in the road. But before my fingers brushed the blacktop I felt Amanda behind me. I stood up and pointed out the shattered pavement.

"No," she said. "Look." She waved her hands under the branch of a bare tree just behind us, and I watched as the cracks on the road disappeared. Of course. It was only shadows. I waved my own hand between the beam of the streetlight and the tree limbs to break the illusion. I was embarrassed at how easily I'd been fooled, and I stepped back onto the sidewalk to sweep the dirt off my pants legs.

"Can you drop me off at my house?" Amanda said then, thwart-ing my moment to suggest she come back to my house for the night, for maybe a couple of days, while I sorted out what to do about her most recent damage to herself; until I could reinvigorate my resolve to stick it out with her; until she was ready to deal with unhappiness in some other way than with pills or drinks or a knife. I shrugged, tacitly agreeing to take her where I didn't want her to go.

We crossed the crooked shadows to the other side of the street, toward the alley that led to the lot where my car was parked. On our way, we passed a couple sitting at a well-lit table on the side-walk outside a closed café, their swaddled baby lying in a plastic infant seat. Tiny pink hands poked out of the blanket, knocking around the cold air. The man on one side of the table jumped up. He thrust out his arms toward us. "Ladies, ladies!" he called out. Amanda stopped, and I did too. My daughter turned to look at me, as if wondering what we should do, then looked back at him.

Teeth were missing from his mouth; he had no coat on, just a thin shirt that fluttered in the breeze. The woman, coatless too, stood up once she realized they had our attention, brown hair col-lapsed over her shoulders, her eyes dull and tired.

"Can you help us?" the man said.

Amanda and I were separated from this family by a waist-high retaining wall of red brick, which I was glad for. It would help us get away when we had the chance. I wanted only to return to the car, to have a few more minutes to talk to my daughter before we lost contact again. She would go to her house and I would go to mine and there was no telling what would bring us together again the next time. But right now I had to deal with this man shout-ing at me. I wasn't sure whether to respond to or ignore him— I glanced at Amanda to see what she wanted me to do. I wondered if it would please her for me to help these people by giving them a few dollars, perhaps even the sweaty twenty in my palm. I tried to read some sign in her, some indication of what would make her happy.

The man broke in again. "Do you have one of those cards?" he said, pointing to an ATM just beyond the sidewalk's edge. "No," I said quickly. Amanda knew I had one, and I waited for her to ex-pose me to these strangers. But she didn't. The man went on as if he hadn't heard me. The baby's godfather had sent a check, he said, pulling a rectangle of paper from his pocket and shaking it toward us. "We're not from here, nobody will cash it."

He wanted me to deposit the check in my account and then withdraw the same amount so he could have the cash.

"I'm sorry," I said, "I don't have a card."

"But we need the money. We need it for our baby," he said, rattling the check again, as if the sound alone would conjure up help and hope and comfort. The woman had already given up on us and sat back down, ignoring her child, who had started crying and whose cries were steadily getting louder.

I turned away as the man stuck the check back in his pocket. He mumbled at my back in frustration. That's when I noticed that Amanda had already gone on. I hadn't felt her leave, but she had. She was twenty or thirty feet away, her torso bent into the starless night under the streetlights. I watched her back get smaller as she moved deeper into the alley. I put my hands around my mouth to call to her—ask her to wait until I could catch up—but I couldn't make any sound. No noise would come out of me.

I dropped my hands and turned to look again at the road we'd crossed and at the way the streetlights made a strange web of cracks that still seemed real. For a moment, in the time it took to take a breath perhaps, I thought about following the jagged shadow lines on the road, letting them decide the end of this night for me. But my hands clenched the car keys in my coat pocket, and my body moved around and began to cut through the same air, the same path, as Amanda. I didn't hurry, though. She was already too far away.

8

I DON'T REMEMBER WHY I THOUGHT STOPPING IN AT A police station in downtown San Francisco was a good idea—the police in Oregon had already told me that a change in state law in the 1990s had decriminalized skipping school and running from home, which meant police would no longer search for missing kids. That is, if the kids went missing of their own accord; not stolen away by strangers but rather having slipped from home lives they didn't want or couldn't tolerate. But something in me hoped that California had different ideas about teenagers who left their families to hit the streets.

After an hour's wait in the dim room, surrounded by others who fidgeted nervously too, worrying about their own dealings with the cops, I found out that the law was basically the same here: as long as the kids didn't get caught committing crimes—big-deal crimes such as theft, drug dealing, assault, not just loitering or trespassing—they could squat in abandoned buildings or sleep on park benches or spend their days on street corners asking for spare change, and most of the time the police would look the other way. The blue-uniformed officer across the counter from me at the station rattled off the statistics, saying that dozens of kids streamed into the city every day; saying that nearly a thousand slept on the streets of San Francisco on any given night; saying that the strain on public dollars had shrunk the number of officers who walked a beat, so there was no way to keep an eye out for one girl. My girl, who wasn't unusual. She was part of a movement, a member of a burgeoning subculture that—if the San Francisco street corners crowded with young panhandlers were any clue, he said—was growing beyond society's control by the hour.

I knew Stephanie had become part of some tribe made up of black-clothed, pierced, tattooed kids with necks seamed with dirt and armpits stuffed with snarled hair, but I hadn't thought all that much about the other children—who they were and where they came from and how many of them there were all together. I'd regarded the others as only strange and foreign and a source of trouble, and I wanted them to stay away from my daughters. Here in the police station I finally realized that Stephanie was, after all, just one among many. I got a glimpse of what she gained from being one among many: anonymity and some warped sense of group protection. I understood too that mine was a common quest and query—the officer informing me in short order that I was just another parent fresh in from some other place looking for a son or a daughter on the road. All he could do was add Stephanie's name to a national database of runaway children. That way she'd be in the computer if she did get arrested or hurt, or if she turned up dead, one of those who fell off the seedy margins of the street life and landed in a hospital or a morgue. As if this should be a comfort to me, her name on that long list.

The officer took my information, pecking it at a keyboard with his index fingers. But he declined to take one of the posters I'd brought along, a photograph and description of Stephanie copied at the Kinko's in downtown Eugene before I'd left and printed on clean, white eleven-by-fourteen paper, HAVE YOU SEEN MY DAUGHTER? its headline. He claimed that too many posters got left at the station and that he had nowhere to hang them. And then he stuck out his hand to shake mine—his indication that our exchange was over.

"I hate to tell you the truth," he said, frowning so that parallel creases appeared on his forehead like faint ski tracks, "but there's nothing we can do to help you find your daughter."

It was spring of 1997, and not even Amanda had seen or heard from Stephanie since the previous November. I'd come to San Francisco thinking that maybe, if everything lined up and I got lucky, if I wasn't out of my mind believing that possibly Stephanie was here instead of in some other town in some other region of the country, I might locate her. I might track her down. I'd even let myself imagine once or twice that she would suddenly appear before me on Geary Street, on Powell, up at the Grace Cathedral Labyrinth, and that this bleak stretch of not knowing where she was and what condition she was in would be over. After talking to the cop, I realized I'd have to go about such a search without help, at least none from authorities who patrolled this city. Finding Stephanie meant looking for her by myself.

Not long after the ill-fated weekend in Portland with my mother, and after Amanda and Stephanie had jumped a train and disappeared, I'd taken a long drive with Barry through the rural parts of the Willamette Valley, just the two of us alone. It was a sunny afternoon in late September, Mary and Mollie off with friends for the day, and the air that streamed in Barry's truck windows and that blew my hair around smelled faintly of fall. Late September: the loveliest time to be in our half of Oregon—summer crops gathered, fields burned, apples ripe on the trees. Fall had always been my favorite season, with my kids freshly back from their dad's. By the first of most Septembers I could rest easy. My lonely summer had ended—I could stop writing daily postcards and letters to my girls in Arizona, and stop sitting through the long evenings in our empty house waiting for them to come home; I could stop listening to Amanda's seventh-grade choir's rendition of "Shenandoah" every time I drove in the car—and all of us could now fit back into the comforting-for-their-predictability schedules of school and work and dance classes and music lessons and evening homework and an hour of TV each night. All that was long ago, but my body still remembered the pleasure of regular life, those ordinary times, and I rode through the valleys of Oregon with Barry, who drove exactly five miles over the posted speed limit, while I fought off an ache that had nowhere to land.

When we got to the town of Woodburn, nearly to Portland,

Barry suggested we head up the hill to a Catholic monastery called Mount Angel. I'd seen the signs for this place dozens of times on the interstate but had never wondered much about its mysterious looming residents, the nuns and priests. When we reached the monastery grounds on a plateau that overlooked the valley and got out of the truck to walk around—the sun on the back of my neck, and my hand in Barry's warm one—we found an assortment of buildings and a courtyard with a perfectly groomed pond in the middle, koi popping the green surface with their round orange mouths. There were no people, so it was exquisitely quiet on the hill. We strolled in the breeze, the golden maple leaves on long branches over our heads rustling like bird wings, until we came to the brink of a cliff. Barry sat on a bench there, pointed in the direction of the vast view, and I settled on the cool ground in front of the bench for no other reason than it seemed like the right thing to do—to feel the damp from the grass seep into my jeans and to feel the hard earth under my bones. In front of us was a rolling, variegated aspect of farmland: in the center, one farmstead with a small, steep-roofed house that was painted white and surrounded by a line of trees and, past that windbreak, acres of plowed ground fresh with tractor stripes.

I looked over at the scene, as empty of humans as the monastery behind us, as if the afternoon had been preserved for Barry and me alone. This hilltop where we'd paused seemed to invite a Sunday-afternoon type of quiet rest, but rest had so long eluded me I didn't know how to accept the offer. I do remember being struck by that farm in the distance. Everything in that setting was in its place, or so it seemed to me: the home and garden, the chicken coops and the horse barn, even the straight lines of broken ground. The house was built mid-hill, as if the slope had been created just for this dwelling and for those who lived there.

What if I had given my daughters this kind of life once I was divorced from their father? It wouldn't have been impossible—I could have moved back to Idaho instead of Oregon and found a house with acreage near one relative or another. We could have had cows and chickens. The girls could have grown up as my cousins had, rising before dawn to milk and feed, and returning home from school to do farm chores. The palms of their hands could have grown calloused from the pitchfork and the rake while their faces became wind-burned pink. The routines of getting by, day after day, would have muted any thoughts of taking off in anger—everyone would have work to do and would know to do it. At least that's how I thought of it for a moment, this split second, as I watched the farm across the valley. The simple life I'd not chosen for my girls.

I realize now that this vision of rural life held no clues for me or for us. All it did was stir a familiar bitterness over the what-ifs, bring on the same old self-berating: for so long I couldn't think of much I'd done right. It was too late to raise my daughters better than I had. It was too late to make up whatever I'd done wrong as a parent. The one thing I'd hoped to get right—being a good mother to my kids—had somewhere along the line gone terribly awry.

There on the monastery grounds, Barry leaned over to put his hand on my shoulder, and I turned away from the farmscape and toward him. He told me every day that I was a fine mom, a loving mom, and though I didn't believe him much at that time, I lapped up his praise, every word. He'd also waited with as much patience as a person on the periphery of a family could muster, concentrating on making a friendship with the younger girls and letting me talk out the million worries a day that cropped up over Amanda and Stephanie. He brought gallons of milk when he came over, and O-rings for the leaky bathroom faucet. He got the oil changed in my car when I forgot all about it. He told me he planned to stick around, to be the person I could most count on in the world.

"What are you thinking about?" he said now, running his other hand down his beard.

"What else," I said. "The girls."

He leaned back against the bench and crossed one leg over the other as if he were ready to listen, though I couldn't help but notice the flinch of the muscle in the leg I rested against—this old subject again, that dead horse we kept beating.

But I took a new tack, one he hadn't heard before. "I'm tired of looking for my own kids," I said. "I can't keep hiring people to find them or signing them up for some treatment that might work or might not. I'm sick of it."

He stared at me for a long time, maybe wondering if this was a test or a trick—I'd not yet voiced such a strong desire to give up, even though I had many times felt that desire keenly. "Do you mean that?" he asked, leaning forward, the hand on my shoulder again.

"I think I do," I told him.

There was a long pause before he said anything else. "Then maybe it's time to let them go," he nearly whispered. His hand lifted from me and I felt suddenly lighter, unyoked, nearly free enough to float.

I twisted around to see once again the house on the hill and the expanse of farmland. "Maybe it is," I said.

But nearly eight months after sitting on that hill with Barry, where I thought I'd reconfigured my heart to begin to accept my daughters' decision to leave me, I went to San Francisco to look for Stephanie. Doing nothing was going to eat me alive—with guilt, with remorse, with resentment. I'd chosen San Francisco for the search even though Amanda couldn't say for sure whether Stephanie had returned to the Tenderloin District. Maybe Stephanie had made her way back to their old hangout on the corner of Sixth and Market, sure. But she could as easily be in LA, New York, maybe New Orleans. She could be anywhere. Yet I'd convinced myself, for all kinds of reasons, that I should look in this big city on the bay.

I arrived on a Friday evening with my friend Sherry, whom I'd talked into coming along to help me look; she was younger, and the girls considered her one of the friendly adults around us. I figured Stephanie might talk to her even if she wouldn't talk to me. Soon after we checked into our hotel, we hit the streets, wanting to fit all the searching we could into our short time—we'd take a Sunday-afternoon plane home. Sherry and I headed from our hotel to the Larkin Street shelter, a place Amanda had said she and Stephanie had gone to now and then for food. As we walked past closed shops and bustling restaurants with a cold spring wind in our faces, it suddenly occurred to me that if Stephanie was in the city on this day and saw me, she'd have to choose to show herself, or I wouldn't see her. She'd have to step out from the gradations of gray and brown, the angles and shadows of downtown San Francisco, and flash her hair, turn her body, in such a way that I'd know without a doubt that it was she.

But if she wanted to stay hidden, she could do that too.

"Boy, could I use a glass of wine," Sherry said, pulling her scarf up to cover her pink chin, slowing down to glance into a busy restaurant where tables of patrons were pressed against the other side of the glass.

"Me too," I said. I followed her look into the café, yearning to be one of these people who slung their jackets and purses on the backs of the chairs and scooped appetizers into their mouths and dangled glowing cigarettes from their lips. I imagined purple wine on their flat tongues and warm food in their bellies. They smiled and laughed as if every concern or worry could easily be set aside for the sake of the evening's good time. They could carry on with their party and not even think about the kids, some of whom were barely teenagers, who had made their way to San Francisco and who were camped now in the grimy recesses of city streets. Why should these people in the restaurant consider for one second the young strangers who'd laid claim to squalid city corners? These patrons could leave their cafés and bars and step over kids huddled against the cold in donated blankets, or over kids too stoned to roll out of the way; they could go home and not think of those children again.

"What are you going to do if you find her?" Sherry said as we picked up the pace, once we'd agreed on getting a glass of wine or even a martini back at the hotel bar when we returned. She'd asked me the same question several times since we'd left home—and even before we'd left, when I'd first brought up the idea of her going with me to search for Stephanie. This time the strain in her voice made me think she was worried I was going to fall apart in front of her if we found my daughter here only to have her run off again.

"I don't know," I said. "I really don't."

And I didn't know. Force Stephanie onto an airplane? Sherry and I both knew that was nonsense; there'd be no forcing her to do anything. Besides, Stephanie would no doubt be surrounded by friends who'd be all about protecting her from me. They wouldn't let me take her away. I didn't have the authority to demand that she whip herself into shape and get her ass back to Oregon. Nor could I charm her with gentle words and nice promises. All I had to offer was our home, her family, school. Amanda. Amanda most of all. None of those things apparently mattered to her anymore, and they made up my entire stash, my whole ball of wax.

So here's what I told myself: If I saw Stephanie for a few minutes, at least I'd know my daughter was still in the world, however distant that world was from mine. Maybe that knowledge, for now, would be enough.

Amanda was back in Eugene, so why was Stephanie still on the road? That's what I couldn't figure out. When they'd first bolted —those early days of slipping off to some downtown haunt right there in our own town, before they'd thought to jump a train and go far away—I was convinced that Stephanie didn't want to be this bad. Not really. She didn't want this much of my disapproval or rebuke. Deep down, I thought, she longed to come home and reconcile with me and her little sisters, to do well in school and have nice friends and take art lessons and get ready for a good college—she was only on the streets with Amanda to be Amanda's companion, her protector, so that each girl would know that she had someone watching over her. But that no longer added up, not with Amanda home for months, raw and aching for some news of Stephanie. Ruined over the lack of any word from Stephanie.

What was out there that allowed Stephanie to forget the rest of us? Especially to forget Amanda, her best friend, her sister, her accomplice, her other half?

Eventually, after a lot of talking around the subject, Amanda had told me that hours after her overdose in Tucson, after Stephanie's amateur resuscitation had restarted Amanda's heart—Stephanie the one, indeed, who'd bent over her sister, breathing into her mouth, thumping her chest, eventually dragging her into an apartment building to make a call and then waiting until the paramedics arrived—and after a shot had counteracted the heroin in Amanda's system, the girls had been hauled to a group home by a cop who'd told them they couldn't run away because he was "too fat and too slow" to catch them. Run away they did. The next morning, after another night sleeping on the streets, the girls were walking around downtown Tucson when, for some reason, they drew the attention of a street officer—maybe a business owner had complained of the girls' loitering; maybe the cop had spotted them trying to buy drugs. Whatever his reason, the officer sidled up to them and asked who they were. Stephanie rattled off the first fake name that came to her, but Amanda—to Stephanie's dismay and surprise—gave her real name. Just blurted it out. The cop radioed in her real identification, and—what? Put together the near death of the night before or found old charges against her? I had no idea, and Amanda wouldn't say. I barely got her to recite the last details: the officer shoving Amanda into the back seat of his car as Stephanie hurried down the sidewalk. "We'll be together soon," Stephanie called from yards away as the cop shut the door on Amanda. "I'll be with you soon."

Since that day, eight months of silence.

Here in San Francisco, in my secret heart, I simply wanted to spot Stephanie in this vast place so she'd know I'd come looking for her. Or maybe she didn't even need to see me, or I her. Maybe I was searching for her in a city that she'd probably left long ago so I could someday claim that I'd done what any good mother would do. I'd looked. I'd pursued. I'd pounded the pavement seeking my daughter. Even though she obviously didn't want to be found, I'd done my best to locate my lost child.

Stephanie, who'd become an inhabitant of the streets and of

the rail yards. Not someone I knew, someone probably even more war-torn than when she'd left. I imagined her, her hair grown out and larger ceramic plugs shoved into her earlobes; the ripped T-shirt and the black jeans with leather patches; the hoodie with cuffs that she stuck her thumbs through to make half-gloves; the stink of her body, the stink of her breath. Not the girl who'd once spent about an hour in the bathroom every morning making sure that the curl in her bangs was neither too tight nor too loose but the perfect soft loop resting against her flawless skin (Stephanie back then had used so much hairspray in the morning that six-year-old Mary once complained, "She's putting a hole in the bozo layer!"). This wasn't the daughter who'd written notebooks full of poetry about the dog that had died and the dad she'd left behind; it wasn't the girl who'd been invited to lunches at her teachers' homes on the weekends.

I would have said she had become a stranger, but strangers have the gift of benign unfamiliarity, a barrier they can choose to break down or keep erect. Stephanie and I had only alienation.

The Larkin Street center, on the northwest corner of the intersection, was unlit when Sherry and I got there, about nine o'clock at night. The windows were black, though a smear of light snuck out from a side door that had been propped open a couple of inches with a shoe. I pushed it open all the way and stepped inside, Sherry behind me.

"Hello?" I called.

"Excuse me?" Sherry shouted.

There was no response, though I heard the soft clatter of friendly talk and dishes from a back room.

"Hello?" I called again.

I moved through the large, chilly area in which folding tables were lined end to end. The room seemed colder because of the empty metal chairs scattered this way and that, as if people had left the room suddenly, abandoning their messes on the long, flat surfaces. The tables were covered with paint kits, pictures cut from magazines, and butcher paper splashed with bold colors, muddied now by the dim light. The rug, avocado green and thin, scuffed up under my shoes.

"Is anyone here?" Sherry shouted more loudly.

Chairs in the next room, behind the wall, erupted in noise then, pulled back with scrapes and bumps, and before I could look in the doorway ahead, five or six men and women in their twenties emerged, rushing toward us. They wove together like a human fence and pushed forward. Sherry and I stepped back. I held up one hand.

"Wait," I said.

"What are you doing here?" one man demanded. He wore an earnest flannel shirt, jeans, and dusty, heavy boots. "Who let you in?"

"I'm looking for my daughter," I said, lowering my hand to my side, yanking my purse strap higher on my shoulder. "Can you help me?"

The man, who had a gangly, long frame and a jolt of cropped hair—and held his napkin still twisted in his hand—walked around Sherry and me to open wide the door we had just come through.

"We'll call a counselor. Maybe she can talk to you," the man said. "But you can't be in here." He ushered us through the door.

A woman behind me repeated it: "You can't come in here!" As if we'd broken into a secret house and spotted contraband.

A few seconds later, the door snapped shut, the shoe having been kicked out of the way, leaving us standing on the street. A lock clicked as a last reminder of how unwelcome we were in there. We waited five minutes or ten, pacing up and down in front of the building, both of us a little nervous about the neighborhood and the hour, our arms wrapped across our chests against the wind.

"Maybe we should come back tomorrow," Sherry said, and I shrugged. She was probably right. Waiting on this sidewalk made no sense. But I couldn't stand the thought of a fruitless first night in the city—hadn't we come here to endure the hardships and challenges of the hunt? Still, Sherry's suggestion was correct: it was getting late and I was hungry and tired, and I knew she was too.

I was about to concede and head back to the hotel when the main door opened and a middle-aged woman beckoned to us. Sherry took a long look at her and whispered that this time she'd stay outside, but could I hurry? I nodded yes and went inside the dingy office, a small brown sofa under a blind-covered window, desk in the center of the room, large chalkboard on the wall scrawled white with names: *Justin, Amy, Steven, Kim.*

"How can I help you?" the woman said. Before I could respond, the phone clipped to her belt burred and she held one finger up to me as a Be Patient sign and answered it. When she returned the phone to its slot a few minutes later, I had a poster I'd brought along unrolled on the desk.

"This is my daughter," I said. "Is she here? Have you seen her?"

The counselor looked over Stephanie's picture—one from the first day of ninth grade, her satchel on her back filled with lunch and notebooks and new pencils. She patted the image as if assuring me that, oh yes, my child was pretty and sweet and worth looking for. Then she told me she couldn't tell me if Stephanie was at this shelter. Even if she'd just seen Stephanie, even if Stephanie was in the next room eating pizza with the other street teenagers and the young-adult human fence who'd volunteered their evenings to help out with the "homeless youth," even if she was sick, addicted, arrested, I couldn't be told.

"I hope you understand, it's our mission to protect the kids," she said, lowering herself into the chair behind her desk.

"If my daughter is here, I want to see her," I said, shaking now, sick to death of this same answer. Suddenly I despised this woman and her position that the best way to protect a fifteen-year-old girl was to keep her from her mother.

"I know," she said, patting the poster again in a way that made me pull it from under her palm and rolled it into a tight tube. "We get dozens of parents in here every month and every one of them tells me the same thing," she went on, scowling, worn thin by me and my touchiness. "They want their children back. But that's not my job. My job is to make a safe place for kids who'd otherwise be on the street."

I opened my mouth but shut it without saying anything. I could see by the look on her face and the way she flipped a pen between her fingers that she was going to hold rigidly to the position granted her. The nonprofit-sanctioned permission to assume she could do better for lost and wandering teenagers than any parent standing before her. She was already done with me—sure that she could provide better for Stephanie, if indeed Stephanie was in her building, than I could.

I had no defense since what she believed was, at least in part, true. It was impossible for me to provide for Stephanie at that moment—Stephanie didn't want me to provide for her—so perhaps, by default, this stranger behind this cheap desk in this unfriendly building was the only provider Stephanie could have right now. If my daughter was even around this city and not traveled on to some distant place that none of us could name: suddenly the country seemed very big and very foreboding.

I slid the poster back into the roll of them I had stashed in my bag and turned for the door.

"Wait a minute," she said, her tone less dismissive. I stopped and watched as she opened the top drawer of her desk. She pulled out a map of the city and drew a circle around one section. "This is Haight-Ashbury," she said. "If your daughter is hanging out on the streets, she's probably around this area."

I took the map but explained that my older daughter was sure Stephanie would be in the Tenderloin District, probably panhandling on the corner of Sixth and Market, if she was in San Francisco at all.

"Oh, I don't think so," the counselor said, standing up again to make sure that this time I made it to the door. "The Tenderloin is full of prostitution and drugs and longtime street people. It's hard core. We don't see runaways from Oregon in the Tenderloin."

She gestured toward the exit as her phone rang again. "Believe me," she said as she pulled the cell out of its holder and punched it on, "drive in Haight-Ashbury, on Pine Street. If there's a chance of spotting your daughter, it'll be there."

I hurried back to the hotel to call Amanda, frantic about this woman's description of the hardest and meanest part of town. Surely Stephanie wouldn't choose such a place on purpose. If she had to run away, if she had to be in San Francisco alone, then she'd find a safe corner to squat in, right? I reached Amanda at our house; she'd come to spend the night with Mary and Mollie and the college student I'd hired to stay with them for the weekend, waiting for word from me. I told her about the woman at the shelter and about her suggestion to look in Haight-Ashbury.

"No way," Amanda said. "Haight-Ashbury is for poseurs. Stephanie would never go there. If she's in San Francisco and she needs money, she'll be in the Tenderloin."

So adamant was my daughter's tone that my heart sank—not only did she insist that Stephanie had purposely aimed for the seediest and most dangerous corner the city had to offer, but Amanda obviously admired this in her sister, and perhaps yearned for it herself. I pinched my eyes shut, refusing to listen to that bravado. I had to believe Amanda was over a need for the streets and for what the streets had to offer. I could only search for Stephanie if I felt sure that Amanda was contained and that she intended to stay put and get better—she had seemed so committed to doing that over the past weeks, the drinking and fighting with her boyfriend ended, her skin shining again. A self-rehabilitation that was becoming more obvious and more sure every day: things had been so good, so hopeful. Amanda was steadier now, and if I did find Stephanie, and if Stephanie would consent to coming home and being done with roaming the country by freight train, we might finally turn a corner on this thing that had been like an animal at our throats for too long. Or was that just one more self-deluding fantasy?

Saturday, Sherry and I went through the Tenderloin, a part of the city I could only describe as gray. Gray sidewalks, littered with flyers for strip shows and free pregnancy and HIV tests, and dingy gray buildings whose windows were streaked with dust and smoke. People were huddled asleep in many of the front alcoves of those buildings, gray cardboard beneath them, smelling of yesterday's beer and someone else's used clothes. Sherry and I wandered past those small encampments and up and down the long lines outside a place called Hospitality House, which Amanda had told us about, searching for Stephanie's familiar face to appear from out of the crowd. Her narrow chin, the almond-shaped eyes, the perfect nose—and the sprinkle of moles across her cheek like a constellation.

On Saturday afternoon, during my wasted trip to the police station, Sherry combed through the shops. I handed out posters while Sherry showed Stephanie's picture to those on the street who looked like they might know her—the ones who weren't too scary or too out of it to talk to.

Then the two of us split up—Sherry went in one direction and I went in another with no firm plan of what to do or exactly who to speak to. Mostly by now we were engaged in abject wandering, and we both knew it. We persevered under sunny skies and against a cold wind as if some sign of a child who wanted nothing to do with me would soon rise up in front of one of us. Of all the cities in all the country I'd chosen this one—and what was it exactly that I believed this one might deliver into my arms?

After parting with Sherry, I made my way to a public square—in front of the library, if I remember right. I sat on the edge of a marble bench and surveyed the scene in the open space. People huddled in blankets and torn sleeping bags, asleep on benches and beneath the eaves of buildings. In a small grassy area not far from me, someone had dumped a pile of clothes—three or four feet high, a tangle of pants, shirts, sweaters, jackets; an unsortable cacophony of color and fabric that were sure to get moldy and thick the first time it rained. A woman walked by and picked at the mass. She held a blue sweatshirt between her finger and thumb, keeping it apart from her as if it were loathsome. She dropped it again.

About then an expensive steel blue SUV pulled into the square and parked next to a concrete abutment under a large NO PARKING sign. Five or six teenagers hopped out of the doors, as did a fortyish woman, mother to one of these kids, who'd done the driving. She opened the hatchback, and the teenagers, jockeying, giggling, pulled out a couple of cardboard boxes and, using the tailgate as a table, began to stack packages of sandwiches and bottles of juice. A roadside cart, a way station for the hungry.

I stood up and walked closer, scanning for some hint of where they were from and what they were doing—community service for their school or some kind of outreach for their church? The need to know their mission was strong in me, though I didn't know why. Maybe for this group it was simply a Saturday afternoon excursion to feed the drug- and booze-addled population of the Tenderloin, nothing more than that. For me, it was a big, fat reminder of the sordid parameters of my life.

Once the meals were stacked and ready, the kids stood around in a circle to talk to and tease one another. The girls had long, straight, shining hair and wore coats from Tommy Hilfiger and J. Crew. The boys' jeans were new, and their shoes were clean and expensive. From my vantage point midsquare, I took in every detail. After a few minutes, the mother noticed me. She looked over and smiled, though warily. What did I want?

What I wanted was a child like hers. I wanted one who feeds, not one who is fed. This was how I'd tried to raise my own daughters—to help those who had nothing and no one. What a bust.

By now, my younger-woman illusions about motherhood were gone. It was true that early on my four daughters had wanted nothing more than to be near me, to hear my voice, to curl in my lap. A caress, a kiss. Now that time between us was a lie. Or maybe this time at the gritty seams of San Francisco looking for a child who'd left me was the lie. I couldn't tell. Nor could I measure where guilt stopped and resentment began—the two emotions had found a perfect lock with each other inside my body, as deep as my bones, where the sensation no longer came and went but stuck like an implanted rod.

I felt, keenly, both emotions at this moment. Guilt and resentment. Guilt for not creating a life where my daughters handed out sandwiches to the needy, and resentment that this mother on the other side of the square, glancing back at me now and then as if worried about what I might do, would never know how bad it felt to be me.

I broke eye contact with the woman and made my way around the group bunched up at the SUV and past the people who'd emerged from blanket or sleeping-bag shelters to go after the free sandwiches and the bright yellow containers of juice. The roll of posters was under my arm—I'd dropped some off at youth shelters, at the cafés willing to take them, and even at an Urban Outfitters store, where the young clerk had given me a long, quizzical look. Why in the world would a girl who'd run away from her middle-class mother venture into a middle-class store like his? And if she did come in with her dirty fingernails and matted hair, smelling like the devil himself, she'd be chased out. He took the poster anyway. He told me he'd hang it in the employees' room, "just in case."

On Sunday morning, Sherry and I were back in the Tenderloin. We walked the litter-ridden sidewalks of Market Street, circled the neighborhood, and—when we were brave enough—lifted the thin hems of blanket tents to look inside them. I stepped close to the sleeping bags on the library steps and on the steel park benches, hoping to see a wisp of hair, the side of a face, an arm hanging loose from the fabric's folds. But after several hours, neither of us had spotted anyone who looked like Stephanie. Droves of teenagers and even more adults stumbled and slumped down the streets around us. The air wrinkled with the smell of stale urine and sticky dust. The downtown traffic, quieter on a Sunday but still there, honked and thumped along with insistence and impatience. A few tattered people stepped out of shadowed alcoves to ask me for money; each time I declined. Kids on street corners smoked cigarettes with their backs up against brick buildings, their knees pulled up to their chests; long lines of the barely conscious formed in front of soup kitchens as morning deepened into afternoon. One man helped another shoot up on a sidewalk bench out in the middle of everything. But I'd seen no one with my daughter's sharp shoulders and elbows. I hadn't recognized her narrow hips or the slope of her long legs under any of the many pairs of sagging, soiled pants. I hadn't found a sign of her anywhere.

And now, two days and some hours after searching San Francisco, we'd reached the hour of going home. We barely had time to get back to the hotel to retrieve our stored bags, catch the shuttle to the airport, and make the plane to Eugene, where Barry would be waiting to pick us up, eager to hear every detail of this last day's fruitless search. Sherry insisted that we get on our way.

"One more look?" I said.

She lifted her hands then dropped them again, giving in. So I stood alone on the corner of Sixth and Market, the very spot Amanda had suggested, keeping watch in the failing afternoon light for any new panhandlers. Sherry headed for the McDonald's behind me—one last time around the tables and through the bathroom.

A few minutes after my friend left, the crowd on the sidewalk cleared enough that I noticed a girl sitting on a concrete bench a few feet from me. Her wool-hat-covered head hung between her parted legs, strands of dirty blond hair sticking out and falling toward the pavement. It was warm that day, the sky was once again blue and bright, but she was shivering so violently that the fabric of her jacket trembled. A boy, maybe sixteen or seventeen, had his left arm around her hunched body. He held a sandwich near her face and he was whispering in her ear. Although I couldn't hear him, I knew he was encouraging her to eat. Both of them wore cargo pants and black sweatshirts, clothing piled on more clothing, bulky, rumpled, falling apart.

I couldn't see her face.

I stepped closer, and closer again. Neither of them noticed me, or if they did, they didn't acknowledge it. Her damp hair stuck to her cheeks like a feathered veil. She moaned and told him in a husky voice to leave her alone. I had no hope from where I stood of getting her eyes in front of my eyes. I moved around them to look from the other direction. That's when—downwind of the couple now—I smelled them, or at least her. Sour, rancid. Not even the rush of traffic and the breeze from Market Street could dissipate the stench of illness. The boy pushed triangles of white bread toward the girl but her head only sank lower and strands of saliva webbed from her mouth and dripped to the ground. She was barely holding on to the bench. I waited for her to fall and wondered if I should try to catch her if she did.

I could have told him that if he kept forcing her to smell food or if he kept talking about eating they'd both soon be covered in vomit. I could have asked him if he knew of a place where she could lie still, warm and safe for a little while. I didn't speak to them. I watched him hold her tighter, reach in to lift her chin, and beg her to take a bite.

Sherry called my name as I took the last step forward. I was inches away from the bent girl. Even though it must have looked ridiculous for me to do so, I held on to a lamppost and squatted low enough that I could peer up at her. The girl's eyes were unfocused, blurred by tears, closing and opening with tremendous effort. Within a second or two, I stood again, because now I knew she wasn't my daughter. She wasn't Stephanie. I stepped to the side; I backed away. Was it sorrow that swelled in my chest or relief? Before I could sort it out, Sherry had reached for me, pulled on my arm until I was next to her. And then I heard her say, "We have to go, we have to hurry," and that's when I realized that I had reached the culmination of this weekend. Now I understood, as I'd not understood before, that Stephanie was gone and that I might not in this lifetime see her again.

Sherry and I went up the street; my friend linked her arm with mine. We moved away from the girl and from the boy helping her, and I began to let my vision take in everything around me. I once again noticed the gray and brown avenues snarled with cars and with people, the streets where some lived like wisps of smoke, seen only if they wanted to be seen. The girl and the boy were far off now, merged with memory, merged with people heading home for Sunday dinner and with others on the street who had nowhere to go. And here was Sherry looking at her watch, urging me to walk faster up the hill, into a bus, onto an airplane, and into the air that would lift and pull us north up the coast.

I was flying already. Gone from the Tenderloin, far above the city. My feet moved ahead but my arms stayed still at my sides, my fingers stretched open. And then hope—a last smidgen of it—vanished as fast as this day.

A few weeks after that weekend in San Francisco, I drove the narrow road next to the McKenzie River. A few miles before the turnoff to Barry's house, I passed the Rennie boat launch on my right. A steep road, maybe twenty yards long, descended from the shoulder of the highway to a paved and U-shaped patch of land just large enough for one or two trucks and their trailers. From the edge of the launch, a ramp stuck out a few feet into the tumbling, splashing river. The idea was to back a trailer down the sloping blacktop until its rear wheels were under water, unlatch the white-water raft or kayak (now tied to the ramp) from the trailer, and then drive out again.

I'd passed the Rennie launch dozens of times on the way to Barry's. Most days it was empty, unoccupied, a few fast-food cups and old leaves blowing across the bare asphalt. In the summer, though, it hummed busily as people in bathing suits and shorts scurried about to get their rafts and coolers and paddles and kids in the water in anticipation of the ride over the white-water rapids ahead.

Now as I drove by the launch it was mid-May, too early yet—too much rain and wind—to put in a raft for a day's float. The water was too cold. No one would last more than a few minutes in it. This evening's dusk had settled over the slate-colored river and the small dock. I didn't want to glance down to the water's edge—*keep your eyes on the road*—but I did, which caused a short burst of fire in my chest and up into my throat as I'd expected, as I'd felt before. If it wanted to, that sinister force in the river could come and get me—it could catch me even in the matter of seconds it took to drive by.

A few months earlier—in January, I think, or maybe February—two middle-aged couples in one car were heading down the McKenzie River Highway toward the hospital in downtown Eugene. Their children, one couple's son, the other couple's daughter, were having a baby. The daughter had gone into labor that morning, and the two sets of grandparents-to-be, who lived on the other side of the Cascades in Bend, had decided to make the trip to the hospital together.

Except they'd never arrived. They'd crossed over the often-slippery Santiam Pass and had only a handful of miles still to travel along the river into town when they got to the Rennie boat launch. For some reason, the driver—the maternal grandfather of the yet-unborn child—aimed the sedan down the short, steep incline and straight into the swift water. The car was found the next day mid-channel with the two women still belted into the back seat, one woman clutching her purse. The men's bodies were discovered floating in downstream eddies.

I couldn't get them out of my mind. Why hadn't the driver realized he'd gone off the road in time to stop? Why hadn't he slammed on the brakes? The police found no skid marks. Something, who knows what, had pulled them to the middle of the frigid current.

After the accident, I thought about the two couples every time I drove the last stretch toward Barry's house. I remembered them in a cloud of sentiment, believing again that life was a cheat and that all of those people, down to the baby, had been cheated. I was tired of feeling cheated. Tired of being afraid. Whatever lurked in those waters might recognize how done in I was, and how defeated, and would soon enough call me into the river.

This May night, as I turned to the wet road again, I felt especially weak, especially alone, as if the water already lapped at my feet. Then the last Rennie sign was behind me, and I was okay. One second, then two, then thirty, then sixty, and I breathed again. A few minutes after that, dry and safe and calmer now, I was in Barry's driveway and out of my car, standing under a starless wet sky and under the canopy of Douglas firs that arched over his house.

I'd left Mary and Mollie alone for the evening—promising to be home before bedtime—because I had to make the hour's drive to where Barry lived. I had to speak to him, face to face.

He'd been standing in the doorway when I pulled in, and he waited for me to take a couple long breaths of the cool country air before he said hello and urged me to come out of the rain. Usually when I drove up I brought a pot of soup or a sack of warm cookies, but this time I had nothing. I didn't need to stay long and I didn't have much to say. But I had to do this thing on this night and only here, in the still woods and to the man I most trusted, with the sound of the river rushing past in the distance.

I followed Barry to the living room, where he had a fire in the wood stove, popping and crackling and emanating waves of heat. He sat down in his favorite blue chair and I stretched out on the Persian rug that lay over the slats of oak flooring. The warmth soaked through my jeans and sweater to my skin. My hair got warm, and the edges of my left ear, the one closest to the fire, turned hot and pink.

"What's on your mind?" Barry finally said with a strain of nervousness. I'd called earlier in the afternoon, while I was still at work, to ask if I could come up and talk something out with him. I hadn't yet mentioned that soon after my return from searching for Stephanie in San Francisco, I'd had an appointment with the therapist who'd been helping me out for several years. I told that counselor about the futile weekend, about having no other ideas about how to find my missing daughter. After a few minutes of us talking it over, he said it was time for me to plan what I was going to do if Stephanie was dead.

"Dead?" I said to the solemn-faced man. "She's not dead." I got up, gathered my coat and my purse. "Why would you say she's dead?"

But he got me to sit back down and hear him out. "I didn't say she's dead," he told me in his rational, soft voice. "I said it would be good to have a plan in case she is."

Mary and Mollie were about to finish a school year on a fairly good note, both doing fine in classes and practicing for their spring band recitals and dance performances. Amanda had taken a job caring for elementary-school children before and after school. She'd been wobbly at times, but she'd made this job work—her self-repair was well under way, the focus of her days now. She arrived at the darkened school building at six thirty A.M. and helped little kids move out of the last memories of sleep and into the day. She poured juice, got their schoolwork together with them, held the smallest ones on her lap while they adjusted to another morning. She was sober in every sense of the word, and had grown into a quiet and serious young woman who hardly ever smiled, but who hardly ever got angry anymore either.

Our lives were starting to feel the slightest bit normal again—even with the endless hole of Stephanie-still-missing in the middle. If Stephanie was gone forever, if she was dead, it would be up to me to keep my other three children from sliding off the edge. That's what the therapist told me. I could only do that if I wasn't clinging to the edge myself. "Get a list together. Who you'd call first. What would need to be taken care of, and who could take care of it," he said.

I shook my head. I wasn't going to do any of that. I thought he was unnecessarily pushy, or anyway, cruel.

I left his office with a million sad and swirling thoughts clogging my head. Two days later I came to realize that if I had to prepare myself, as he'd said, the first step for me was to say the words out loud to the person who'd gather me up if I needed him to. So I drove to Barry's house and sat up on his rug, woven reds and purples and blues. I turned my body so that my back was against the fire and I was facing him, and I said what I'd come to say. "I think Stephanie might be dead."

The previously unthinkable ending to this trouble with my daughters—that one of them would not make it out alive—was in the room now, and it would in the days ahead gush through my dreams and my waking thoughts. Ever since the therapist had brought up the possibility, I'd been turning it over and over and over again. It couldn't be true, but maybe it was. Why else would this silence have stretched on so endlessly? Why else would Stephanie let so much time pass without contacting us, without contacting Amanda? Too many months had gone by for this absence to make any kind of sense. And pretty soon I was convinced: the worst news could arrive, a black package on my doorstep, and I would have to open it.

Barry didn't say anything once my sentence was out. He waited for me to go on. I muttered a few more words, but they didn't mean much. Making the one statement was all I'd come for. Getting it out of my mouth and hearing my own voice in my own ears.

I curled on the rug again, rolled sideways toward the warmth of the fire. Barry stood up to add more wood and to poke the embers that had already burned down to near ash, then he knelt beside me to put his hand on my back. I closed my eyes and let the heat cover me like a blanket.

A little more than a week later, while I was cooking dinner, the phone rang. The voice on the other end was Stephanie's. I moved down the hallway, away from Mary and Mollie, who were doing homework at the dining room table, and into my bedroom. I closed the door.

"Where are you?" I said, my voice quaking. My hands quaking, my legs quaking.

She sounded far away, a tinny strain to her voice. "It doesn't matter," she said.

"It does matter," I told her. "Where are you?"

But she wouldn't say. She had called to ask me for money. She'd adopted a dog, a puppy from a box outside a grocery store, and had named it Kaw-Liga, after a Hank Williams song. Now the dog was dying of the parvovirus and Stephanie wanted five hundred dollars to pay the vet to try to save him.

I didn't have five hundred dollars or anything close to that in my account, but even if I had, I wasn't going to send money to her for a sick dog, and I told her so.

Wait, were we really talking about money? Were we actually discussing a dog? Stephanie and I were embroiled in an argument this fast? This was not the phone call from her that I had banked on for months. That phone call, the one I'd hoped for and planned on, had her asking for my forgiveness, begging to come home. And it had me opening my heart to her and letting her back in, just like that. With Stephanie's hard voice in my harder ear, that's not the way our first talk in eight months' time was going. Where was the cry of relief from either of us? Where were words of reconciliation or apology? The conversation was brief, tense, and difficult. The most difficult conversation of my entire life: how could that be?

I realize now that her voice couldn't pierce me. All I could acknowledge was the deflation, the frustration and grief between us during our few-minute talk. I couldn't, or wouldn't, hear Stephanie's need; I couldn't let in that she was scared out of her wits at the other end of the phone. She wanted—or at least some part of her wanted—for me, her mother the adult, to fix this, to make it better. To provide the opening, the possibility of hope. But I was too shut down to do that for her.

Stephanie's words were rushed, trailing off. She didn't know what she wanted exactly, but she needed to get her dog cared for and she'd talked to her father, who'd told her to get the money from me. I owed her at least five hundred dollars from the child support I'd accepted while she was gone, she told me. I'd better send it to her, she said, because it belonged to her and she was going to use it for her dog.

I couldn't respond. I couldn't say a single word. I searched in myself again for some sense of relief. I wanted it; I ached for it and can only imagine that she ached for it too. For one second, I thought I detected the skeleton of relief pressed up against my ribs—Stephanie was alive and that was cause for the dead part of me to come to life again too—but there was no bursting, all-consuming glory of reconnection.

I had no idea what to do next.

"Are you sending me the money?" Stephanie pressed.

"No," I said, leaning against my bed, hearing Mary call me from the other side of the house, saying that the soup on the stove was boiling over. "But I'll send you a plane ticket to come home."

That's when I heard a click and a dial tone. She had hung up.

9

AFTER STEPHANIE HUNG UP ON ME ON THAT SUNDAY
evening in May 1997, the first thing I did was push the zero on my
phone until a human voice came on. I wanted to know where my
daughter had called from, and after a ten-minute runaround from
the phone company, I got someone to tell me: Stephanie was in
Austin. I dialed Barry to let him know she was alive. After that brief
conversation, I called Amanda, who by then had a telephone in her
house and who had to get up early the next morning for her job at
the elementary school, but who most likely wouldn't sleep a wink
after this news.

"Austin," I said.

"I know," she replied.

It turned out that Stephanie had contacted her before she'd
called me — and that Stephanie had called her father before she'd
phoned either of us. I'd been the last on her list, a fact that settled
too heavy on me even while I tried to shake off what I took as a
slight, already letting myself slide into the old pattern of competition with Tom.

"Did she say she wants to come home?" I asked Amanda. I'd
slumped to the floor, my back resting against the closet door, and
I'd crossed my legs so they'd started to throb. I heard Mary and
Mollie out in the dining room asking each other where I'd gone.
What was going on with the overcooked dinner? How come the
laundry was left half folded on the sofa? "Mom!" Mary called out.
"Where are you?"

"Not really," Amanda said on the phone, her voice subdued, sad. "She said she has a job and a place to live and that her dog is sick and she needs money." If Stephanie had given Amanda a telephone number or an address in Austin, Amanda was keeping that knowledge from me. Actually, I didn't think she had. Stephanie had made a peep of a noise in our direction and now we were reeling, each in her own way, from what that might mean. She was alive, she was okay. Now what?

The next day at work—a Monday morning in late spring—I called the three youth shelters I'd found listed in Austin. I'm not sure why I started that way because I was already aware of the answer: they existed for the kids, not for the parents, and could offer me nothing. Maybe I wanted the rejection—maybe it was taking me a while to warm to the idea of finding my missing child, and the old pattern of no help to parents was right if only for its familiarity. I didn't bother with the police. Instead, in the middle of the day, done now with the shelters, I was struck by the idea of one institution I had yet to turn to—the church. I called directory services and asked for a handful of Austin, Texas, church numbers, and then I started dialing. Each time I asked to speak to the youth pastor. Even if there was indeed such a minister to talk to, my request was inevitably turned down. "I have choir practice in an hour," one man told me. "That's lousy," another said, pausing for a small throat-clear of sympathy before he added, "but not something I can help with."

I'd asked the few pastors who'd heard me out to please look for my daughter—take a couple of hours one day to see if she was findable, figure out where she was living and if she was safe and fed. Stephanie had mentioned to Amanda that she was working at a pizza restaurant near campus. That was a pretty good clue, wasn't it? How many pizza shops could be harboring a fifteen-year-old runaway? Mostly, I realize now, I wanted these representatives of God to discover some way to ask my daughter to come home so I wouldn't have to.

But they said no, one minister after the other. "Do we know

you?" one man asked me. "I don't understand why you've called here."

Which leads to the obvious question: why didn't I go myself? Why didn't I find a babysitter and hop on a plane that night to do my own digging through college cafés in search of my child, instead of asking strangers to do that for me? No doubt I could find her—the chances of coming upon her in Austin were a thousand times better than those of my lost weekend in the Tenderloin District of San Francisco. What was keeping me in my chair at work, so afraid to trust this recontact with Stephanie that all I could do was curse the unhelpful reverends?

That night at home I phoned Richard and Jane in Montana —their having taken Stephanie into their home and family for half a year giving them claim, I thought, to hear even sketchy news of my daughter's whereabouts. Maybe I tried to explain my state of mind: stunned. My state of inaction. I don't remember. Whatever I said, a few days later Richard was on a plane to Austin, doing what I wasn't ready to do. He walked around the streets near the university, scouring the restaurants until he ran right into Stephanie at a Pizza Hut. She'd lied about her age and was waitressing full-time, bustling around the tables, arms loaded with trays of hot sausage and cheese pies.

She was, Richard said when he called me from his Austin hotel room, nonplussed at seeing him standing in the doorway of her workplace. She stared and stammered. Her boss let her off early, and Stephanie took Richard to meet her friends, casting sidelong glances his way as they walked along the street as if trying to decipher his sudden appearance in Texas. One friend turned out to be a theater student who'd allowed Stephanie to crash at her apartment until she could start paying part of the rent. "It's filthy," Richard said of that crowded place. "They're squatting in filth. Stephanie's teeth are brown."

The visit was short and sometimes tense, though Richard got Stephanie talking about what she was going to do next. By the end of Richard's stay, my daughter had agreed it was probably about time to return to Eugene. But not yet. In the weeks to come, my brother Ron would appear at her door to take her to dinner. My mother, in Texas on business, would see Stephanie too and would do her best to persuade my daughter to come home. But I stayed away, only later realizing why. After two years of going after my child, reeling her back home again and again, this time I wanted her to choose to return to me.

By early summer, I'd talked to Stephanie several times on the telephone and had begun to understand her tentative plans: she wanted to go first to Tucson to see her father, then I would buy her—and the dog—a ticket to fly to Eugene. We could start to put small parts of this into motion, though much was not yet firm. Ours was a standoff that would be weeks in breaking, either toward some sense of reconciliation or toward more alienation, who knew.

While Amanda worked on college applications and found a job at a daycare camp that summer, and with Mary and Mollie off for the annual visit with their father, I prepared for Stephanie to finally come home. I borrowed five thousand dollars against my mortgage, an unheard-of move for me. I convinced a contractor friend to give me a good deal on remodeling our backyard storage shed into a small cottage for my returning child. I'd forgotten, I suppose, how outraged I was when Tom and Ellen stuck Amanda in a made-over outbuilding in their own backyard when she'd gone to live with them all those years ago. In my mind, this backyard construction project of mine made perfect sense: Stephanie had been gone too long and had seen and done too much to simply move back into her old room and take up a ninth-grader's life. That was my justification, anyway—though there was another part to it. I wanted to have her a good distance from my bedroom in the rear of the house so I wouldn't have to notice her comings and goings, which were sure to get under my skin like some itchy rash.

By the end of August, the little house was finished, its walls painted periwinkle blue and filled with garage-sale furniture—bed, chest of drawers, dressing table with mirror, and a big overstuffed chair in the corner. An extra bathroom was beyond my means, so she'd have to share the one in the house with Mary, Mollie, and me.

But everything else felt as right as it could feel for this once-lost daughter's return home.

One night in November, after Stephanie had been living at home for eight weeks, living in that remodeled shed, I made my way across the dark patio behind our house and around the corner to the wet backyard, the last of the evening's rain dripping off the eaves, to peer in the window of her small place. The cottage sat smack in the middle of our backyard, just east of the garden and about ten feet south of the main house, a window on each of its three sides. I had to stand on a stepstool, which I'd pulled over from the patio, to see into her bright room. Stephanie had left on every lamp when she'd taken off to join her friends. The day before, maybe, or the day before that. Though irritated about what she was doing to my electricity bill, I was also glad for the light, because I needed to know two things: if the whining dog inside was suffering from hunger and thirst, and how much damage that dog was doing to a cottage for which I'd taken out a big, fat loan.

Kaw-Liga was a gangly tan Lab mix, with a lolling spotted tongue and huge paws. I hadn't wanted him to live with us—adding a dog to the tricky mix of estranged daughter and wary family seemed too much—but Stephanie had bluntly informed me that where she went, the dog went. So I'd given in and here he was, scratching the new molding around the door to splinters, peeing on the rugs I'd bought from the carpet store's remnant pile, tearing the pillows off Stephanie's bed into clouds of floating feathers, and rolling on his back to moan in loneliness and boredom.

Mary and Mollie had been pleading with me all evening to break the glass out of a locked window so one of them could slip a skinny body through the opening to release Kaw-Liga. Now, instead, I put my hands to the sides of my face, blinder-like, seeking some clue to the schedule of Stephanie's appearances and disappearances. After a few seconds, I made out the shimmer of water in one bowl and a meal's worth of fresh kibble in the other: a relief. Stephanie had been there in the past few hours to feed her dog and to play with him while I was at work and the little girls at school.

Still. The dog was miserable. Mary, Mollie, and I had heard his barks and cries when we got home that evening, before we'd even opened the car doors. Mary ran to the backyard with Mollie on her heels to stand on the stepstool and try to see what shape he was in. As soon as Kaw-Liga spotted the girls in the window he went even wilder, yipping and leaping, believing release was near. I went in the house to retrieve messages off our machine, all of which were from neighbors asking me to please do something about the dog that never shut up.

That night at dinnertime, as I'd been finishing up a pot of beans and rice, which we'd top with cheese and sour cream and eat with salad and cornbread, the phone had rung. It was someone from the county's youth services—"baby jail," as Stephanie called it. Stephanie had been arrested for drinking wine in the park, the woman on the other end of the line had told me. But not just underage drinking with her old friends and a new group of pals she'd found on Eugene's streets—for that mere transgression she might have been given a ticket and a ride home. Instead, she'd battled with the cops, calling them names, and she'd shoved one while trying to wriggle out of his grip. That made the charge assault and worth a trip to a holding cell.

"Do you want to come get her?" the woman said.

"What's my other choice?" I asked.

"You could leave her here for the night and come get her tomorrow."

"I'll see you tomorrow," I'd said, and hung up.

With Stephanie locked up until morning, I had to do something about the dog. And so I was standing next to the cottage considering my choices when Mary came outside in her pajamas and robe, fresh from a shower. She stayed at the edge of the patio and out of the damp grass. "Are you going to do it, Mom?" she asked me.

A couple of days earlier, the extra key to Stephanie's cottage, a room she had dubbed "the shack" on her first day home, had been in the top drawer in the kitchen. Now that key was gone, and so was Stephanie. If I wanted to get in, I'd have to do what the girls had suggested earlier: put a brick through one of the expensive Pella windows, bought to be extra-safe and extra-sturdy.

I paused for a minute, Mary's still, small frame bundled in a furry pink robe a beacon from the patio. "I guess I have to," I finally said. I walked over to the side of the house to a small pile of bricks I stored there for garden use and picked one up, rough and cold and heavy in my hand. I hauled back and gave it a hurl.

A few months before, in the middle of summer while Stephanie was still with her father, I'd had a couple of meetings at the local evening alternative school, whose population was about twenty-five near dropouts and a few harried teachers. Classes met at a suburban high school at night, hours after the regular students went home. At our second meeting, the head teacher told me there were no spaces left—Stephanie was out of luck for the fall semester. But by the time I'd left his office that day, she was in. When I'd mentioned what I did for a living, he'd said that some of the kids had been asking to start their own newspaper. I promised to teach a journalism class for free every Tuesday night if he'd find my daughter a slot, and he agreed.

Stephanie quit attending that school after the third or fourth week. She didn't like it and I shouldn't have assumed she would, she told me. True enough: I had assumed. I couldn't imagine a better choice for her in our town if she wanted to finish high school. My problem now, once she'd ditched the plan for good, was that I'd made a deal with the head teacher. I couldn't see how I could drop out as my daughter had, so every Tuesday evening after work, Mary, Mollie, and I drove out to the school so I could repeat a few simple ideas about leads and nut graphs and sources to about ten kids and get them to write little spurts of stories for our version of an alternative school newspaper that we'd put together before Christmas break. My daughters sat in the back row doing their homework or reading—or staring at a boy clad in black and metal who typically fell asleep, snoring into his forearm. I saw Mary gaze at the clock now and then; I felt her wishing we could just go home.

Home, where we rarely saw Stephanie, or even heard from her. Upon her arrival in Eugene, this daughter had needed only a couple of days to reconnect with kids on the street from past years and to get hooked up with new ones. At first when she stopped coming home at night, I was astonished—but why was I? My practical side couldn't make sense of this surprise and disappointment. Wasn't this exactly what I should have expected? The same old, same old. Nothing had changed since she'd last been with us, except that my heart was even harder toward her. We were simply starting again where we'd left off, one angry woman versus one angry teenager. I continued to pick fights with her because I'd grown oh-so-comfortable with that mode of communication and only that mode of communication when it came to Stephanie. She didn't get why I was so adamant about addressing matters she felt were finished, done with—school, curfews, drinking—and I couldn't begin to get her fury or her stubbornness toward me. It hadn't sunk in yet that Stephanie took the remodeled cottage not as an offer of private space and a gesture of forgiveness but as one more sign, along with my distance and silence in her presence, that she didn't quite belong in our family or in our house.

The day after Stephanie's arrest, I took the morning off work to appear at the baby jail. It felt strange that, given all our teenager troubles, I hadn't been there for five years, not since the last session in front of the judge regarding Amanda's arson charge. Now I sat in a small bunkerlike room, the office of the youth services counselor, posters about not doing drugs and not having unprotected sex attached to the walls with wads of pale green adhesive that stuck out the sides like old chewing gum. After a few minutes, Stephanie was led in by a woman whose round face was already drooping even though it was not yet nine A.M.

Stephanie plopped in an institutional chair across from mine, legs sprawled out in front of her as if she intended to take all the room available. Her clothes were wrinkled and her hair gritty and tousled. She reeked of dried sweat and stale alcohol. She crossed her arms over her chest and refused to look at me, probably knowing that I'd had the option of getting her the night before and had declined, though maybe she was just going to act—just going to be—furious no matter what. I was going to be angry no matter what too. Any sympathy or desire to start again with this daughter—which I'd weakly brought around in myself in the days before she came home—had been pounded out like dirt from a rug since her return.

The youth services counselor brought out a pile of papers for both of us to sign, and also began to stack on the desk in front of me brochures about various county and state programs that Stephanie could enroll in. Drug rehab, alcohol rehab, or the free school for runaways. Et cetera. We'd tried most of them years before; we'd passed on others years before. The girls had long ago collected their shares of free blankets, pizza on the mall, warm chicken dinners in exchange for an AIDS prevention class at some downtown center. Without access to my bank records, this woman couldn't have tallied the thousands and thousands of dollars I'd doled out for counseling, was doling out even then to the new therapist who was seeing Stephanie when Stephanie bothered to show up. This youth services counselor couldn't have known what pros we were at this business, Stephanie and Amanda and I, how I could list the programs as easily as she did, and how I was so far beyond the solutions she'd laid out that I nearly bounced one hard laugh around her concrete block of an office, where our voices kept landing with a thud on the floor.

Stephanie, who apparently agreed with my sense of futility, had her head cocked with an oh-this-old-crap-again expression on her face. We both knew the truth: no one could instruct us how to get to the other side of our own private sea of hurt and bitterness. We had to swim our way toward forgiveness ourselves, discover it ourselves, whatever that meant and however distant the possibility seemed that day at the juvenile center. Until then, this would be about two people making each other miserable.

Ten minutes later in the car, with Stephanie in the passenger seat, I started toward the bridge that led to our home. I planned to stop first at the hardware store to pick up a pane of window glass and some putty and then get Stephanie to help me replace the window I'd broken the night before. I'd knocked out the shards, packed blankets around the jagged edges, and slid Mollie through so she could open the door and release bounding, happy Kaw-Liga into the yard. I couldn't stand that dog, who triggered the wrath that lived right under my surface, but I'd still let him sleep in Mary and Mollie's room. I woke in the morning to the smell of his musty damp fur and the clicketing sound of his toenails on our wood floors.

Halfway to the hardware store, I suddenly couldn't bear it: going back to the cluttered house, the needy dog, the torn-up cottage. Our same old rhythms, the arrhythms, I should say, the *thump-thump*ing along to the next catastrophe that would bring only distress to the younger girls and to Amanda.

I was aware that a good number of the hours Stephanie spent away from our house were spent at Amanda's small rental house, which was shared with five or six others. Neither girl talked to me much about the other, but I could tell—even from a distance—that some dimension of cool remained between them, although they were trying to get back together, the way they used to be. They couldn't get over what had happened that last day on the streets, when Amanda gave her real name and Stephanie went on; they have been years getting over that day.

Now, with Stephanie beside me in the car, I pulled over to the side of the road, turned off the engine. I was fed up enough that I hurt everywhere, as if I'd stood up fast and banged my head into the corner of a kitchen cupboard—in pain and pissed off deep into my back muscles and down my thighs, and so full of the need to scream that nothing could keep the sound in. I didn't yell, though, even though that outburst might have been better, might have released some of the heavy tension between us. I stared straight at my daughter and focused all the anger I could muster.

"I'm done with this," I told her.

"What do you mean?" she said, scowling at her faint reflection in the windshield.

"I mean I'm done, finished. I give up. We can't live together anymore." My hands held the steering wheel at ten and two exactly. "I am so fucking done with you."

She didn't answer, but lifted up her own hands for a second and then dropped them in her lap. Her eyes straight ahead out the windshield, her lips a flat line even in profile.

I'd had lunch earlier in the week with a woman I was interviewing for a story, and after the right quotes and facts were gathered and my notebook put away, we entered into the subject of our kids. I hadn't meant to, but I'd blurted out the worries drilling a hole in my brain—Stephanie. Stephanie home and as aimed for trouble as she'd ever been. I had no idea what to do next. The woman, Vicki, told me it so happened that her ex-husband ran a school in Colorado, a one-of-a-kind boarding school where bright but troubled kids who couldn't get along in public school lived and worked together. And, better yet, the school was funded entirely by an auto company, Honda. It was one of the company's philanthropic projects, and so there were no costs to the students' families other than their children's travel and medical expenses. I ate the last leaf of lettuce in my salad without believing such a place actually existed. I thought Vicki must have at least some of the story wrong, that a school couldn't be that accommodating. But I went home that evening and called Vicki's ex-husband, the school's headmaster, Robert, and he explained Eagle Rock in pretty much the same way. He also told me that parents couldn't send their kids there. The only way for a teenager to get in was to write her own application, her own essays about why she needed a different place and a different kind of education. It would be Stephanie's promise of commitment, not mine, that he'd need if he was going to consider her.

There in the car I told Stephanie, just freed from baby jail, she had two choices: either apply to Eagle Rock School or move on to wherever. If she took the second option, I was done being her mother. Any bond left between her and me would be chopped apart. It's hard for me to remember myself as this shut down, this distant from a daughter who, in her own way, was still sending out a coded call for help I couldn't interpret. She needed me, and she needed me to break through whatever was keeping us parted. But all I could register then was that Stephanie spent most of her nights either on the floor at Amanda's or at a crusty dive called the Warehouse, an old storage building where a dozen or so kids like her holed up to do whatever holed-up kids do. Drinking and drugs; I figured she was back into both. If that was how she wanted it to go, so be it. I'd give her up to those people and to this way of grinding through her teenage days, with no education and no plan for one. I couldn't have her coming and going whenever she wanted from our house anymore. I couldn't let her do that to Mary and Mollie. And though I'd given her a variation of this ultimatum many times before, this time I meant it. And this time she heard me.

Stephanie chose the school. She wrote and sent in pieces of the application, survived a tough series of elimination interviews, and then went with me to buy long johns and wool socks and sweaters and snow boots; three months after our talk in the car, I put my second daughter on a plane to Denver. She and I battled up to the moment of her departure, and I thought I couldn't wait until she was gone, yet once I was in that blue and gold waiting room at the same airport I'd been in dozens of times to send off and reclaim my children, I found no pleasure at her leaving. Not one bit of happiness. What settled in me was a deeper sense of defeat, the endless sorrow of irreplaceable loss.

I knew that day that we'd not live together ever again. Stephanie was a little girl when she first hit the streets with Amanda, still a child. The ways we needed each other would never be fulfilled, or at least not in the manner that mothers and daughters usually borrow and collude and give and take from each other before they part for good. It was out of habit that Stephanie and I spent fury on each other in the weeks before she left for Colorado. We didn't know how to show each other joy or relief, and we'd forgotten how to be sad; we'd lost the ability to show the plain, aching sadness of separation. We flung anger at each other every hour because we couldn't remember how not to. We couldn't remember what to replace it with.

10

EAGLE ROCK SCHOOL, TUCKED IN THE FOOTHILLS OF
Rocky Mountain National Park just outside Estes Park, Colorado,
is made up of a scatter of log buildings connected by meandering
gravel paths. Most of the ground around the ten or so metal-roofed
classrooms and dormitories is bare. A dash of pink and gold wild-
flowers pop up in the spring, but otherwise growth is sparse between copses of stunted pine trees. In the winter, which lasts from
about October to April, the place is buried under piles of drifting
snow.

This Colorado landscape was unfamiliar to me, beyond my
imagination as a place to turn to during the conflagration that was
my family's life. The night we finally heard from Stephanie after
eight months of silence, and in the subsequent weeks and months
of getting her home from Austin, it would never have occurred
to me that a school in a Rocky Mountain town was the place she
would finally flourish. But that's what happened.

About eighty-five students from everywhere in the country
board at Eagle Rock. They live in sturdy houses that have names
like Piñon and Spruce and Lodgepole, and each house is designed
to accommodate sixteen students, eight girls in one wing and eight
boys in another. The two wings are separated by a common area,
and students are watched over by two resident adults in each house.
At six thirty A.M., fleece-bundled students show up in front of the
main lodge for an hour of required exercise, which is led by Robert
the headmaster. Most days that means running a three-mile loop

at first light, down the hill to the gate and then back up the steep and winding blacktop drive in a communal cloud of frosty breath. By eight each morning, Robert is holding the daily gathering in front of the lodge's massive fireplace, tossing out paperback novels as door prizes of sorts to teenagers sprawled on the floor, a number of whom are braiding the hair of a boy or girl in front of them, most dressed in baggy sweatpants and sweatshirts. Robert makes announcements and sets forth the plan for the day and allows students far from home one brief free-for-all gripe session — *Someone stole my stereo and I want it back; There was too much noise in the commons last night; I was the only one to show up for KP again.* To me, when I visited, this was the sound of ordinary teenage banter — obnoxious and joyous at once — which happily included my daughter.

Until the summer after her nineteenth birthday, a nearly three-year period, Stephanie was a student at Eagle Rock. Each of the five or six times Barry and I drove over from Oregon to visit her, the tires of our car squealed through the hairpin turns leading to the ten-thousand-foot-elevation compound, and my head got dizzy as my heart beat harder. My mouth became sticky and dry, the moisture in my body wicked away by an altitudinal wind.

In August 2001, Barry and I were at the school for the last time — we'd made a final trip to watch Stephanie graduate. Nine students would receive diplomas, making my daughter's graduating class the second largest in the school's history. A small group — yet I still wanted Steph to feel like the day was as big a deal as the graduations at schools that paraded five or six hundred students across the stage. I'd ordered announcements off the Internet, bundles of small cards with Stephanie's name printed on them in formal script, just like those from regular high schools. Before I mailed them, I tucked a picture of her, taken during her last visit home, into each envelope. Stephanie seemed happy enough about the graduation extras, the announcements and ad hoc senior photos, but maybe they didn't matter as much to her as they did to me. Maybe she went along with the trappings because she knew how attached I was to the unspoken message that went with them: *See how normal we are after all? See how much she's over being a bad girl on a bad road?*

During her years at Eagle Rock, Stephanie threatened to quit at least a dozen times—plenty of nights I'd lie awake in my bed at home convinced that she wasn't going to finish, but instead to toss herself again into the raw tumble of the streets. But she didn't quit. And in the end, the final stretch of months before she graduated, she was among the students chosen for a weeklong class in politics in Washington, D.C., and for trips with teachers to national conventions where she spoke as one of the turned-toward-a-brighter-future kids. She was the Eagle Rock student selected by the staff to get the Rotary Club funds that allowed her to live in Thailand for a summer and teach kindergarten in a small village called Pha Lariet. She put in her required eight hundred hours of community service, cleaning and repairing forest service cabins, shoveling the snow from elderly folks' driveways, picking up garbage in the city's park. Stephanie had squeaked by in math and science classes, and she'd excelled in every art class she could get into. She'd finished glass-blowing workshops with enough glistening bowls and vases to line a bookcase, and she'd learned how to develop her own distinctively grainy photographs in the school darkroom. She wrote poetry and made books with artfully sewn bindings. She taught herself to play the accordion so she could pump out Tom Waits's "Closing Time," among other songs of his, and in the school's bulletin she dedicated her graduation not to me or her father but to her favorite singer, "the man who's gotten me through the worst of times."

Stephanie did these things, made these changes, a thousand miles away from me. It was Robert and the other teachers at the school who got to look on at this young woman who'd come to charm them (who was once again the girl who adults loved to love). They saw her shed the Sno-Cone-colored hair and the dirty clothes and the plugs in her earlobes. The snarl on her face, the one she'd come back from Austin with, faded. Her skin settled into its former translucent glow. The anger and the need to run once molded to her skin—like a waxy rind on cheese—fell away during these Eagle Rock years. All those many miles from the rest of us, with adults other than me guiding her, she put an end to her time on the streets.

Graduation weekend. We were all there—the three other girls, their father, my mother, Barry, and I—sitting in metal seats on a Friday afternoon while the girl wearing a silky spaghetti-strapped peach dress and a shine of pink on her lips gave her final senior presentation in the Eagle Rock gymnasium. After her last words and a squeaky sendoff from the school band, which consisted of about eight kids and Robert (on trombone), Barry and I wandered out to the grounds outside the gym. I stood in the afternoon air looking at the grayish mountains, still trying to adjust to the altitude's pinch across my forehead and waiting for Stephanie to come out and find us. She'd been surrounded by her sisters and by Tom—and teachers and friends—right after her talk, so Barry and I thought it best to step away. Robert, tall and ruddy-cheeked, with a spry patch of sand-colored hair on his head, came out the main doors with trombone case in hand and walked over—he knew Barry had to leave at dawn the next day, hours before the actual cap-and-gown ceremony took place, to catch a plane to an East Coast appointment. Robert quietly asked us now if we'd like to have a private showing of the slides he'd collected since these nine kids had arrived at Eagle Rock. Each teenager had been some version of war-torn and lost back at the beginning; many had been like Stephanie when she landed on the school's doorstep: still itching for a fight, daring the Eagle Rock adults to throw her out. She'd been exploding out of corners for so long by then, she didn't understand for years how to do anything but explode.

After the graduation ceremony, which would culminate in the most sophisticated dinner the school kitchen could put together for the hundred or so of us on campus—aluminum vats of chicken and whipped potatoes and chocolate mousse for dessert—Robert planned to bring out the projector and, accompanied by a loop of sentimental pop music, flash before the onlookers the transformations of Stephanie and the eight other kids. Now he leaned toward

Barry and me to ask again in a low voice: did we want to meet him in the administration building later for a preview so Barry could see the slides? I told him yes, we did, and I made note of the room and the hour, but even then—even in my eagerness to see evidence of my daughter growing out of what she had been and growing into what she had become—I wondered if I could handle being walloped with these images of what I'd missed, with all that had gone on without me, all I hadn't seen or heard or experienced because I'd sent Stephanie away to this school instead of sticking it out with her, instead of being the one who'd helped her forge her way to this change.

At this same time, Amanda—who'd flown in for Stephanie's ceremony—was in the middle of her own metamorphosis. She was going to school at Prescott College in Arizona. She'd taken on big student loans to attend that private school, but she'd set her heart and mind on Prescott and now was there, allowed in with her GED scores and the offer of extra help from teachers to make up for lost high-school years. She was, for the first time since the age of fifteen, actually creating a future for herself rather than remaining stuck in the flattened possibility of each single day at a time.

I'd traveled to Prescott with Amanda the summer before Stephanie's graduation, for a first visit of the school. Amanda, who was nineteen years old then, and I wandered around the town of Prescott and then drove to the campus to pick up paperwork and look at classrooms and eat at the small student café that served deep bowls of lentils and brown rice along with piles of organic kale and spinach. The student body was dressed, to a one it seemed to me, in earth-tone variations on the color brown. Sweaters and wool hats, Dickies or Carhartt's pants, and big work boots. Amanda would fit in with the no-makeup, tousled-hair crowd, with these mountain hikers and kayakers and bikes-not-cars drivers. She was still shaky in ways, and had just begun to separate herself from Billy. She felt ready, she told me, to leave Eugene behind for a few years. We'd gone to Prescott to see exactly how she might do that.

All that day, as we met college folks here and there and saw the kinds of classes the school offered, I watched Amanda brighten, felt her lighten. In the middle of the day, it occurred to me that she was a steady young woman who'd finally left adolescence behind and not the person I'd made her out to be for too long: an ageless just-off-the-street waif.

We stayed a few hours in Prescott, then drove back down the mountain to the valley to spend the night in an upscale Scottsdale resort, all dreamy pink architecture, translucent fountains, and manicured cacti. We'd live it up for a few hours; for the first time since she was a toddler, just Amanda and me for a whole night. Once in our room, we pulled the stiff polyester covers from our queen-size beds and lolled around on the cool sheets and checked out cable television, which neither of us had back home. I decided that before having dinner in the hotel dining room we should each take advantage of one service from the resort's spa. I moved to Amanda's bed, sitting thigh to thigh with her, and together we read over the thick brochure I held in my hands. It described massages, manicures, mud baths, hot rocks, facials, the hour with a personal trainer, the class with a nutritionist. "Can people actually afford this?" I said, running my finger down the prices column, my nail scraping one hundred-dollar-plus charge after the other. Amanda giggled. Amanda fell backward on the covers.

Though it had seemed like a good idea when I'd suggested the treatments, five minutes after pondering the brochure I wasn't so certain. Suddenly I was picturing myself in a strange room naked except for a stranger's sheet, facedown in one of those dough-nut pillows with soft music humming overhead and a stick of incense burning in the corner, and I wanted nothing more than to talk Amanda into staying put in our room. She wouldn't be surprised by my sudden switch, my mild panic. She'd seen me act this way when I got around people I didn't know. The parent meetings at the middle school, for instance, where I sat in the back believing that every whisper and glance in my direction had to do with me and my bad-girl daughters. I'd wander to the perimeter of the room during punch-and-cookies time, pretending to read the book titles on a teacher's shelf or look at the art on the wall, and I'd hurry to the parking lot as soon as possible once the meeting was finished, before someone could say, *Aren't you Amanda's mother? And Stephanie's?* Over a seven-year period I showed up regularly at the school that all four of my daughters eventually attended, but I never bothered to learn one other mother's name.

I felt acutely out of place at this resort, as much — or more — than I did at the girls' schools or at the few parties and social affairs I'd been unable to skip after my daughters had started running off. While they were gone, I avoided others' scrutiny, avoided others in general, not yet understanding that I was only deepening the girls' alienation by hiding away from people myself.

The brochure, printed on thick adobe-colored paper and embossed on the front with the hotel's insignia, grew heavy in my hands. The spa was beyond me — and, I thought, beyond Amanda. We couldn't show up in this locker room in our old jeans shorts and T-shirts and worn sandals and undress with the wealthy guests of the desert. I didn't see how it would be good for us to squirm in discomfort in a place we didn't fit.

I was on the verge of saying that we should stay in and watch movies, order room service, and forget about the other half of our plan as well, which was to get dressed up for dinner in the resort's restaurant — but before I could say much of anything, Amanda started to push. Sweetly push.

"When are we going to have another chance?" she asked, sitting up and taking the brochure out of my hands. "Let's just do one thing each. It'll be fun." She linked her arm with mine. "You deserve it, Mom," she said, smiling and bumping her shoulder against my shoulder.

A few minutes later, I picked up the phone to order our treatments — moving back into a world alongside my daughters; yes, I could try that. I decided I'd have a plain massage, the standard fifty-minute type that might get out some of the potato-size knots that had formed in my shoulder muscles in the wake of Stephanie's return, and Amanda would get her long, thick hair cut for the first time in over a year.

• • •

By the time I'd finished my treatment in the jasmine-scented room and then enjoyed the fifteen minutes in the sauna I was allowed as a bonus, twilight had fallen. The blue sky was dusky now out the high windows in the women's locker room. I pulled on old sweats that were rough against my tingling legs, my skin hot and hair wet against my neck. Out in the hallway—where the salon had for some reason shut down early, its shades drawn and a CLOSED sign in the window—I looked around for Amanda, a damp towel and my swimsuit rolled up under my arm. After a few minutes of wandering, I found her outside. She was sitting on a concrete bench, legs crossed, smoking a cigarette under the golden arc of the exterior light. Her hair was shoulder length now, with a gently curved bounce at the perfectly snipped ends. I reached out to touch those soft locks.

"Wow," I said. "You look good."

But when she glanced up at me, her face was dark, closed down. Since the time we'd gone our separate ways, about an hour earlier, she'd retreated inside herself, and I had no idea why.

"What's going on?" I said, heart sinking already. "What happened?"

Amanda shrugged and stood up, twisting the bottom of her flip-flop on the cigarette butt to put it out. "Nothing," she said. "No big deal."

We started back to the hotel room in silence, and only after we were away from any other people on the path and walking in dusk's dimness did she let me in on the scene with the hairdresser. Amanda's hair had been washed and trimmed, and the woman was starting to blow it dry—running a fine-tooth comb through the wet strands and using a sharp pair of scissors to catch any stray hairs—when she found first one nit, then another, then a bunch of them at the base of Amanda's skull. Tiny lice eggs that had no doubt been passed to her from one of the children she watched every morning and every afternoon.

I felt my own face turn beet red as she told the story. Every fall the four girls had come home from school with the itchy bugs in their hair—damp western Oregon turned out to be a perfect breeding ground for the crawling parasites, and a classroom the ideal place to encourage their spread. But a resort in Scottsdale, Arizona, is not the place anyone would expect to find even a single shiny white lice egg, and I writhed in discomfort for my daughter.

"She freaked out," Amanda went on. "She called the other woman over and they started throwing the brushes and combs and everything else in the sink and pouring disinfectant all over them. Then they told me I had to get out of there."

The hairdresser had yanked the plastic covering from around Amanda's neck and hustled her to the front door. Once Amanda was on the other side, the woman flipped the lock, pulled down the shades, and slapped up the sign to close the place down.

"I'm so sorry," I said, reaching over to touch her. She veered away from me, clasping her arms tight to her chest.

"I don't care. It's nothing. I'll never see them again," she said, shrugging her shoulders, but everything about her body—the way her back bent slightly as she walked under the path lights, the set of her jaw, as she'd held herself in the old days—were sure signs that it did matter. I pressed the damp towel in my arms against my own chest, frustrated and silent.

We put our few things away in the room and I picked up my purse and the keys to our rental car. With Amanda in the passenger seat, I drove out of the resort and into the more residential part of town, where we fairly soon found a strip mall full of ordinary shops. At a chain drugstore, I bought a container of lice shampoo nearly identical to the dozens of others I'd purchased since my children had started school. Back in our room, we took the sheets off Amanda's bed and the cases off her pillows and wadded up any towel and washcloth she might have used, shoving the bundle under the bathroom counter. Amanda knelt on the floor and hung her head into the bathtub, and I scrubbed the thick gray liquid through her freshly washed and cut hair, the long strands of it smooth between my fingers. The water from the bathtub faucet roared, steam wafted around my wrists, and a familiar medicinal smell rose in the air—the sting of insecticide—that devoured the dainty scents of Amanda's new shampoo and rinse and of the rich oils a masseuse had rubbed into my skin. I wrapped Amanda's soapy hair in a clean towel and we went out to watch television for the few minutes the chemicals needed to sit on her head, to soak in and do their killing. Then we did the rinse.

By eight o'clock I was finishing the treatment—she in the desk chair, me standing behind her working through small sections of wet hair with the metal comb included in the box with the shampoo. I scraped the teeth against each area of her scalp, raking out the dead nits, dead lice, wiping the comb clean with tissue, and starting again. Drips of water traveled down the sides of her face and fell off the edge of her chin and now and then she'd reach up to wipe one away—but she didn't say anything. She didn't make any sound. She didn't complain about the rough metal against her head or the harsh chemicals on her recently softened hair. Mostly, she didn't say a word about being embarrassed or humiliated or hurt.

A short while later, Amanda and I made our way to the outdoor Jacuzzi in the middle of the hotel grounds, next to the long, blue, and very still pool. We'd decided to sit in the hot water and relax for a bit, then go back to the room and order hamburgers from room service and watch a movie on cable television. She and I were the only ones around the water and for that I was thankful—the other guests in for the night, or busy with other plans. I took off my sandals, tossed my towel across the back of a webbed patio chair, and slipped into the bubbly hot water, Amanda coming in after me, her damp hair bunched in a knot on top of her head.

The stars—even competing with the hectic lights of Phoenix —were brilliant, popping into the black cloth of the sky one after the other. The air was a perfect temperature, not too hot, and I pressed into the jets of water that kneaded the muscles of my back. I closed my eyes and listened to Amanda sigh next to me. We floated in the absolute quiet of the evening for a few minutes, until the sound of a man's voice boomed out over a loudspeaker. I sat up and looked through rows of cultivated saguaro and strands of ocotillo cactus bursting with orange blossoms toward the hotel's ballroom, trying to figure out what was going on. Earlier, when we'd returned from the store, Amanda had noticed the parking lot jammed full; we'd spotted gaggles of teenagers and their parents dressed to the hilt—tuxedos and formal gowns and glittery tiaras nestled into piles of hair—sweeping into the hotel's lobby. We figured it was a prom, but now, as the loudspeaker man began his introductions, I realized he was announcing a debutante ball.

"Rebecca Rowe, daughter of Dr. and Mrs. Wilson Rowe," the voice trilled in that *Masterpiece Theatre* accent.

"Heather Jenkins, daughter of Dr. and Mrs. Frederick Jenkins."

Doctors to the wealthy retirees of Phoenix now led their pretty daughters to the dance floor; even though we couldn't see it happening, only heard the sounds of music and controlled frivolity, Amanda and I should have burst out laughing. But we didn't. From across the pool, she grinned at me, and I grinned back, but there were no guffaws or cackling parodies of the announcements. A raw, strange vulnerability had come up in both of us. All evening Amanda had glanced at the phone, expecting the front desk to call and say that the hairdressers had reported in and we should gather our things and leave. Or maybe an army of housekeepers was about to pound on our door and douse us and everything we'd touched with disinfectant. I'd worried about the same—about this small incident in the salon ballooning into a reason for Amanda to shut down again, maybe for a long time. But such a phone call hadn't come, and it seemed that until we checked out the next morning, the hotel would leave us alone and we would leave the hotel staff alone. Until it was time to return to the airport and make our way home, Amanda and I would keep to ourselves and take care of each other.

We got out of the tub and went back to our room for sandwiches and television, the final announcements of coming-out girls following us down the path. Later that night, and for the first time since she was a toddler, we crawled into the same bed—a big bed that allowed us to keep our sleeping distance. I lay awake, thinking about the day—about the college that made her happy and the resort that made her miserable. I wanted to make sense of it all, but whatever lesson I was to take away from our brief stay in the posh hotel didn't fully come that night.

Maybe it's as simple as Amanda allowing me to mother her again, and me allowing myself to mother her. I've wondered too if that day marked the moment that she and I could finally be on the same side, protecting each other from whatever force was trying to humiliate us, or to make us feel small.

Amanda was mostly silent during the graduation days at Eagle Rock—wandering away by herself into the forested grounds or reading a book on Stephanie's top bunk. Staying clear of her dad and of me. I'd been concerned about her since we'd arrived and would stay concerned—though I wasn't thinking about Amanda the night Barry and I made our way to the room at the back of the administration building. At this moment, my mind was fully consumed with Stephanie. We sat down on folding chairs, and Robert soon started flashing photos on a wavy white screen, images of Steph mixed with hundreds of images of the other graduates. Stephanie playing intramural football. Stephanie in the lodge eating. Stephanie dressed up for one of the rare Eagle Rock dances. My daughter helping repair a bridge in the city's park; shoveling snow from the school's walks; standing in front of a class to give a paper. Interwoven with the life of the campus, this girl who'd finished growing up without her mom.

In the shadows of the room, with Robert and his own eleven-year-old daughter behind us running the show, I hunched in my chair and pulled my jacket tighter around me. Barry set his open hand on my thigh, *I'm here.* We laughed at the funny slides, the ones we were supposed to laugh at, but mostly I swam in a kind of grief the room couldn't contain, and I suddenly felt very far from my daughters who were just yards away on the other side of the school grounds. I grieved deeply for the time I'd missed with Stephanie. I was wrung out, too, over the post–Eagle Rock plan, a grief that I'd kept from poking at me until this moment. Amanda would return to Prescott, and Stephanie had decided to move to the Berkshires in Massachusetts to do a yearlong internship at a magazine before she started college. Neither girl was coming home, or anywhere near home. This time they'd be settled, directed, more mature, and I could release myself from the day-to-day fussing about their safety. But none of us would be in the same town, making up for lost time. Whatever was going to happen among us would have to happen at a distance. I didn't much care for that.

In the months and years that followed, with no immediate crisis concerning my oldest daughters exploding in front of me, I spent a lot of time alone. Mary and Mollie went off with their own friends as they finished high school, dabbling in the most innocuous acts of rebellion (or so they seemed to me): getting caught with a beer at a party, skipping school to go sledding with friends, things like that. Then they, too, started taking college classes, getting apartments of their own, finding boyfriends with whom to spend most of their time. Home by myself many days, before Barry and I were married and living together, I often ground away at one question: where had we gone so wrong? I'd cast back to the past to try to sort out what had torn us up, the train wreck of their teenage years. I'd ask myself again, and again: What happened? And how do I ever get over what happened?

How do I forgive myself for what happened?

Not long ago, I visited Stephanie's house in the Berkshires, a small rented cottage on a large parcel of land where (in the spring) a garden grew and, beyond the barbed wire fence, cattle grazed. It was mid-January when I arrived this time, and fifteen degrees below zero. Everything—trees, roads, water pipes, windowpanes—was ice caked, encased in winter's stony glass. Stephanie had fixed up for me the tiny attic room that she usually used as an art studio, and she'd bought, on her meager budget, a small radiant heater to warm the room's scant square footage, which was just big enough for a bed, a desk, and a bookcase.

I woke up the morning after I'd arrived and crawled out from under the mound of blankets—*down comfortables*, Mollie called them as a kid—and into my own thick robe. The room was still dim, the sun not yet high enough to provide full light through the one frosty window. Against the far wall, Stephanie's desk was precisely arranged. Neat, as they say, as a pin. Every pencil, paintbrush, roll of film in its place. A gray manual typewriter sat in the middle of the wood surface, and on the paper rolled into it was a half-finished poem.

I couldn't help but think she had left out these items for me to see. A pile of her photographs. The letter from her college telling her that she'd made the dean's list. I picked up a calligraphy pen, set it back down. I opened a sketchbook leaning against another wall to look at a drawing of one of the backyard cows. Everything in the room was a reintroduction to my daughter, to the young woman she'd become, and I shuddered with a bittersweet pleasure. Had she meant for me to do this, to touch and see everything that was hers? I held in my hand the things she'd held in her hands.

Stephanie called out to me. I pulled my robe tighter against the cold and, shutting the small bedroom door behind me so as not to spill the heat, started down the stairs. My daughter was waiting at the bottom, hip cocked in that way she has so that her lean body nearly takes on the shape of the first letter of her name, and she held two cups of coffee from which white steam waved and unfurled. The furnace had yet to warm up the drafty old house, which had grown cold through the long night—a sheen of ice formed on the inside as well as on the outside of the windows—and Steph saw me shiver.

"Come here, Mom," she said, handing me a cup and pulling me toward the living room. She yanked two wool blankets from the top shelf of her coat closet, and, setting our coffee on a table for a few seconds, we each wrapped up in an extra layer. I stood bundled and sipping hot coffee in the middle of the room while she walked over to switch on the radio. I recognized Garrison Keillor's voice filling the room from the speakers. This was his morning show about poetry. It wasn't broadcast in Eugene, but Stephanie had told me about it many times. She often wrote down the names of the poets and the titles of the verses and sent them to me. Now she moved back so we could stand side by side and listen, our separate breaths puffing white into the still air of the room. We waited through the announcements of birthdays and the few historical occasions of this day, and then the host finally came to the program's daily poem.

I have many times since read over the last stanza of the poem Keillor recited that morning, his broadcast voice the same timbre as the rumble of the furnace that had kicked on by then, both voice and heater beginning to warm the air around my daughter and me. It's not that I believe the universe, or God, produced the perfect couplets for reconciliation. Robert Frost's lines didn't then or now offer the shape of what Stephanie and I needed if we were going to close the space that remained between us; these words weren't going to wash away the residue of our history. We'd have to find a way to do that ourselves during the days she returned to Eugene for visits and in the times I stayed with her over the summers and winters to follow. Stephanie and I walked the streets of her town, hiked in her woods, swam in her river, cooked in her kitchen, drank cold beer in her favorite cafés, and somehow we found our way back to each other without the explanations I once thought would be required. I've not asked why and she's not said why, and month after month, the why of our once-separation becomes less important.

But this day, in her cold-to-the-core house, the Robert Frost poem filled me with both sadness for the life not lived and with a glimmer of the peace that could come from repair between us. Before the last of the poem rose out of her radio, I looked over at Stephanie's face. Her cheeks the pink of spring's first camellia blossom, and her eyes clear and ready. She looked back at me and smiled, her hand emerging from under her blanket to take mine as Garrison Keillor read to us.

> It's when I'm weary of considerations,
> And life is too much like a pathless wood
> Where your face burns and tickles with the cobwebs
> Broken across it, and one eye is weeping

From a twig's having lashed it open.
I'd like to get away from earth awhile
And then come back to it and begin over.
May no fate willfully misunderstand me
And half grant what I wish and snatch me away
Not to return. Earth's the right place for love:
I don't know where it's likely to go better.

Seven years after she and Stephanie ran off to live on the streets, Amanda gave birth to a son, just minutes after midnight on the sixth day of July. Earlier that night, I'd sat in a worn-out patio chair outside the small apartment nearby where Stephanie was staying, along with her boyfriend, who'd traveled with her from Massachusetts. They'd come for the baby. We all waited for the baby: she on the concrete porch smoking a cigarette and pressing the cell phone to her ear, me in a plastic lawn chair sipping a beer and watching stars glittering in a moonless sky. Amanda's water had broken at eight in the evening. At about ten thirty, the phone rang, and Stephanie answered it. I tried to listen in and tried not to listen in at the same time. Gabriel, the baby's father, had informed me earlier that Amanda didn't want me hovering around her through the early stages of her labor—they wanted to be alone for those hours. I'd be summoned, along with Steph, when Amanda could endure company; when birth seemed imminent.

Now in quick succession Stephanie shut off the phone, stood up, threw her cigarette to the ground, and reached for my hand. "He said to hurry," she said. But I stood slowly, suddenly clenched with an anxiety that was new to me.

I hadn't been keen on the idea of a home birth when Amanda had told me about their plan; on this sultry evening, weirdly silent after the Fourth of July fireworks and restless activity the evening before, I was even more worried about my daughter giving birth in her own bed, with candlelight, soft music, and one midwife. Once Stephanie and I were at their house just a mile or so down the street, Gabriel seemed to read these doubts as if they were listed across my forehead. He gave me a hard look at the front door before I stepped in.

"She doesn't want any noise," he said, whispering. "And nobody can say one negative thing, so keep those opinions to yourself."

I pushed a little to get past him, staying as quiet as he'd asked but also letting some old claims of motherhood take hold: if I wanted to make noise, I'd make noise. Who was he to tell me not to make noise? With Stephanie behind me, I padded through the blackened house, through the quiet kitchen, and into the bedroom, lit only by dozens of scentless candles, already dripping wax down the sides of the bookshelves and the front of the dresser.

Amanda was nowhere.

"She won't come out," Gabe said, words that propelled Stephanie and me a few steps to the doorway of the bathroom in the corner of the master bedroom. As soon as we got close, Amanda's voice burst from the darkness. "Get away from me! Don't come in here!"

We scurried to the kitchen, and Gabe switched on the dim light over the sink. That's when I saw how scared he was. Steph noticed it too, and reached over to take my hand. He told us that she'd let him in the bathroom a few minutes earlier and that he'd had a good look. She was bleeding, a lot, and the contractions, one right after the other, were each lasting two minutes. The midwife was driving back from an appointment in Portland as fast as she dared but wouldn't arrive for at least half an hour.

"Did she tell you what to do?" I asked him.

"Find clean washcloths. Put some blankets in the oven on low. Boil water," he said.

Boil water? That was it?

"Let's get her to the hospital," I said. "She needs to be in the hospital."

Gabe intensified his stare about tenfold. "She wants to have the baby here," he said. "It's going to be fine."

To keep my hands away from the phone, to prevent myself from taking over and punching 911, to stop myself from canceling this man and his anti-hospital birth plan, I opened the cupboard door to look for a pot.

Just when I'd set the water on the stove to simmer, Amanda called out for me. I hovered in the kitchen, wondering if I'd imagined hearing her say *Mom*. Then she said it again. I went back into the bedroom alone, this time dropping to my hands and knees and crawling the last few feet through darkness to the open bathroom door. I stayed on my side of the wood threshold, at least smart enough not to venture onto the towel-covered linoleum, where she had rolled herself into a tight ball. I glanced back toward the door and saw that Gabe was still in the kitchen talking with Steph. Perfect. Now I could insist to Amanda that we get her to a doctor and a hospital; now I could make her listen to me. I mumbled sounds, looking for words, then reached out to touch her damp hair. When she didn't jerk back or tell me to leave her alone, I moved my fingers through one long, loose strand.

"It hurts," she said as she leaned into my shoulder for just a second—the last time she would let me touch her that night. "It hurts so much worse than I thought it would."

I stayed quiet—my protest over this choice of a home birth suddenly swallowed by the ache in her, and also by the strength that poured from her naked body. Maybe it was in this moment that I figured out that I had to trust her—that I had to trust her and Gabe, as a couple—as impossible as that could feel from one moment to the next. Even if I thought I saw danger and doom ahead, I had to let them make their own choices about this baby and then live with those choices.

From the moment she found out she was pregnant, Amanda had taken on the mission of growing a healthy baby with a fervor I hadn't known was in her. She didn't just quit smoking and drinking, she weighed and considered everything that went into and onto her body—the organic fruit and the steamed vegetables; the herbal teas that she mixed up in quart jars and sipped all day;

the creams made of cocoa butter and hemp oil that she rubbed on her belly. Now, in the candlelight, I looked around the room: Stacks of cotton diapers she'd washed and folded, topped with new, sharp safety pins. Baskets of soft blankets she'd made herself and tiny baby clothes she'd found at used-clothing stores. She had cleaned every inch of the space, washed the sheets, vacuumed the rug, scrubbed the walls. Amanda had made this bedroom ready for her baby. And maybe all I could do now was assure myself that she knew what she was doing.

The candles on the table above me cast both light and shadow on her skin—in the tiny bathroom, she rocked back and forth, squatted, rose straight and still, then squatted again, while I knelt on the other side of the bathroom door, silent. Her skin was a color described in fairy tales: alabaster. I hadn't known such a shade until I saw it on my daughter. Marble white and smooth. Every inch of her was taut. Her breasts, her belly. Face, thighs. I was in such awe of this transformation from girl to mother that for a second I could almost release myself from the wild worries about my child giving birth when no one in the house had the experience to make sure it went well. But then a contraction took hold, the rocking started up again, and she groaned as deep as an old tree hit by a freezing wind. I closed my eyes, wishing this could just be over.

And soon enough, it was. Amanda's midwife, Elena, arrived a few minutes after eleven and found the baby's head had crowned. She coaxed Amanda out of the bathroom and onto the bed, while Stephanie and I stood next to the bedroom's French doors, open wide to the patio, holding hands, whispering to each other, trying not to be in the way. Trying not to panic.

Despite the midwife's prediction of a quick birth, the baby refused to come out. Not by eleven thirty, not by a quarter to twelve. The midwife pulled an oxygen tank and mask from her Mary Poppins bag of endless stuff, and she told Gabriel that the infant had been too long in the birth canal and that the heart rate had dropped too low. Elena leaned over the bed and put her hands on each side of Amanda's face, which was streaked bright pink from effort and exhaustion. "Your baby has to come out now," she said.

"I'm too tired," Amanda whispered, her eyes closed, heavy and wet. "I have to rest."

"Too bad," Elena said. "You're the only one who can do this."

So Amanda pushed. Elena examined again, then shook her head. The baby hadn't budged: a brown patch of hair no larger than a half-dollar was still all that showed.

I looked at the phone on its cradle across the room and felt my hands itching for it. What kind of mother wouldn't get herself on it to call for help? Yet I didn't move. This was a decision that wasn't up to me, and though I didn't want to accept that, some stern part of me knew I had to.

Seconds before midnight, Elena—worried now, trembling herself, I noticed, and curt in answering the questions we threw at her —pulled Amanda to her feet to let "gravity do the work."

"This is it, Amanda," she said. "This has to be it. One last try."

She called the rest of us over. Stephanie, Elena explained, was to kneel on the bed and wrap her arms around Amanda's chest to hold her upright. Gabriel was to squat to the floor to catch the baby when he came. I hung back as Elena delivered staccato directions, thinking that all the jobs were taken and I could at least have the phone in my hands if things got even a tiny bit worse. If the baby hadn't come in two more minutes, I promised myself, I was going to make the call whether I was deemed meddler or not. But then Elena reached for my arm and pointed to the floor. She told me to sit still between my daughter's legs and hold the beam of a flashlight on the emerging baby.

Before I could think about the position this would put me in, I did what I'd been instructed. I sat at Amanda's bare feet with the metal shaft of the flashlight in my hand, the wet-earth smell of childbirth enveloping me, the pot of recently boiled water—full of clean washcloths—steaming the back of my shirt, and I tried not to think about how deep I was into my daughter's privacy. In a back corner of my mind was the fear that she'd someday consider my position at this moment an invasion, a lit firecracker to lob in my direction next time she was fed up with something I'd said, something I'd done. I pushed that concern away and flipped on the light.

"One more, Amanda," Elena said as she turned toward the tight mound of belly, pressing the cup of the stethoscope into its steepest slope. Amanda groaned, bearing down. "No noise!" Elena shouted. "Put it all in the push. Everything you've got."

I trained the beam on the purple bulge between my daughter's legs. Instead of thinking about Amanda's own birth, instead of thinking about how much her body had changed since that day she was born or the change it was going through on this day, instead of thinking of all we had gone through as a mother and daughter to get here, I thought of the dozens of times I'd held the flashlight for my father while he fixed a broken pipe under the sink or a radiator hose in the car. "Give me my light!" he'd say if my arm drooped. I gave Elena her light, careful not to let my arm fall, while she pulled at the tissue around the baby's head, trying to release him from the grip of his mother's body.

There was a soft murmur of noise in the room, and from my spot on the floor I added to it, saying to Amanda what I thought needed to be said. That she could do this. That her baby needed her now. That I believed in her. "Amanda, Amanda," I said. She whimpered, a rabbit sound that hadn't come out of her since she was tiny. I held the flashlight steady with my right hand, and I laid my left hand over my daughter's cool, bare foot. Did she feel me there? I didn't know until, in one quick move, she raised her toes and lowered them again.

I heard a pop a second later, and a squished white-masked and tiny face appeared in front of me. From behind the flare of the light, I was the first one to see a forehead, eyes, a nose, a crop of hair. Elena reached around and wiped the baby with a soft swab, clearing mucus. His eyes squeezed tight against her touch, then opened to tiny slits. Even before his shoulders, before his arms and body, were born, Amanda's baby boy opened his eyes.

The next morning, Barry and I went to Amanda and Gabe's house early, after we thought they'd all be awake. We brought juice and rolls and flowers. When I walked into the bedroom, I found Stephanie stretched on the bed with her sister, the sleeping newborn boy between them. Stephanie beamed up at me from the other side of the baby, both sisters delirious in their happiness, and they silently welcomed me into the first hours of this boy's life. Gabe was in the kitchen, making coffee and, now, chatting with Barry, and Amanda was recalling her labor, going over every detail of the long night we'd all just been through.

"When Elena got me on my feet," she said as I moved to the edge of the bed, "I couldn't go on anymore. I've never wanted to quit so bad in my life." She reached over to pick a fleck of dust off her baby's cheek, and his forehead wrinkled for a second before he sighed and settled back to deep sleep. Amanda rolled herself flat on her back and looked up at me standing next to her. The smell of her rose up to my face, startling me a little with the memory of my own first hours with newborn babies—the scent was of the first clean, sweet milk of motherhood and the last musky hint of childbirth. "At the end, I just made myself concentrate on Mom's voice," she said. "I kept telling myself to listen to what you were saying, Mom."

"What did I say?" I asked her, sitting down now. I couldn't remember anything but the most ordinary statements of encouragement—the same words everyone in the room was saying, Gabe and Stephanie and Elena.

Amanda reached over to put her hand around my wrist, wrapping her fingers and tugging at me a little. I leaned closer to my family on the bed. I breathed them in, children, grandchild, and then Stephanie reached over to hold me too, her hand just above Amanda's on my arm.

"Don't you remember?" Amanda asked me there in the soft hum of morning and in the glow of this first day, a day of change and possibility for every one of us. "You said, 'Amanda, do it for your baby.'"

Acknowledgments

This book has been a long time coming, so it's impossible to acknowledge here the many people who have helped along the way—

I am thankful for the support of my mother, Barbara Strickfaden, and her husband, Ed, and my father, Mike Gwartney, and his wife, Tore. Thanks, too, to siblings Cindy, Ron, Rebecca, and John. Dear friends Alice Tallmadge, Cheryl Crumbley, and Kathleen Kochan have kept me upright during difficult times—I'm indebted to them and others who befriended my family: Kathleen Holt and Alex Dupey, Abigail Gripman Capalby, Molly Hollister and Jerry Andrus, Mary and Brian Doyle, Megan Breen Leigh, Tom Gerald and Frances Scott, and "Richard and Jane," as they're called in the book (to protect their privacy), all loving adult friends to my daughters.

Thanks to Sandy Tolan, who produced our *This American Life* radio show and whose love and humor have often sustained us —the same for Alan Weisman and Beckie Kravetz.

My old writers' group allowed me to get first stories on paper, and other friends have offered support, particularly Magdalene Smith, Dan Raeburn, Anna Mills, Tracy Miller, and Barbara Ras. Elisabeth Ceppi and Sandra Morgen read early drafts and offered keen insight. Phillip Lopate and Sven Birkerts pushed me to dig in, do better. I am privileged to know them. Much gratitude to Bob Shacochis and Catfish, who offered just the right advice and who've many times buoyed me with their faith in the book.

Jon Garlinghouse provided years of good counsel, and I'm grateful that we could turn to the Catherine Freer Wilderness Therapy Program, Northwest Youth Corps, and especially to Robert Burkhardt and everyone else at Eagle Rock School. Thanks to Michael Collier and the Breadloaf Writers' Conference; the Hedgebrook Writing Colony; the Wurlitzer Foundation of Taos, New Mexico; Literary Arts of Portland. And to the students and faculty at Portland State University.

It's been my great fortune to work with Gail Hochman and Deanne Urmy.

Thanks to Gabriel, Otis, Erik, and Nick—young men who've become members of our family. And I am deeply grateful for the joy my grandchildren bring every time they walk in the door.

Not one word of this book would have been written if I hadn't felt my daughters' support behind me—behind this effort to get a complicated family story on paper. Amanda, Stephanie, Mary, and Mollie asked only that I be honest in the telling, and I have tried my best to do that. I hope all four girls consider this book a tribute to their strength and character, and a recognition of the friendship we've formed, dearest to me in the world.

Most of all, thanks to my husband, Barry Lopez, who has believed in me and in this book for eight years of writing and revising. He watches over me, and over the children and grandchildren, reminding me daily what it means to be protected and truly cherished.